MEANING-BASED
TRANSLATION WORKBOOK

Biblical Exercises

MEANING-BASED TRANSLATION WORKBOOK

Biblical Exercises

Mildred L. Larson

with

Ellis W. Deibler
Marjorie Crofts

University Press of America,® Inc.
Lanham • Boulder • New York • Toronto • Plymouth, UK

Copyright © 1998 by

University Press of America,® Inc.
4501 Forbes Boulevard, Suite 200
Lanham, Maryland 20706

Co-published by arrangement with
The Summer Institute of Linguistics

Library of Congress Cataloging-in-Publication Data

Larson, Mildred L.
Meaning-based translation workbook : Biblical exercises / Mildred
L. Larson, with Ellis W. Deibler, Marjorie Crofts.
p.   cm.
Includes bibliographical references.
l. Bible—Translating—Problems, exercises, etc. I. Deibler, Ellis,
II. Crofts, Marjorie, III. Title.
BS449.L373   1997   418'.02—DC21   97-41214 CIP

ISBN 978-0-7618-0948-7

⊖™ The paper used in this publication meets the minimum
requirements of American National Standard for information
Sciences—Permanence of Paper for Printed Library Materials,
ANSI Z39.48—1984

Contents

III. Propositional Structure

x

Preface

This exercise book has been designed as a companion manual to be used along with the textbook *Meaning-Based Translation: A Guide to Cross-Language Equivalence* by Mildred L. Larson. Each chapter of the exercise book provides Biblical drill material for the content taught in the same chapter of the textbook.

The material in the exercises has accumulated through the years as members of the Summer Institute of Linguistics have taught the course to prospective translators. Some of the material first occurred as "Drills on Linguistic Adjustments in Translation." This material was further expanded by Larson in a 1975 volume called *A Manual for Problem Solving in Bible Translation*. In 1988 Ellis W. Deibler edited a manual called *Exercises in Bible Translation* using much of the material from Larson 1975, adding some new material. However, Deibler's arrangement did not follow the chapters of the material in Larson's 1984 textbook. Also Deibler did not use all of the material in Larson 1975. While teaching the textbook and using the Deibler arrangement of the exercises, Marjorie Crofts and Mildred Larson worked on a reorganization which would make the exercises compatible with the text. They also added new exercises for chapters that had inadequate drill material.

This work has resulted in the current volume. The authors have been listed to include the three main contributors. For the few exercises by others added to this volume, the source is indicated. It is hoped that this new arrangement will be of special help to those training prospective translators.

It cannot be overemphasized that these drills are for the purpose of learning principles of translation. They do not presuppose that all of the adjustments discussed will be made in any given translation. The need of a particular adjustment in the translation process will depend on the receptor language.

Actually doing the drills will give the students practice in applying translation principles, but there is always the need to understand and to emphasize the translation theory that underlies each drill. In the broader context of theory, the students learn to make judgments as to which, if any, adjustments need to be made in a specific translation. It is hoped that, by focusing their attention on one type of translation problem at a time, the students will gain an awareness of the variety of problems facing a translator and thus be better prepared to anticipate and uncover problems as they translate.

A set of possible solutions to the problems is being prepared for staff teaching the course or for persons who wish to teach themselves through reading the text and doing the exercises. In the second case, it is especially important to read the text carefully, prepare written answers to the exercises, and only then compare those answers with the answer book. Anyone grading assignments selected from this book should attempt to determine whether the sense is the same as that of the "official answer," rather than demanding the exact answer in the answer book.

A teacher will need to select from these exercises according to the academic and cultural background of the students and the time available for working on these assignments. In some cases, the teacher will want to assign only part of a given exercise or one of the two or more exercises under any given topic. Many of the exercises are suitable for classroom use as well.

The solutions to these exercises do not necessarily represent actual adjustments that were made in specific languages either during the process of or as a result of checking a translation, though some examples have been selected from the files of various field branches of the Summer Institute of Linguistics.

Quotations of Scripture verses used in these exercises are from the Revised Standard Version unless otherwise stated. Often only part of a verse is quoted, i.e., the part illustrating the potential problem. The abbreviations from other English versions cited are:

GNB	Good News Bible
JB	Jerusalem Bible
JBP	J.B. Phillips "New Testament in Modern English"
KJV	King James Version
LB	Living Bible
NASB	New American Standard Bible
NIV	New International Version
RSV	Revised Standard Version
TEV	Today's English Version

Additional reading is also suggested at the beginning of each chapter. It is not essential to read the suggested material before doing the drills, but it will provide more detail for the student on each topic.

The authors would like to express gratitude to Teresa Bunge and Ray Stegeman for the many hours they spent keyboarding and updating the material, and to the students of Asia SIL, Singapore, for their diligence in looking for errors in the exercises or finding ways to improve them. It is hoped that this manual will be of service in training many more Bible translators around the world.

Mildred L. Larson

Additional Reading

Barnwell, Katharine. 1974. Introduction to semantics and translation. Horsleys Green, England: Summer Institute of Linguistics.

———. 1980. Introduction to semantics and translation, second edition. Horsleys Green, England: Summer Institute of Linguistics.

———. 1983. On planning a Bible translation project. Notes on Translation 95:10–19.

———. 1986. Bible translation: An introductory course in translation principles, third edition. Dallas: Summer Institute of Linguistics.

Beekman, John. 1966. "Literalism" a hindrance to understanding. The Bible Translator 17:178–89.

———. 1968. Eliciting vocabulary, meaning, and collocations. Notes on Translation 29:1–11.

———, and John C. Callow. 1974. Translating the Word of God: With Scripture and topical indexes. Grand Rapids: Zondervan.

———, ———, and Michael Kopesec. 1981. The semantic structure of written communication. Dallas: Summer Institute of Linguistics.

Blight, Richard C. 1970. An alternative display of Jude. Notes on Translation 37:32–36.

Callow, Kathleen. 1974. Discourse considerations in translating the Word of God. Grand Rapids: Zondervan.

Crofts, Marjorie. 1987. Some considerations in translating "body" in 1 Corinthians. Notes on Translation 19:40–49.

Deibler, Ellis W. 1988. Exercises in Bible translation. Dallas: Summer Institute of Linguistics.

Edgerton, Faye. 1965. Relative frequency of direct discourse and indirect discourse in Sierra Chontal and Navajo Mark. In John Beekman (ed.), Notes on translation, with drills, 228–31. Santa Ana, Calif.: Summer Institute of Linguistics.

Glassman, Eugene H. 1981. The translation debate: What makes a Bible translation good? Downers Grove, Ill.: Intervarsity Press.

Greenlee, J. Harold. 1962. "If" in the New Testament. The Bible Translator 13(1):39–43.

Hawkins, Robert E. 1962. Waiwai translation. The Bible Translator 13(3):164–66.

Larson, Mildred L. 1965. Drills on linguistic adjustments in translation. In John Beekman (ed.), Notes on translation, with drills, 245–346. Santa Ana, Calif.: Summer Institute of Linguistics.

———. 1967a. Back-translations: A tool for checking one's own translation. Notes on Translation 28:17–18.

———. 1967b. Making a useful back-translation. Notes on Translation 28:19–20.

———. 1969. Making explicit information implicit in translation. Notes on Translation 33:15–20.

———. 1975. A manual for problem solving in Bible translation. Grand Rapids: Zondervan.

———. 1978. The functions of reported speech in discourse. Summer Institute of Linguistics and the University of Texas at Arlington Publications in Linguistics 59. Dallas.

———. 1984. Meaning-based translation: A guide to cross-language equivalence. Lanham, MD: University Press of America.

Nida, Eugene A. 1964. Toward a science of translating. Leiden, Netherlands: E. J. Brill.

———. 1965. Problems in translating the Scriptures into Shilluk, Anuak and Nuer. The Bible Translator 6:55–63.

———. 1970. Formal correspondence in translation. The Bible Translator 21:105–13.

———, and Charles Taber. 1969. The theory and practice of translation. Leiden, Netherlands: E. J. Brill for the United Bible Societies.

Pallesen, A. Kemp. 1970. More on elicitation. Notes on Translation 36:20–26.

Peeke, M. Catherine. 1965. The Gospel of Mark in Auca. In John Beekman (ed.), Notes on translation, with drills, 47–54. Santa Ana, Calif.: Summer Institute of Linguistics.

Shaw, R. Daniel. 1988. Transculturation: The cultural factor in translation and other communication tasks. Pasadena, Calif.: William Carey Library.
Toussaint, Stanley D. 1967. A methodology of overview. Notes on Translation 26:3–6.

NOTE: *The Bible Translator* is a journal prepared by the United Bible Societies and published by Headley Brothers Ltd., The Invicta Press, Ashford, Kent, TN24 8HH, United Kingdom. *Notes on Translation* is published by the Summer Institute of Linguistics, 7500 W. Camp Wisdom Rd., Dallas, Texas 75236, U.S.A.

Scripture References

Beck, William F. 1963. The New Testament in the Language of Today. St. Louis: Concordia Publishing House.
Good News Bible: The Bible in Today's English Version. 1976. New York: American Bible Societies.
The Jerusalem Bible New Testament. 1968. Garden City, New York: Doubleday & Company, Inc.
Phillips, J. B., trans. 1972. The New Testament in Modern English. New York: The MacMillan Company.
The New English Bible New Testament. 1970. Oxford University Press and Cambridge University Press.
The New Testament of our Lord Jesus Christ, King James Version.
The Living Bible paraphrased New Testament. 1971. Wheaton, Ill.: Tyndale House.
Marshall, Alfred. 1960. The Interlinear Greek-English New Testament. London: Samuel Bagster 2nd and Sons Limited.
Moffat, James. 1935. A new translation of the Bible. New York: Harper and Brothers Publishers.
The New American Standard Bible New Testament. 1972. Lakara, Calif.: The Lockman Foundation.
New International Version of the New Testament. 1973. Grand Rapids, Mich.: Zondervan Bible Publishers.
The Revised Standard Version of the Bible. 1952, 1971. The Division of Christian Education, National Council of Churches of Christ in the United States of America. New York: Thomas Nelson and Sons.
Today's English Version of the New Testament. 1966, 1971. New York: American Bible Society.
Weymouth, R. F. 1908. The New Testament in modern speech. London: James Clark and Co.
Williams, Charles B. 1950. The New Testament. Chicago: Moody Press.

Acknowledgements

Unless otherwise indicated, Scripture quotations are from the Revised Standard Version of the Bible, copyright 1946, 1952, 1971 by the Division of Christian Education of the National Council of the Churches of Christ in the USA. Used by permission.

I. Overview of the Translation Task

Chapter 1
Form and Meaning

Additional Reading:
Barnwell 1974: Chapters 1 and 2.
Nida 1970:105–13.
Nida and Taber 1968: Chapter 1.

A. Analyzing "work of..."

> Surface structure is what may be termed "multifunctional." That is to say, a given grammatical construction may signal different meanings, depending on the context; a lexical item may also have a number of senses. Further, and more significant, a given word or expression may be fulfilling several functions simultaneously. (Beekman and Callow 1974:270–71)

Each of the following quotations contains a prepositional phrase containing the words "work of" or "works of." Reword each of these phrases so as to eliminate the word "of" and express unambiguously the meaning of the construction. You will need to study the context to formulate an answer which is semantically correct.

Example: John 9:4
We must work *the works of him who sent me.*
Answer: We must do what the one who sent me wants us to do.

(1) John 6:29
This is *the work of God*, that you believe in him whom he has sent.

(2) John 9:3
It was not that this man sinned, or his parents, but that the *works of God* might be made manifest in him.

(3) John 10:37
If I am not doing *the works of my Father*, then do not believe me...

(4) Rom. 14:20
Do not, for the sake of food, destroy *the work of God.*

(5) Gal. 2:16
...yet who know that a man is not justified by *works of the law* but through faith in Jesus Christ...

(6) Phil. 2:30
...for he nearly died for *the work of Christ*...

(7) 2 Thess. 1:11
...that our God may make you worthy of his call, and may fulfill every good resolve and *work of faith* by his power...

(8) 1 John 3:8
The reason the Son of God appeared was to destroy *the works of the devil.*

B. Analyzing "love of..."

In each of the following passages the phrase "love of" occurs. Reword the passage so as to give the meaning clearly. You may need to study the context.

Example: Rom. 8:35

Who shall separate us from *the love of Christ?*

Answer: Who shall separate us from the love which Christ has for us?

(1) Luke 11:42

But woe to you Pharisees! for you...neglect justice and *the love of God...*

(2) John 5:42

But I know that you have not *the love of God* within you.

(3) Rom. 5:5

...and hope does not disappoint us, because *God's love* has been poured into our hearts through the Holy Spirit...

(4) Rom. 15:30

I appeal to you, brethren, by our Lord Jesus Christ and by *the love of the Spirit...*

(5) 2 Cor. 5:14

For *the love of Christ* controls us...

(6) Eph. 3:19

...to know *the love of Christ* which surpasses knowledge...

(7) 1 John 5:3

...for this is *the love of God...*

(8) 2 Cor. 13:14

The grace of the Lord Jesus Christ and the *love of God...*

C. Identifying the underlying meaning of identical grammatical structures

In each of the following, two or three verses are cited in which the same grammatical construction is used but the underlying meaning is distinct. Reword as many of the examples in each set as necessary to show the difference in meaning.

Example: Luke 18:27

The things which are impossible *with men* are possible with God. (KJV)

Answer: Things which men are not able to do, God is able to do.

Example: 2 Pet. 3:8

With the Lord one day is as a thousand years, and a thousand years as one day.

Answer: The Lord has determined when he will do something (judge ungodly people), whether he will do it right away or wait a long time to do it.

(1) Acts 21:21

...they have been told...that you teach all the Jews who are *among the Gentiles* to forsake Moses...

Rom. 2:24

The name of God is blasphemed *among the Gentiles* because of you.

Acts 15:12
they related what signs and wonders God had done through them *among the Gentiles.*

(2) Philem. 13
I would have been glad to keep him *with me.*

Matt 26:23
He who has dipped his hand in the dish *with me...*

(3) Luke 1:59
And *on the eighth day* they came to circumcise the child...

Luke 13:7
...I have come seeking fruit *on this fig tree...*

(4) Matt. 14:26
But when the disciples saw him walking *on the sea,* they were terrified....

Matt. 27:25
And all the people answered, "His blood be *on us and on our children!"*

Acts 4:5
On the morrow their rulers and elders and scribes were gathered together in Jerusalem...

D. Types of adjustments

In producing idiomatic translations, often there are adjustments made in form which still convey the meaning of the original. Some of those adjustments may be:

- a. A grammatical shift, using a different phrasal or clausal construction but basically the same parts of speech (e.g., changing a passive verb into an active one);
- b. Use of a phrase to convey what one word conveys in the original, or vice versa;
- c. Changing the order of elements within a phrase or clause;
- d. Changing the parts of speech used (e.g., changing a noun into a verb or a full clause); and
- e. Replacing an idiom or figure of speech in the original with a nonidiomatic or nonfigurative expression in the translation.

In the following passages there is a word-for-word translation from *The Interlinear Greek-English New Testament* (Marshall 1960) and another English translation. Indicate which of the above best describes the type of adjustment the italicized portion has made, using the appropriate letter from the list above. In some cases more than one type of adjustment may apply.

Example: Luke 9:44
        Original: Lay ye in the ears your the saying these
        Translation: *Don't forget* what I am about to tell you! (GNB)
Answer: e

(1) Matt. 5:1–2
        Original: And seeing the crowds he went up into the mountain and sitting him approached to him the disciples of him and opening the mouth of him he taught them...
        Translation: Now when he saw the crowds, he went up on a mountainside and sat down. His disciples came to him and, *he began* to teach them... (NIV)

(2)   Acts 3:19
      Original: turn again for the to-be-wiped-away your sins
      Translation: turn to God, so that *he will wipe away* your sins... (TEV)

(3)   Acts 4:12
      Original: There is not in another any salvation
      Translation: No one else who *can save us.* (Beck)

(4)   Acts 4:23
      Original: And being-released...
      Translation: *As soon as they were set free...* (TEV)

(5)   Acts 4:30
      Original: by the hand of you stretching for cures
      Translation: send *your healing power...* (LB)

(6)   Acts 4:31
      Original: was shaken the place in which they assembled
      Translation: ...the building where they were meeting *shook...* (LB)

(7)   Acts 5:28
      Original: you intend to bring on us the blood of this man
      Translation: ...you want to *make us responsible for* his *death!* (GNB)

(8)   Acts 5:31
      Original: to give repentance to Israel and forgiveness of sins
      Translation: to give to the people of Israel *the opportunity to* repent and have their sins *forgiven.* (GNB)

(9)   Rom. 7:19
      Original: For not what I wish I do good, but what I wish not evil this I practice.
      Translation: *For I do not do the good I want,* but the evil I do not want is what I do. (RSV)

(10) Col. 4:7
      Original: The things about me all will make known to you Tychicus the beloved brother...
      Translation: *Tychicus,* our much beloved brother, *will tell you* how I am getting along. (LB)

Chapter 2
Kinds of Translations

Additional Reading:
    Beekman 1966:178–98.
    Beekman and Callow 1974: Chapters 1 and 2.
    Glassman 1981.

A. Comparing literal and idiomatic translation

Compare each of the following pairs of translations. For each pair state which one is more literal, and which one is more idiomatic. (The title of the version being quoted is not given, as it might influence the answer.)

Example: Matt. 3:15
     a. ...thus it becometh us to fulfill all righteousness.
     b. ...we do well to conform in this way with all that God requires.
Answer: a is more literal, b is more idiomatic: "becometh us" and "fulfill righteousness" are not natural in present day English.

(1)   Matt. 3:8
     a. Bear fruit that befits repentance...
     b. Do the things that will show that you have turned from your sins.

(2)   Rom. 12:17
     a. If someone does evil to you, do not pay him back with evil.
       Try to do what all men consider to be good.
     b. Repay no one evil for evil, but take thought for what is noble in the sight of all.

(3)   1 Cor. 15:20
     a. ...He has become the very first to rise of all who sleep the sleep of death.
     b. Christ has been raised from the dead, the first fruits of those who have fallen asleep.

(4)   Titus 2:13
     a. looking forward to that wonderful time we've been expecting, when his glory shall be seen—the glory of our great God and Savior Jesus Christ.
     b. looking for the blessed hope and the appearing of the glory of our great God and Savior, Christ Jesus.

(5)   James 3:13
     a. Who is wise and understanding among you? By his good life let him show his works in the meekness of wisdom.
     b. If there are any wise or learned men among you, let them show it by their good lives, with humility and wisdom in their actions.

B. Comparing various versions

In each of the following, several versions are quoted. Classify the kind of translation for each. Where on the continuum from very literal to unduly free does each translation fall? Use the following classifications:

    L   literal
    M   modified literal
    I   idiomatic
    UF   unduly free

(The passage is first quoted from the glossary in Marshall's *Interlinear Greek-English New Testament*. The titles of the versions which follow are not given lest this information influence the answer.)

Example: 1 Cor. 8:1 Now about the idolatrous sacrifices...
    a. Now about working on Sunday...
    b. Now concerning food offered to idols...
    c. Next is your question about eating food that has been sacrificed to idols...
    d. Now about the food that has been sacrificed to idols...

Answer: a. UF
    b. L
    c. I
    d. M

(1) Luke 20:47 who devour the houses of the widows
    a. who swallow the property of widows
    b. they are planning schemes to cheat widows out of their property
    c. who devour widows' houses
    d. who take advantage of widows and rob them of their homes

(2) Acts 7:38 This is the one having been in the church in the desert with the angel speaking to him in the Mount Sinai and with the fathers of us, who received oracles living to give to you.
    a. He it was who, when they were assembled there in the desert, conversed with the angel who spoke to him on Mount Sinai, and with our forefathers; he received the living utterances of God, to pass on to us.
    b. How true this proved to be, for in the wilderness, Moses was the go-between—the mediator between the people of Israel and the Angel who gave them the Law of God—the Living Word—on Mount Sinai.
    c. He is the one who was with the people of Israel assembled in the desert; he was there with our ancestors and with the angel who spoke to him on Mount Sinai; he received God's living messages to pass on to us.
    d. This is the man who was with the congregation in the wilderness and who was the go-between between the angel who spoke to him on mount Sinai and our fathers. He also received the living Word of God to be handed down to us.
    e. This is he, that was in the church in the wilderness with the angel which spake to him in the mount Sina, and with our fathers: who received the lively oracles to give unto us.

(3)   Rom. 8:12 So then, brothers, debtors we are, not to the flesh according to flesh to live.

    a. So, brothers, we are under obligation, but not our lower nature to live by the standard set by it... (Williams)

    b. ...my brothers, we owe a duty—but it is not to the flesh! It is not to live by the flesh. (Moffatt)

    c. So, dear brothers, you have no obligations whatever to your old sinful nature to do what it begs you to do.

    d. It follows, my friends, that our lower nature has no claim upon us; we are not obliged to live on that level.

    e. Therefore, brothers, we are debtors—but not to the flesh, to live after the flesh.

(4)   1 Cor. 10:32 Without offense both to Jews be ye and to Greeks and to the church of God.

    a. Give no offense to Jews or to Greeks or to the church of God.

    b. So don't be a stumbling block to anyone, whether they are Jews or Gentiles or Christians.

    c. Set a good example for both whites and Negroes—for God's whole church.

C. Identifying naturalness

A faithful translation must communicate the same meaning as the original. At the same time it must communicate clearly. Which of the two passages, a or b, seems to you to communicate more clearly? What differences between the passages make one easier to understand than the other?

(1)   Luke 7:44

    a. I entered your house, you gave me no water for my feet... (RSV)

    b. I came into your house but you provided no water to wash my feet. (JBP)

(2)   Luke 18:13

    a. But the tax collector, standing far off, would not even lift up his eyes to heaven, but beat his breast, saying, "God, be merciful to me a sinner!" (RSV)

    b. But the corrupt tax collector stood at a distance and dared not even lift his eyes to heaven as he prayed, but beat upon his chest in sorrow, exclaiming, "God, be merciful to me, a sinner." (LB)

(3)   Mark 12:14

    a. Tell us, is it against our Law to pay taxes to the Roman Emperor? Should we pay them, or not? (TEV)

    b. Is it right to pay taxes to Caesar or not? (Moffatt)

(4)   Mark 1:2

    a. It began as the prophet Isaiah had written: "'Here is my messenger,' says God; 'I will send him ahead of you to open the way for you.'" (TEV)

    b. As it is written in Isaiah the Prophet, 'See I am sending my messenger before thy face, who will prepare thy way.' (Weymouth)

(5)   1 Cor. 10:1

    a. Our fathers...all passed through the sea. (RSV)

    b. Our ancestors...all of them passed through the Red Sea. (NEB)

    c. Our ancestors who followed Moses...all passed safely through the Red Sea. (TEV)

(6) Luke 12:5
    a. I will show you whom to fear: fear God who, after killing, has the authority to throw into hell. (TEV)
    b. But I will warn you whom to fear: fear him who, after he has killed, has power to cast into hell. (RSV)

(7) Matt. 22:32
    a. " 'I am the God of Abraham, and the God of Isaac, and the God of Jacob?' He is not God of the dead, but of the living." (RSV)
    b. " 'I am the God of Abraham, and I am the God of Isaac, and I am the God of Jacob.' Since God is now the God of those ancestors of ours, it means that they are not just dead bodies, they are still alive." (Aguaruna back-translation)

(8) Rom. 3:27
    a. So what becomes of our boasts? There is no room for them. What sort of law excludes them? The sort of law that tells us what to do? On the contrary, it is the law of faith, since, as we see it, a man is justified by faith and not by doing something the Law tells him to do. (JR)
    b. Where then is there room for boasting? It is shut out. On what principle? On that of merit? No, but on the principle of faith. For we deem that a man is accounted righteous by faith, apart from fulfillment of the law. (Weymouth)

(9) Luke 17:26
    a. As it was in the days of Noah, so will it be in the days of the Son of Man. (RSV)
    b. In the time of the coming of the Son of Man, life will be as it was in the days of Noah. (JBP)

(10) Rom. 2:4
    a. Do you think so little of the riches of God's kindness, forbearance, patience, not conscious that His kindness is meant to lead you to repentance? (Williams)
    b. Don't you realize how patient he is being with you? Or don't you care? Can't you see that he has been waiting all this time without punishing you, to give you time to turn from your sin? His kindness is meant to lead you to repentance. (LB)

D. Historical fidelity

In the following drills the RSV is compared with the Koinonia "Cotton Patch" version, which contains violations of historical fidelity (sometimes called anachronisms). List the words which involve historical inaccuracies in the b part of each example.

Example: 1 Cor. 1:2
    a. To the church of God which is at Corinth, to those sanctified in Christ Jesus.
    b. To God's people in Atlanta—those whom Jesus Christ has set apart by calling them together.

Answer: Atlanta—violates the historical fact that Paul wrote to the people in Corinth.

(1) 1 Cor. 1:13
    a. Is Christ divided? Was Paul crucified for you? Or were you baptized in the name of Paul?
    b. Tell me this, since when did Christ get so split up? And was Paul lynched for you? Or were you given Paul's name when you were initiated?

(2) 1 Cor. 1:19

    a. For it is written, "I will destroy the wisdom of the wise, and the cleverness of the clever I will thwart."

    b. It's just like the Scripture says, "I will tear to bits the dissertations of the Ph.D.; I will pull the rug from under those who have all the answers."

(3) 1 Cor. 3:2

    a. I fed you with milk, not solid food; for you were not ready for it; and even yet you are not ready.

    b. I gave you a bottle, not solid food. That's all you could take. And you still don't seem to be doing much better.

(4) 1 Cor. 8:5–6

    a. For although there may be so-called gods in heaven or on earth—as indeed there are many "gods" and many "lords"—yet for us there is one God, the Father, from whom are all things and for whom we exist...

    b. Even though there are also many special days on both Catholic and Protestant calendars, such as those to saints and special events, still for us God alone is supreme, our Father, the source of all things; we are his.

(5) 1 Cor. 16:1

    a. Now concerning the contribution for the saints: as I directed the churches of Galatia, so you also are to do.

    b. Now a few words about that fund for sharing with the church members. I'd like for you all to follow the same plan I recommended to the Alabama churches.

E. Accuracy of meaning

Following the quotations from RSV, a proposed translation is given for each verse below. These are not published translations but made up to illustrate this topic. Check each verse carefully to see if it has (1) omitted information, (2) added information, or (3) different information. List the type of inaccuracy which is illustrated, and then explain specifically what is wrong. Note that there may be more than one of these three illustrated in a given example.

Example: Acts 2:37

    a. Now when they heard this they were cut to the heart, and said to Peter and the rest of the apostles, "Brethren, what shall we do?"

    b. When the people heard this, they were deeply troubled, and they said to Peter, "What shall we do, brothers?"

Answer: omitted information—"rest of the apostles" is not included.

(1) John 17:9

    a. I am praying for them; I am not praying for the world but for those whom thou has given me, for they are thine.

    b. I am praying for those who are mine. I'm not praying for the other people in the world. I'm just praying for those who are mine, for they are thine.

(2) Acts 1:12

    a. Then they returned to Jerusalem from the mount called Olivet, which is near Jerusalem, a sabbath day's journey away.

    b. They left the mount called Olivet and returned to Jerusalem which was nearby, the distance they were permitted to walk by the Jewish law.

(3) Acts 5:7
   a. After an interval of about three hours his wife came in, not knowing what had happened.
   b. Three hours after they carried Ananias out his wife came running in. She didn't know that her husband had died.

(4) Acts 6:10
   a. But they could not withstand the wisdom and the Spirit with which he spoke.
   b. Stephen spoke with the power of the Holy Spirit and the people were amazed at what he said.

(5) Acts 8:36
   a. And as they went along the road they came to some water, and the eunuch said, "See, here is water! What is to prevent my being baptized?"
   b. When Philip finished speaking, and the chariot came along the road to some water, the eunuch said, "Look, there is some water here! Could I be baptized now?"

F. Comparing versions

In each of the following, there is given (a) the NASB translation of that portion, and (b) the English in a proposed translation into a certain receptor language. Consider each carefully to decide whether the (b) rendering illustrates omitted information, added/extraneous information, or different information.

Example: Mark 2:18
   a. Now John's disciples and the Pharisees were fasting...
   b. Well, there were some companions of John who used to baptize people. And the Pharisees' companions were not eating because like that was their custom. You see, two days each week they did not eat, because they were thinking God would do his goodness to them for it. But they were just adding things to God's word.

Answer: The words "who used to baptize people" are not added because they identify which John is meant. The words "because like that was their custom" are not added because one needs to clarify what fasting was for. The words "two days each week they did not eat" are interesting background information, but probably extraneous information and unnecessary. The words "because they were thinking God would do his goodness to them for it" are not extraneous, but needed to show the implied purpose of fasting, which is unknown in the receptor culture. However, the words "but they were just adding things to God's word" are not necessary and should be considered extraneous/added information.

(1) Gal. 1:1
   a. Paul, an apostle, (not sent from men nor through the agency of man, but through Jesus Christ, and God the Father, who raised him from the dead)...
   b. From Paul, a delegate, not from any human organization nor appointed by any human being, but by Jesus himself and by the Father-God who raised him from the dead three days after he was crucified.

(2) Gal. 1:2
   a. ...and all the brethren who are with me, to the churches of Galatia...
   b. ...and from all the brothers here with me; to the churches of the Georgia Convention.

(3) Gal. 1:3
   a. Grace to you and peace from God our Father, and the Lord Jesus Christ...
   b. Warm greetings to you and peace from our Father-God and from the Lord Jesus Christ.

(4) Gal. 1:4
   a. ...who gave himself for our sins, that he might deliver us out of this present evil age, according to the will of our God and Father...
   b. ...who willingly got into our sinful mess with us to pull us out of this present-day wickedness. Such was the eternal intent of our Father-God

(5) Gal. 1:5
   a. ...to whom be the glory forevermore. Amen.
   b. ...to whom the credit is due throughout all ages.

(6) Gal. 2:1
   a. Then after an interval of fourteen years I went up again to Jerusalem with Barnabas taking Titus along also. It was because of a revelation that I went up...
   b. Fourteen years later, because of an insight I had, I went again to Atlanta with Barnabas, taking Titus with me.

(7) Gal. 2:2
   a. ...I submitted to them the gospel which I preach among the Gentiles, but I did so in private to those who were of reputation, for fear that I might be running, or had run, in vain.
   b. There I laid before them the message which I preach among Blacks. (I did this privately before the executive committee, so that what I was doing might not be wasted.)

(8) Gal. 2:3
   a. ...but not even Titus who was with me, though he was a Greek, was compelled to be circumcised.
   b. But not even my right-hand man Titus, the Greek who was with me, was compelled to submit to their Southern ritual of circumcision which they thought necessary to salvation.

G. Comparing versions

Compare the following translations of 1 Cor. 1:17–18. Which translation do you feel expresses the accurate meaning most clearly? In light of the principles of accurate, clear, and natural, do you think any of the translations given are not completely accurate, clear, or natural (English)? State your reasons.

(1) For Christ sent me not to baptize, but to preach the gospel: not with wisdom of words, lest the cross of Christ should be made of none effect. For the preaching of the cross is to them that perish, foolishness; but unto us which are saved, it is the power of God. (KJV)

(2) For Christ did not send me to baptize but to preach the gospel, and not with eloquent wisdom, lest the cross of Christ be emptied of its power. For the word of the cross is folly to those who are perishing, but to us who are being saved it is the power of God. (RSV)

(3) For Christ did not send me primarily to baptise, but to proclaim the gospel. And I have not done this by the persuasiveness of clever words, for I have no desire to rob the cross of its power. The preaching of the cross is, I know, nonsense to those who are involved in this dying world, but to us who are being saved from that death it is nothing less than the power of God. (JBP)

(4)   For Christ didn't send me to baptize, but to preach the Gospel; and even my preaching sounds poor, for I do not fill my sermons with profound words and high sounding ideas, for fear of diluting the mighty power there is in the simple message of the cross of Christ. I know very well how foolish it sounds to those who are lost, when they hear that Jesus died to save them. But we who are saved recognize this message as the very power of God. (LB)

(5)   Christ did not send me to baptize. He sent me to tell the Good News, and to tell it without using the language of men's wisdom, to keep Christ's death on the cross from being robbed of its power. For the message about Christ's death on the cross is nonsense to those who are being lost; but for us who are being saved, it is God's power. (TEV)

Chapter 3
The Semantic Structure of Language

Additional Reading:
   Beekman and Callow 1974:267–74.

A. Semantic classes

Each italicized word in the examples below represents skewing between the semantics and the grammar. Identify the grammatical class and the semantic class for each. Then rewrite the given phrase or clause using grammatical forms which eliminate the skewing.

Example: Isa. 1:21
   Righteousness used to dwell in her...
Answer: *Righteousness* is a noun grammatically but an attribute (or quality) semantically. It could be rephrased as "Righteous people used to live there," or "People there used to live righteously."

(1)   Isa. 1:4 ...a people loaded with *guilt*...

(2)   Isa. 1:4 ...a brood of *evildoers*...

(3)   Isa. 1:5 ...you persist in *rebellion*...

(4)   Isa. 1:6 There is no *soundness*...

(5)   Isa. 1:8 ...like a city under *siege.*

(6)   Isa. 1:11 ...the *multitude* of your *sacrifices*...

(7)   Isa. 1:13 Stop bringing *meaningless offerings!*

(8)   Isa. 1:13 Your incense is *detestable* to me.

(9)   Isa. 1:23 Your *rulers* are *rebels, companions* of *thieves*...

(10)   Isa. 1:23 ...they all love *bribes*...

B. Skewing between semantics and grammar, examples from the Psalms

Each of the following has at least one example of skewing between the deep and surface structure. Words which represent this skewing are italicized. Rewrite the clause, eliminating the skewing.

Example: *Forgiveness* is important.
Answer: It is important to forgive (or, it is important that we forgive people). ["Forgiveness" is grammatically a noun, but semantically an Event.]

(1)   Ps. 1:2
      ...his *delight* is in the law of the Lord... (NIV)

(2)   Ps. 5:7
      ...the abundance of thy steadfast *love*... (KJV)

(3)   Ps. 5:9
      ...there is no *truth* in their mouth...

(4)   Ps. 6:5
       ...in *death* there is no *remembrance* of thee... (KJV)

(5)   Ps. 7:8
       ...judge me, O Lord, according to my *righteousness*...

(6)   Ps. 7:16
       ...on his own pate his *violence* descends...

(7)   Ps. 8:4
       ...what is man that thou *art mindful* of him?

(8)   Ps. 10:7
       His mouth is *filled with cursing and deceit and oppression*...

(9)   Ps. 16:11
       ...in thy presence there is *fullness of joy*...

(10)   Ps. 18:1
       I love thee, O Lord, my *strength.*

C. Skewing between semantics and grammar, examples from Romans

The passages cited from each of the following verses (NIV) have at least one example of skewing between major classes of the semantics and the grammar (see chart on page 29 of Larson 1984). List the word or words that exemplify this type of skewing. Then rewrite these clauses to eliminate the skewing.

Example: Rom. 12:12
        Be...faithful in prayer.
Answer: "prayer" illustrates skewing because it is a noun representing an Event. *Pray faithfully.*

(1)   Rom. 13:4
       ...to bring punishment on the wrongdoer.

(2)   Rom. 13:10
       Love is the fulfillment of the law.

(3)   Rom. 14:19
       Do what leads to peace and to mutual edification.

(4)   Rom. 15:4
       Through...the encouragement of the Scriptures we might have hope.

(5)   Rom. 15:13
       May the God of hope fill you with all joy...

(6)   Rom. 15:14
       I myself am convinced...that you yourselves are full of goodness, complete in knowledge.

(7)   Rom. 16:17
       Watch out for those who cause divisions and put obstacles in your way that are contrary to the teaching you have learned.

(8)   Rom. 16:18
       By smooth talk and flattery they deceive...naive people.

(9)   Rom. 16:24
       May the grace of our Lord Jesus Christ be with all of you. (JB)

(10)   Rom. 16:26
       The mystery...is now disclosed and through the prophetic writings is made known to all
       nations, according to the command of the eternal God, to bring about the obedience of faith...
       (RSV)

D. Eliminating skewing between semantic and grammatical classes

In each of the following, determine the semantic class or classes of the italicized words. Then
rewrite the portion of the verse given, using a grammatical part of speech that corresponds to the
semantic class(es) you have given to each italicized word. Use an active form of the verb for Events.

Example: Luke 2:47
               ...all who heard him were amazed at his *understanding* and his *answers.*
Answer: "Understanding" and "answers" are Events semantically. Rewrite: All who heard him
               were amazed because he understood and answered well.

(1)   John 4:22
       ...for *salvation* is from the Jews.

(2)   John 8:51
       ...he will never see *death.*

(3)   Acts 8:32
       As a sheep led to the *slaughter...*

(4)   Acts 16:26
       ...suddenly there was a great *earthquake...*

(5)   Rom. 3:5
       But if our *wickedness* serves to show the *justice* of God, what shall we say? That God is
       unjust to inflict *wrath* on us?

(6)   Rom. 5:10
       ...reconciled to God by the *death* of his Son...

(7)   2 Cor. 7:10
       ...godly *grief* produces a *repentance* that leads to *salvation* and brings no *regret...*

(8)   2 Cor. 9:15
       Thanks be to God for his *inexpressible gift!*

(9)   Col. 3:12
       ...put on a heart of...*kindness, humility, gentleness* and *patience...* (NASB)

(10)   2 Thess. 1:11
       ...fulfil every good *resolve* and *work* of *faith* by his power...

Chapter 4
Implicit Meaning

Additional Reading:
   Beekman and Callow 1974: Chapter 3.
   Larson 1969:15–20.
   Nida 1964:227–29.

A. Ellipsis

Though ellipsis occurs in all languages, the particular structures which permit such "omitted" words are by no means identical from language to language. Accordingly, in an expression almost obligatory elliptical in one language, an ellipsis may not be permitted in another. Hence, a clause such as "he is greater than I" may require expansion into "he is greater than I am great." (Nida 1964:227)

For many passages in which ellipses must be filled out in the translation the parallelism of the structure supplies the information needed to fill out the ellipses, as in the illustration given above. In the following there are similar ellipses which often must be filled out. Rewrite filling out the elliptical expression, after looking at the context.

Example: Matt. 26:5
   But they said, "Not during the feast, lest there be a tumult among the people."
Answer: But they said, "Let's not arrest him during the feast, lest there be a tumult among the people."

(1)   Mark 6:38
   And he said to them, "How many loaves have you? Go and see." And when they had found out, they said, "Five, and two fish."

(2)   Mark 12:27
   He is not the God of the dead, but of the living...

(3)   John 1:21
   And they asked him, "What then? Are you Elijah?" He said, "I am not."

(4)   John 2:10
   ...and said to him, "Every man serves the good wine first; and when men have drunk freely, then the poor wine..."

(5)   John 4:12
   ...Jacob, who gave us the well, and drank from it himself, and his sons, and his cattle...

(6)   John 7:46
   "No man ever spoke like this man!"

(7)   1 Cor. 2:8
   None of the rulers of this age understood this; for if they had, they would not have crucified the Lord of glory.

(8)   1 Cor. 7:35
   I say this...not to lay any restraint upon you, but to promote good order.

B. Linguistically obligatory additions in the receptor language

Often the language into which one is translating demands that information be made explicit to avoid wrong meanings, but there is not an easy parallelism from which to find what must be added. However, the context of the sentence itself or of the entire passage may give the information. Some verbs require that an object be made explicit in order to avoid wrong meaning, others require a location, etc. In each of the following the passage is given and then a note as to what is required by the receptor language. What addition would you make to fulfill this requirement? Base your answer on the context. Rewrite the passage with the needed addition.

Example: Acts 5:16

The people also gathered...bringing the sick and those afflicted with unclean spirits, and they were all healed. (In Cuicateco, "healed" can be used only to talk about "sickness," not to talk about "casting out evil spirits." To be sure that these people were helped as well, an obligatory addition was made.)

Answer: The people also gathered...bringing the sick and those afflicted with unclean spirits, and they were all healed *and the evil spirits left them.*

(1)   Acts 16:11–12

...we made a direct voyage to Samothrace, and the following day to Neapolis, and from there to Philippi... (In a language that never has a clause consisting of only time and location what verb would you add in the last two clauses?)

(2)   Matt. 26:6

...in the house of Simon the leper...(Without an addition this would mean that Simon was not yet cured of leprosy. What modification would you add to "leper"?)

(3)   John 4:20

Our fathers worshipped on this mountain; and you say that Jerusalem is the place where men ought to worship. (The verb "worship" requires an object.)

(4)   Mark 1:21

And they went into Capernaum; and immediately on the sabbath he entered the synagogue... (If translated literally it means that the disciples did not go to the synagogue.)

(5)   1 Cor. 7:26

I think that in view of the present distress, it is well for a person to remain as he is. ("Remain" when used by itself about people can only mean to stay in one place. What addition is needed to give the right meaning to "remain"?)

(6)   Mark 8:20

"And the seven for the four thousand, how many baskets full of broken pieces did you take up?" (Numbers that are attributives occur only as modifiers. Add the nouns that they modify.)

C. Implied identification of a referent

Sometimes a reference is made to some thing, event, attribute, or relation implicitly, without actually stating in the source language what is being referred to. However, for clarity in the receptor language it may be necessary to make this information explicit. For each of the following tell what information is implied by the italicized word or phrase.

Example: Matt. 4:5

...the devil took Him to the *holy city*...

Answer: the holy city, *Jerusalem*

(1) John 1:21
And they asked him, "What then? Are you Elijah?" He said, "I am not." "Are you the *prophet?*" And he answered, "No."

(2) Matt. 26:14
Then one of the *twelve,* who was called Judas...

(3) Matt. 16:4
...no sign shall be given to it except the sign of *Jonah.*"

(4) Acts 2:14
But Peter, standing with the *eleven,* lifted up his voice and addressed them, "Men of *Judea* and all who dwell in *Jerusalem,* let this be known to you..."

(5) James 5:11
You have heard of the steadfastness of *Job,* and you have seen...

D. Implied contextual information

In each of the following some information is left implicit which may need to be made explicit in some languages. Supply the information by rewriting the text to make it explicit. After each reference the implied information to be supplied is identified.

(1) Matt. 4:4 (The word "written" requires that the place be made explicit.)
But he answered, "It is *written,* 'Man shall not live by bread alone...' "

(2) Matt. 6:29
...yet I tell you, even Solomon in all his glory was not arrayed like one of *these.*

(3) Matt. 15:21 (person accompanying Jesus, or it may imply he went alone)
...Jesus went away...

(4) Matt. 16:22 (What is he rebuking him about?)
And Peter took him and began to *rebuke* him...

(5) Matt. 27:46 (language source)
...Jesus cried with a loud voice, "Eli, Eli, lama sabachthani?" that is, "My God, my God, why..."

(6) Mark 1:10 (person accompanying Jesus)
...Jesus came up out of the water... (TEV)

(7) Mark 5:21 (person accompanying Jesus)
...Jesus had crossed again in the boat...

(8) Mark 10:17 (person referred to)
And as *he* was setting out on his journey, a man ran up and knelt before *him,* and asked *him...*

(9) Mark 14:55 ("Found" requires an object more explicit than "none.")
...the whole council sought witness against Jesus to put him to death; but they found none.

(10) Luke 2:24 (person who is to provide the sacrifice and person who is to offer the sacrifice)
...and to offer a sacrifice according to what is said in the law of the Lord, "a pair of turtledoves, or two young pigeons."

(11)   Acts 7:17 ("Promise" needs an explicit content of what was promised.)
       But as the time of the *promise* drew near, which God had granted to Abraham...

(12)   Acts 7:35–36 ("Led out" needs a location, that is, out of where?)
       "This Moses whom they refused...He led them out, having performed wonders and signs in
       Egypt..."

E. Implied cultural information

Often a biblical writer counted on the readers being able to supply some information from their culture, their background and experiences, their knowledge of Scriptures, or of the world in general, to provide a correct comprehension of what he wished to communicate. In many instances speakers of a different receptor language will not be able to supply some of that information, or they may, from their experiences and culture, sometimes supply information which is very different from what the original author expected his readers to supply. In such cases the translators may have to supply, in some way or other, the correct information to make the intended meaning of the passage clear.

Example: Matt. 27:27
               Then the soldiers of the governor took Jesus into the *praetorium,* and they gathered the
               whole *battalion* before him.
Answer: governor's palace, called the praetorium
               battalion of soldiers (large group of soldiers)

(1)   Acts 1:12
       Then they returned to Jerusalem from the mount called Olivet, which is near Jerusalem, *a
       sabbath day's journey away...*

(2)   Acts 10:9
       The next day, as they were on their journey and coming near the city, Peter went up on the
       housetop to pray, about the *sixth hour.*

(3)   Acts 11:8
       But I said, 'No, Lord; for nothing *common or unclean* has ever entered my mouth.'

(4)   Acts 11:28
       ...and this took place *in the days of Claudius.*

(5)   Acts 14:13
       And the priest of Zeus...*brought oxen and garlands* to the gates and wanted to offer sacrifice
       with the people.

F. Old Testament quotations

The information given in the introduction of an Old Testament quotation may need to be expanded to make explicit the writer, speaker, or persons spoken to in order to avoid wrong meaning or ambiguities that are confusing to the reader. For example, Mark 1:2 says, "As it is written in Isaiah the prophet, 'Behold, I send my messenger...' " Unless the information that God is the speaker is added, the impression may be left that Isaiah himself is sending the messenger. And so the verse might be translated, "The prophet Isaiah wrote what God said, 'Behold, I send my messenger...' "

For each of the following quotations used in the New Testament the reference in the Old Testament is also given. Study each passage to determine if information concerning the speaker, writer, or persons spoken to or about needs to be added to avoid potential wrong meaning. Check the Old Testament reference in order to supply this information where needed. Rewrite only the introduction to those verses in which you see a possible need for making explicit one or more of these participants.

Example: Matt. 4:4

But he answered, "It is written, 'Man shall not live by bread alone'." (Deut. 8:3)

Answer: But he answered, "Moses wrote that God said, 'Man shall not live by bread alone'."

(1)   Matt. 2:23

...that what was spoken through the prophets might be fulfilled, "He shall be called a Nazarene."

(2)   Matt. 5:21

You have heard that it was said to the men of old, "You shall not kill..." (Exod. 20:13)

(3)   Matt. 5:31

...saying; "It was also said, 'Whoever divorces his wife, let him give her a certificate of divorce.'..." (Deut. 24:1)

(4)   Matt. 7:23

And then I will declare to them, "I never knew you; depart from me, you evildoers." (Ps. 6:8)

(5)   Matt. 12:7

And if you had known what this means, "I desire mercy, and not sacrifice..." (Hos. 6:6)

(6)   Matt. 12:17–18

This was to fulfil what was spoken by the prophet Isaiah: "Behold, my servant whom I have chosen,...I will put my spirit upon him..." (Isa. 42:1–3)

(7)   Matt. 15:7

You hypocrites! Well did Isaiah prophesy of you, when he said: "This people honors me with their lips..." (Isa. 29:13)

(8)   Matt. 21:4–5

This took place to fulfil what was spoken by the prophet, saying, "Tell the daughter of Zion..." (Isa. 62:11)

(9)   Matt. 21:16

And Jesus said to them, "Yes, have you never read, 'Out of the mouth of babes and sucklings thou hast brought perfect praise'?" (Ps. 8:2)

(10) Matt. 26:31

Then Jesus said to them, "You will all fall away because of me this night; for it is written, 'I will strike the shepherd, and the sheep of the flock will be scattered'." (Zech. 13:7)

G. Review

The following is a literal word-for-word back-translation of Acts 16:11–15 in a Nigerian language. Compare this back translation carefully with the Revised Standard Version of this passage. List any information that was implicit in the RSV but which has been made explicit in the translation. Explain in each instance why you think the information has been made explicit.

[11]We got-into boat, got-up left from Troas, went straight traveled crossed the big-river, until we came reached to Samothrace. When next-day came, we again traveled, came landed at Neapolis. [12]We got-up left from Neapolis, we walked by land, came reached to Philippi, which is the foremost-town in the region of Macedonia. It is also the place where the people of Rome made a settlement. We stayed in that town for a few days. [13]It came reached to the Resting-day, we went outside the town, walked to river-side-bank, because we thought that the Jews would come gather in that place pray. When we reached there we sat seat there, we spoke word with some women who had come gathered there. [14]In the midst of those women who listened to our words, a certain person was there who was called Lydia, who was a person who was-habitually-selling red-cloth. That woman, she-came from Thyatira, she-was-habitually-worshipping God. God opened her heart so that she should repair ear listen to words of Paul. [15]She and all her people, they came baptized water. Then she called us to her house, she said thus, "If you think that I place the Lord Jesus as true (i.e., believe truly in the Lord Jesus), come stay at my house." She persuaded us that we should go there.

Acts 16:11–15 RSV

[11]Setting sail therefore from Troas, we made a direct voyage to Samothrace, and the following day to Neapolis, [12]and from there to Philippi, which is the leading city of the district of Macedonia, and a Roman colony. We remained in this city some days; [13]and on the sabbath day we went outside the gate to the riverside, where we supposed there was a place of prayer; and we sat down and spoke to the women who had come together. [14]One who heard us was a woman named Lydia, from the city of Thyatira, a seller of purple goods, who was a worshiper of God. The Lord opened her heart to give heed to what was said by Paul. [15]And when she was baptized, with her household, she besought us, saying, "If you have judged me to be faithful to the Lord, come to my house and stay." And she prevailed upon us.

Chapter 5
Steps in a Translation Project

Additional Reading:
Barnwell 1974: Chapter 24.
Barnwell 1983:10–19.
Larson 1967a:17–18.
Larson 1967b:19–20.

There are no exercises in addition to the ones in the textbook for this chapter.

II. The Lexicon

Chapter 6
Words as "Bundles" of Meaning

Additional Reading:
   Barnwell 1974: Chapter 3.
   Beekman and Callow 1974: Chapter 4.

A. Identifying the semantic class of a word

Words are surface structure lexical forms which represent four main semantic classes: Things, Events, Attributes, and Relations. Consider the italicized words as they are used in the following examples. To which class or classes does each of the italicized words belong semantically? Some may include more than one class, and some may include an implied semantic class.

Example: Rom. 3:24
   ...*through* the *redemption* which is in *Christ Jesus*...
Answer: "through" is a Relation
   "redemption" is an Event (redeem) but there are also implied Things
   (God as agent, and people as the goal). The meaning is "God redeems people," i.e., it
   contains an Event and two Things, T-E-T.

(1)   Matt. 3:8
      Bear fruit that befits *repentance*...

(2)   Matt. 5:7
      Blessed are the *merciful,* for they shall obtain *mercy.*

(3)   Mark 12:9
      He will come and destroy the *tenants* and give the vineyard to *others.*

(4)   Mark 12:25
      For when they arise from the *dead,* they neither marry nor are given in *marriage*...

(5)   John 11:4
      This *illness* is not unto *death;* it is for the *glory* of God.

(6)   Acts 9:12
      ...*so that* he might regain his *sight.*

(7)   Acts 13:38
      ...through this man *forgiveness* of sins is proclaimed to *you*...

(8)   Rom. 2:4
      Do you not know that God's *kindness* is meant to lead you to *repentance?*

(9)   2 Cor. 5:19
      ...not counting their *trespasses* against *them,* and entrusting to us the *message* of *reconciliation.*

(10) Col. 1:14
      ...in *whom* we have *redemption*...

B. Identifying semantic classes

To which semantic class (Things, Events, Attributes, Relations) do the italicized words belong in each of the following examples? (Events would include processes, states, and experiences.)

Example: Gen. 39:23

  ...gave him *success* in whatever he did. (NIV)

Answer: Event

(1)   Gen. 40:14 ...show me *kindness*...

(2)   Gen. 40:16 ...saw that the *interpretation* was favorable...

(3)   Gen. 41:9 ...I am reminded of my *shortcomings*. (NIV)

(4)   Gen. 41:29 ...years of *abundance*... (NASB)

(5)   Gen. 41:54 ...years of *famine*... (NASB)

(6)   Gen. 42:25 ...gave them *provisions*... (LB)

(7)   Gen. 43:9 ...guarantee his *safety*. (LB)

C. Identifying Event words

Identify the Event words in each of the following passages.

Example: Philem. 5

  ...because I hear of your love and of the faith which you have toward the Lord Jesus and all the saints...

Answer: Events are: hear, love, faith, have

(1)   Matt. 16:28

Truly, I say to you, there are some standing here who will not taste death before they see the Son of man coming in his kingdom.

(2)   Matt. 18:14

So it is not the will of my Father who is in heaven that one of these little ones should perish.

(3)   John 7:38

He who believes in me, as the scripture has said, 'Out of his heart shall flow rivers of living water.'

(4)   Acts 3:14

But you denied the Holy and Righteous One, and asked for a murderer to be granted to you.

(5)   Rom. 7:8

But sin, finding opportunity in the commandment, wrought in me all kinds of covetousness. Apart from the law sin lies dead.

(6)   Col. 1:23

...provided that you continue in the faith, stable and steadfast, not shifting from the hope of the gospel which you heard, which has been preached to every creature under heaven, and of which I, Paul, became a minister.

(7)   2 Thess. 2:16–17
       Now may our Lord Jesus Christ himself, and God our Father, who loved us and gave us
       eternal comfort and good hope through grace, comfort your hearts and establish them in every
       good work and word.

(8)   Heb. 5:7–8
       In the days of his flesh, Jesus offered up prayers and supplications, with loud cries and tears,
       to him who was able to save him from death, and he was heard for his godly fear. Although
       he was a Son, he learned obedience through what he suffered...

(9)   1 Pet. 5:1–2
       So I exhort the elders among you, as a fellow elder and a witness of the sufferings of Christ
       as well as a partaker in the glory that is to be revealed. Tend the flock of God that is your
       charge, not by constraint but willingly, not for shameful gain but eagerly.

D. Identifying implicit Events

In the following passages identify the Event words and then look for other events that are
implicit in the passage and therefore part of the semantic structure even though there is no lexical
item in the surface structure.

Example: Matt. 2:1
       ...in the days of Herod the king...
Answer: implicit-ruled
       ...in the days when Herod the king ruled...

(1)   John 6:11
       Jesus then took the loaves, and when he had given thanks, he distributed them to those who
       were seated; so also the fish, as much as they wanted.

(2)   Matt. 26:5
       But they said, "Not during the feast, lest there be a tumult among the people."

(3)   John 2:10
       ...said to him, "Every man serves the good wine first; and when men have drunk freely, then
       the poor wine..."

(4)   Matt. 2:7
       Then Herod summoned the wise men secretly and ascertained from them what time the star
       appeared...

(5)   Acts 21:13
       Then Paul answered, "What are you doing, weeping and breaking my heart? For I am ready
       not only to be imprisoned but even to die."

(6)   Matt. 26:25
       Judas, who betrayed him, said, "Is it I, Master?"

(7)   2 Tim. 1:7
       ...for God did not give us a spirit of timidity but a spirit of power and love and self-control.

(8)   John 15:4
       As the branch cannot bear fruit by itself,...neither can you...

(9)   Mark 4:28
      The earth produces of itself, first the blade, then the ear, then the full grain in the ear.

(10) Col. 1:2
      To the saints and faithful brethren in Christ at Colossae: Grace to you and peace from God
      our Father.

Chapter 7
Some Relationships between Lexical Items

Additional Reading:
   Beekman and Callow 1974: Chapter 4.

A. Identifying the meaning components of a word

Meaning components and concepts are classified as Things, Events, Attributes, and Relations. In each of the following, what are the meaning components of the italicized word in the passage? Which is the nuclear or most generic component?

Example: Acts 27:16
                And running under the lee of a small *island* called Cauda...
Answer: The meaning components are "land," "surrounded by," and "water." "Land" is a Thing, "water" is a Thing, and "surrounded by" is a Relation. The nuclear component is "land."

(1)   Acts 7:27
      Who made you a *ruler* and a *judge* over us?

(2)   Acts 7:36
      He led them...in the *wilderness* for forty years.

(3)   Acts 7:44
      Our fathers had the *tent* of witness in the wilderness...

(4)   Acts 8:13
      ...seeing signs and great *miracles* performed...

(5)   Acts 9:10
      The Lord said to him in a *vision*...

(6)   Acts 9:40
      But Peter...knelt down and *prayed*...

(7)   Acts 9:43
      ...he stayed...with one Simon, a *tanner*.

(8)   Acts 10:42
      ...he commanded us to *preach* to the people...

(9)   Acts 12:16
      ...they saw him and were *amazed*.

(10) Acts 13:2
      And while they were worshiping the Lord and *fasting*...

B. Identifying generic-specific changes

Study the translation made for the italicized word in each of the following passages. Was the change from (a) specific to generic, (b) generic to specific, or (c) one specific substituted for another specific?

Example: Matt. 6:28
                Consider the *lilies of the field...*

                Aguaruna back-translation:
                Think about the *flowers.*

Answer: a

(1)   John 1:32
      ...and *it* remained on him.

      Amuzgo back-translation:
      the Holy Spirit remained with him

(2)   John 10:12
      ...*the wolf* snatches them and scatters them.

      Aguaruna back-translation:
      The savage-animal grabbing at them causes them to scatter.

(3)   Acts 1:10
      ...two *men* stood by them in white robes...

      Aguaruna back-translation:
      Two people dressed in white clothes appeared by the side of those who stood looking.

(4)   Acts 2:1
      ...*they* were all together in one place.

      Tenango Otomí back-translation:
      The believers were all gathered.

(5)   Acts 2:46
      ...breaking *bread* in their homes...

      Alekano back-translation:
      ...eating ordinary food and Communion food in their houses

(6)   Acts 3:6
      I have no *silver* and *gold...*

      Isthmus Mixe back-translation:
      I don't have any money.

(7)   Acts 3:10
      ...and amazement at *what had happened* to him.

      Huave back-translation:
      when they saw that the man with the crippled feet had been cured

(8)   Acts 13:6
       ...they came upon a certain *magician*...named Bar-Jesus.

       Aguaruna back-translation:
       There they saw a witch doctor named Bar-Jesus who lived there.

C. Using a more generic word

What is a more generic word that includes the specific word italicized in each of the following?

Example: 1 Thess. 2:7
               ...like a *nurse* taking care of her children.
Answer: A more generic word for "nurse" is woman.

(1)   Matt. 10:31
       ...you are of more value than many *sparrows.*

(2)   John 10:12
       He...sees the *wolf* coming and leaves the sheep and *flees...*

(3)   1 Pet. 5:8
       ...like a roaring *lion,* seeking some one to devour.

(4)   Rev. 8:13
       ...I heard an *eagle* crying with a loud voice...

D. Using a more specific word

There are words and phrases in Scripture that substitute for a previously stated referent. Certain pro-verbs such as "do," "happen," "make," and "act" may need to be translated by the more specific action referred to instead of the word in italics. You will need to check the context.

Example: Acts 3:17
               ...I know that you *acted* in ignorance...
Answer: I know that you killed Jesus because you did not know that he was really the Son of God.

(1)   Mark 5:32
       ...he looked around to see who *had done* it.

(2)   Mark 11:28
       By what authority are you *doing these things...?*

(3)   Luke 24:14
       ...talking with each other about *all these things that had happened.*

(4)   John 8:40
       ...*this* is not what Abraham did. (Abraham did not do this.)

(5)   Acts 12:4
       ...intending after the Passover to bring him out to the *people.*

(6)   1 Tim. 4:16
       ...*by so doing* you will save both yourself and your hearers.

Chapter 8
Discovering Meaning by Grouping and Contrast

Additional Reading:
> Barnwell 1974: Chapter 5 and 6.
> Nida 1964: Chapter 5.

A. Taxonomies

Whenever one can say of two terms "X is a type of Y," those terms fall on two levels of a lexical hierarchy and form part of what is known as a taxonomy. Knowing such information is important in translation if, for instance, one must substitute one term for another which is more generic or less generic.

Arrange the terms below according to which ones function on the same level and which on different levels, and draw a chart showing all the terms and their levels. Then add one more item to each of the levels except the topmost level, and encircle the new items. Use a dictionary if necessary.

Example: See Larson 1984:85, display 8.9.

(1) announce, ask, beg, command, demand, implore, plead, exclaim, question, speak.

(2) Make a chart of "ways of walking" in your mother tongue.

(3) Make a chart of "ways of talking" in your mother tongue.

(4) Make a chart of the domain of "spirit world" that reflects the terms used in your culture.

(5) Make a display of the kinship terms used in your mother tongue, label the contrasting components of meaning.

Chapter 9
Mismatching of Lexical Systems between Languages

Additional Reading:
   Beekman and Callow 1974: Chapter 5.
   Crofts 1987:40–49.

A. Son

In Mark 2:5 Jesus addresses the paralyzed man as "My son"; but to do so in some languages could only mean that the man was Jesus' own son. The translation would have to use some other term, such as "young man."

In a language in which "son" means only "the actual male child of a man" and is not used in any general (extended) way, how might you translate the following to express the meaning more accurately?

Example: Mark 3:17
   ...sons of thunder...
Answer: those who are like thunder

(1)   Ps. 77:15
      ...thy people, the sons of Jacob and Joseph.

(2)   Matt. 1:20
      ...Joseph, son of David...

(3)   Matt. 8:12
      ...the sons of the kingdom will be thrown into the outer darkness...

(4)   Mark 10:47
      "Jesus, Son of David, have mercy on me!"

(5)   John 17:12
      ...none of them is lost but the son of perdition...

(6)   Acts 4:36
      ...Son of encouragement...

(7)   Eph. 3:5
      ...which was not made known to the sons of men in other generations...

B. Daughter

In a language in which "daughter" means only "the actual female child of a man" and is not used in any general (extended) way, how might you try translating the following?

(1)   Matt. 9:22
      ...he said, "Take heart, daughter..."

(2)   Mark 5:34
      "Daughter, your faith has made you well..."

(3)   Luke 13:16
      "...this woman, a daughter of Abraham..."

(4)   Luke 23:28
       "Daughters of Jerusalem, do not weep for me..."

(5)   John 12:15
       "Fear not, daughter of Zion..."

C. Brother

Assume you are translating into a language in which "brother" is not used in an extended, general way nor to mean "fellow Christian." How might you try translating the following?

(1)   Acts 9:17
       So Ananias...said, "Brother Saul..."

(2)   Rom. 14:10
       Why do you pass judgment on your brother?

(3)   Rom. 14:15
       If your brother is being injured by what you eat...

(4)   1 Cor. 16:12
       As for our brother Apollos...

(5)   James 4:11
       He that speaks evil against a brother or judges his brother...

D. Older brother and younger brother

In Biangai (Papua New Guinea) one cannot simply say "brother." There are two words from which to choose. One means "older brother" and the other means "younger brother."

Assuming you are translating into one of the many languages that make this distinction between older and younger brother, which do you think you might use in the following passages?

Example: John 1:41
              He first found his brother Simon...
Answer: He first found his *older brother,* Simon...

(1)   Matt. 10:2
       The names of the twelve apostles...James the son of Zebedee, and John his *brother*...

(2)   Matt. 22:24
       If a man dies...his *brother* must marry the widow...

(3)   Mark 3:32
       Your mother and your *brothers* are outside.

(4)   Mark 6:3
       Is not this...the *brother* of James and Joses and Judas and Simon?

(5)   Mark 6:17
       For Herod had sent and seized John,...for the sake of Herodias, his *brother* Philip's wife...

(6)   Luke 12:13
       One of the multitude said to him, "Teacher, bid my *brother* divide the inheritance with me."

(7)   Luke 15:32
       It was fitting to make merry and be glad, for this your *brother* was dead, and is alive...

(8)   Luke 16:28
       ...for I have five *brothers*...

(9)   Luke 21:16
       You will be delivered up even by parents and *brothers*...

(10)   Jude 1
       Jude, a servant of Jesus Christ and *brother* of James...

(11)   Gen. 4:8
       Cain said to Abel his *brother*, "Let us go out to the field."

(12)   Gen. 24:29
       Rebekah had a *brother* whose name was Laban...

(13)   Gen. 32:3
       And Jacob sent messengers before him to Esau his *brother*...

(14)   Gen. 37:2
       Joseph, being seventeen years old, was shepherding the flock with his *brothers*.

(15)   Gen. 42:4
       But Jacob did not send Benjamin, Joseph's *brother*, with his *brothers*, for he feared that harm
       might befall him.

(16)   Gen. 42:38
       But he said, "My son shall not go down with you, for his *brother* is dead, and he only is left."

E. Obligatory possession

In Alekano (Papua New Guinea) most kinship terms have an obligatory possessive suffix (or prefix and suffix). Hence, it is impossible to say "a father" or "the father"; one must say "my father" or "your father" or "some person's father."

So in translating John 3:35 it was necessary to translate "His father was pleased with his son" because there was no way to say "*The* father loved *the* son."

Similarly, in John 14:9 for the two occurrences of the expression "the father" (Jesus speaking) and "our father" (the disciples speaking) the first one was translated "my father" and the second one "our father."

Similarly, just as body parts do not go around unattached, so the terms representing them must have an obligatory possessive morpheme attached. Hence, in translating 1 Cor. 12:15 one must say "our foot cannot say to our hand." Similarly, in Matt. 5:38 instead of saying "an eye for an eye" one must translate "If someone gouges out your eye, gouge out his eye."

Assuming that you are translating into a language like Alekano described above, rewrite each of the following phrases, adding either a possessive pronoun or possessive noun or noun phrase to indicate the possessor of all body parts and all kinship terms (father, son, child, etc.). Check the context if necessary.

Example: Rev. 1:7
        ...every *eye* will see him...
Answer: All people will see him with their eyes.

(1)   Matt. 10:28
      And do not fear those who kill *the body*...

(2)   Luke 1:59
      ...they came to circumcise *the child*...

(3)   Luke 15:13
      ...*the* younger *son* gathered all he had...

(4)   John 14:13
      ...that *the Father* may be glorified in *the Son*...

(5)   Gal. 4:6
      Because you are *sons*, God has sent the Spirit...

(6)   Heb. 10:5
      ...but *a body* hast thou prepared for me...

(7)   James 3:10
      From *the* same *mouth* come blessing and cursing.

(8)   Rev. 4:6
      ...four living creatures, full of *eyes* in front and behind...

(9)   Matt. 6:22
      The eye is the lamp of *the body*.

(10) Matt. 6:25
      ...and *the body* more than clothing?

(11) Matt. 10:37
      …he who loves *son* or *daughter* more than me…

(12) Matt. 11:27
      …no one knows *the Son* except *the Father*…

(13) Matt. 27:59
      …Joseph took *the body*…

(14) Mark 8:18
      Having *eyes* do you not see, and having *ears* do you not hear?

(15) Luke 1:13
      …Elizabeth will bear you *a son*…

(16) Luke 1:80
      …*the child* grew and became strong…

(17) 2 Cor. 4:10
      …always carrying in *the body*…

(18) 1 John 2:22
      …he who denies *the Father* and *the Son*.

F. Obligatory possession and kinship terms

Rewrite John 14:8–14, indicating the possessor of all kinship terms.

[8]Philip said to him, "Lord, show us the Father, and we shall be satisfied." [9]Jesus said to him, "Have I been with you so long, and yet you do not know me, Philip? He who has seen me has seen the Father; how can you say, 'Show us the Father'? [10]Do you not believe that I am in the Father and the Father in me? The words that I say to you I do not speak on my own authority; but the Father who dwells in me does his works. [11]Believe me that I am in the Father and the Father in me; or else believe me for the sake of the works themselves.

[12]"Truly, truly, I say to you, he who believes in me will also do the works that I do; and greater works than these will he do, because I go to the Father. [13]Whatever you ask in my name, I will do it, that the Father may be glorified in the Son; [14]if you ask anything in my name, I will do it."

G. Obligatory possession and body parts

Rewrite 1 Cor. 12:12–27, indicating the possessor of all body parts mentioned, including the word "body."

[12]For just as the body is one and has many members, and all the members of the body, though many, are one body, so it is with Christ. [13]For by one Spirit we were all baptized into one body—Jews or Greeks, slaves or free—and all were made to drink of one Spirit.

[14]For the body does not consist of one member but of many. [15]If the foot should say, "Because I am not a hand, I do not belong to the body," that would not make it any less a part of the body. [16]And if the ear should say, "Because I am not an eye, I do not belong to the body," that would not make it any less a part of the body. [17]If the whole body were an eye, where would be the hearing? If the whole body were an ear, where would be the sense of smell? [18]But as it is, God arranged the organs in the body, each one of them, as he chose. [19]If all were a single organ, where would the body be? [20]As it is, there are many parts, yet one body. [21]The eye cannot say to the hand, "I have no need of you," nor again the head to the feet, "I have no need of you." [22]On the contrary, the parts of the body which seem to be weaker are indispensable, [23]and those parts of the body which we think less honorable we invest with the greater honor, and our unpresentable parts are treated with greater modesty, [24]which our more presentable parts do not require. But God has so adjusted the body, giving the greater honor to the inferior part, [25]that there may be no discord in the body, but that the members may have the same care for one another. [26]If one member suffers, all suffer together; if one member is honored, all rejoice together.

[27]Now you are the body of Christ and individually members of it.

H. Tense

Certain languages have many finer distinctions of tense than English has. In Bali, for example, there are three levels of past tense and three levels of future tense. One level covers events immediately connected with the present tense. A second level covers events farther separated from the present, but still occurring the same day. A third level covers events separated from the present by at least one night.

Assuming you are translating into Bali, which of the following seven tenses would you choose for each of the verbs italicized in the exercise? Check the context for the time sequence. In narration, the point of reference is the time when the Bible book was written, but in direct quotes it may be found by studying the context.

present:	right now
past 1:	present but completed, immediate past
past 2:	recent past, within the same day
past 3:	further past, earlier than the same day
future 1:	present but not yet complete
future 2:	near future, within the same day
future 3:	more distant future, later than that same day

Example: Acts 5:3

But Peter *said,* "Ananias, why *has* Satan *filled* your heart to lie to the Holy Spirit and to keep back part of the proceeds of the land?"

Answer: said—past 3, because it was said long before Luke recorded it has filled—past 2

(1)   Mark 10:32–34
      And taking the twelve again, he *began to tell* them what *was to happen* to him, saying,
      "Behold, we *are going* up to Jerusalem; and the Son of man *will be delivered* to the chief
      priests...and after three days he *will rise.*"

(2)   John 10:25
      Jesus *answered* them, "I *told* you, and you *do not believe.*

(3)   John 18:26
      One of the servants...asked, "Did I not *see* you in the garden with him?"

(4)   John 18:38
      ...he...*told* them, "I *find* no crime in him."

(5)   John 19:15
      Pilate *said* to them, "*Shall* I *crucify* your King?"

(6)   John 20:15
      ...(Mary) *said* to him, "Sir, if you *have carried* him away, tell me where you have *laid* him."

(7)   John 20:25
      So the other disciples *told* him (Thomas), "We *have seen* the Lord." But he *said* to them,
      "Unless I *see* in his hands the print..."

(8)   Acts 1:11
      This Jesus, who *was taken up* from you into heaven, *will come* in the same way...

I. Aspect

Bali has a further problem in the aspects of verbs. One verb form indicates an action which
occurs only once, another form describes an action which continues over a period, and a third form
is used for an action which was repeated several times. Which verb form would you use for each of
the verbs or verb phrases italicized in the exercise below?

> a. unit action (happened once)
> b. repeated action (happened several time in sequence)
> c. continued action (one action but extended over a period of time)

Example: Mark 1:39
           And he went throughout all Galilee, *preaching* in their synagogues and *casting out*
           demons.

Answer: Repeated action (Jesus preached in various synagogues and cast out demons several
           times.)

(1)   Mark 1:40–41
      And a leper came to him *beseeching him*...Moved with pity, he *stretched* out his hand and
      touched him...

(2)   Mark 2:1
      ...it *was reported* that he *was* at home.

(3)   Mark 2:3
      ...*bringing* to him a paralytic *carried* by four men.

(4)   Mark 2:17
      And when Jesus *heard* it, he *said* to them...

(5)   Mark 2:18
Now John's disciples and the Pharisees *were fasting.*

(6)   Mark 3:13–14
And he *went up* on the mountain, and *called to* him those whom he *desired;* and they *came* to him. And he *appointed* twelve...

(7)   Mark 4:2
And he *taught* them many things in parables, and in his teaching he *said* to them...

(8)   Mark 4:37–38
And a great storm of wind *arose,* and the waves *beat* into the boat...but he was in the stern, *asleep* on the cushion; and they *woke* him...

(9)   Mark 5:27
She had *heard* the reports about Jesus, and *came up* behind him in the crowd and *touched* his garment.

(10) Mark 5:36
But *ignoring* what they said, Jesus *said* to the ruler...

J. "Dead" suffix in Amuesha

In a number of languages, including Amuesha of Peru, there is an obligatory morpheme that must be suffixed to the name of any person referred to after his death. An interesting problem arises in the transfiguration account as to whether or not Moses' name should have the "dead" suffix. The translators have decided to leave the suffix off the name of Moses in the transfiguration story, since his obvious physical presence would be contradictory to the reference to his death. They are using it with the names of the characters of the Old Testament when they are mentioned in the New in other contexts and with the names of characters of the New Testament only if they have reason to believe that the person was dead *when the record was written.*

Following their way of handling this problem, on which of the following italicized names would you put the "dead" suffix?

(1)   Matt. 2:7
Then *Herod* summoned the wise men secretly...

(2)   Acts 1:5
...for *John* baptized with water...

(3)   Acts 1:16
...concerning *Judas* who was guide to those who arrested *Jesus.*

(4)   Acts 5:1
...a man named *Ananias* with his wife *Sapphira,* sold a piece of property...

(5)   Acts 7:1–2
And the *high priest* said, "Is this so?" and *Stephen* said...

(6)   Acts 8:1
And *Saul* was consenting to his death.

(7)   Acts 8:9
There was a man named *Simon*...

(8)   Acts 9:36
Now there was at Joppa a disciple named *Tabitha,* which means Dorcas. She was full of good
works...

(9)   Acts 12:1–2
About that time *Herod* the king laid violent hand upon some who belonged to the church. He
killed *James,* the brother of *John* with the sword...

(10)   1 Cor. 16:19
The churches of Asia send greetings. *Aquila* and *Prisca*...send...greetings.

Chapter 10
Multiple Senses of Lexical Items

Additional Reading:
    Barnwell 1974: Chapter 4.
    Beekman and Callow 1974: Chapter 6.

A. Multiple senses of "church"

Identify the meanings of the word "church" in the following passages. In the light of the different senses how might you translate "church" into our own language in each passage. How many words did you use for "church?" What does each mean?

(1)   Acts 8:1
    And on that day a great persecution arose against the *church* in Jerusalem; and they were all scattered...

(2)   Acts 11:26
    For a whole year they met with the *church,* and taught a large company of people; and in Antioch the disciples were for the first time called Christians.

(3)   Eph. 5:23
    ...as Christ is the head of the *church,* his body, and is himself its Savior.

(4)   Gal. 1:13
    ...I persecuted the *church* of God violently and tried to destroy it...

(5)   Acts 7:38
    This is he [Moses], that was in the *church* in the wilderness with the angel which spake to him in the mount Sina, and with our fathers. (KJV)

(6)   Rev. 2:1
    To the angel of the *church* in Ephesus write...

B. Multiple senses of "arms"

Identify the meanings of the words "arm" or "arms" in the following passages. Rewrite the sentence so that only primary meanings are used.

Example: Num. 11:23
          Is the Lord's *arm* too short?
Answer: Does the Lord not have authority/power to do this?

(1)   1 Pet. 4:1
    Since therefore Christ suffered in the flesh, *arm* yourselves with the same thought . . .

(2)   Heb. 12:12 (NIV)
    Therefore, strengthen your feeble *arms* and weak knees.

(3)   Mark 10:16
    And he took them in his *arms* and blessed them...

(4)   Ps. 18:32
    It is God who *arms* me with strength and makes my way perfect. (NIV)

(5)   Isa. 40:11
      He gathers the lambs in his *arms*... (NIV)

(6)   Prov. 31:20
      She opens her *arms* to the poor... (NIV)

(7)   Deut. 33:27
      ...underneath are the everlasting *arms*. (NIV)

(8)   Ps. 44:3
      ...nor did their *arm* bring them victory... (NIV)

C. Multiple senses of "bless"

Identify the meanings of the words "bless," "blessed," and "blessing" in the following passages.

(1)   Gen. 49:28
      ...this is what [Jacob] said to [his sons] as he *blessed* them...

(2)   Mark 10:16
      [Jesus] took [the children] in his arms and *blessed* them...

(3)   Luke 1:64
      ...[Zechariah] spoke, *blessing* God.

(4)   Luke 2:28
      ...[Simeon] took [the child] up in is arms and *blessed* God and said...

(5)   Acts 3:25
      As [God] said to Abraham, "Through your descendants I will *bless* all the people on earth."
      (GNB)

(6)   Eph. 1:3b
      For in our union with Christ, [God] has *blessed* us by giving us every spiritual *blessing* in the
      heavenly world. (GNB)

(7)   Luke 2:34
      ...and Simeon *blessed* [the father and mother of Jesus] and said to Mary his mother...

(8)   Luke 24:50
      ...and lifting up his hands [Jesus] *blessed* [the disciples].

(9)   Matt. 5:8
      Blessed are the pure in heart, for they shall see God.

(10) James 1:12
      Blessed is the man who endures trial, for...he will receive the crown of life...

(11) Luke 1:68
      Blessed be the Lord God of Israel...

(12) Gen. 17:16
      [God said to Abraham] "...I will *bless* [Sarah], and she shall be a mother of nations..."

(13) Rev. 5:13
      ...to the Lamb be *blessing* and honor and glory...

D. Secondary senses of "body"

Study the context in which the word "body" occurs in each verse below. Is the usage a primary or secondary sense? If secondary, what is the secondary meaning of "body?"

Example: Luke 17:37
He said to them, "Where the *body* is, there the eagles will be gathered together."
Answer: 1) secondary
2) corpse/carcass

(1) Rom. 12:1
...present your *bodies* as a living sacrifice...

(2) Mark 5:29
...and she felt in her *body* that she was healed...

(3) Matt. 6:25
...do not be anxious...about your *body,* what you shall put on.

(4) Col. 2:11
...you were circumcised...by putting off the *body* of flesh in the circumcision of Christ...

(5) Eph. 5:28
...husbands should love their wives as their own *bodies.*

(6) 1 Cor. 15:40
There are celestial *bodies* and there are terrestrial *bodies...*

E. Secondary senses

Study each of the following passages. Identify any word that is being used in a secondary sense. Rewrite the passage so that words are used only in their primary senses.

Example: Gal. 4:27
Shout and cry with joy... (TEV)
Answer: "Cry" is used in secondary sense.
Shout and rejoice.

(1) Heb. 9:4
...which contained a golden urn holding the manna, and Aaron's rod that budded, and the tables of the covenant...

(2) Acts 27:33
...Paul urged them all to take some food, saying, "Today is the fourteenth day that you have continued in suspense and without food, having taken nothing.

(3) Acts 4:8
Then Peter, filled with the Holy Spirit, said to them, "Rulers of the people and elders..."

(4) Acts 10:30
And Cornelius said, "Four days ago, about this hour, I was keeping the ninth hour of prayer in my house; and behold, a man stood before me in bright apparel...

(5) Acts 10:45
And the believers...were amazed, because the gift of the Holy Spirit had been poured out even on the Gentiles.

(6)   Acts 12:10
      When they had passed the first and the second guard, they came to the iron gate leading into
      the city.

(7)   Titus 1:9
      ...he must hold firm to the sure word as taught, so that he may be able to give instruction in
      sound doctrine...

(8)   Titus 2:10
      ...but to show entire and true fidelity, so that in everything they may adorn the doctrine of
      God our Savior.

(9)   Titus 3:3
      For we ourselves were once foolish...passing our days in malice and envy, hated by men and
      hating one another...

(10) 2 Tim. 4:3
      For the time is coming when people will not endure sound teaching, but having itching ears
      they will accumulate for themselves teachers to suit their own likings...

Chapter 11
Figurative Senses of Lexical Items

Additional Reading:
    Barnwell 1974: Chapter 12.
    Beekman and Callow 1974: Chapter 7.

A. Various senses

In each of the following sets of verses, the same word is used but in only one of each set is it used in its primary sense. In the others it is used in secondary, or figurative.

Example: a. Luke 16:24
            ...send Lazarus to dip the tip of his finger in water and cool my *tongue*...
        b. 1 Pet. 3:10
            ...let him keep his *tongue* from evil...
Answer: a. primary
        b. figurative

(1)   a. Matt. 8:8
        Lord, I am not worthy to have you come under my *roof*...
    b. Mark 2:4
        And when they could not get near him because of the crowd, they removed the *roof* above him...
    c. Ps. 137:6
        Let my tongue cleave to the *roof* of my mouth...

(2)   a. Matt. 15:11
        ...not what goes into the *mouth* defiles a man...
    b. Luke 19:22
        I will condemn you out of your own *mouth,* you wicked servant!
    c. Gen. 42:27
        ...he saw his money in the *mouth* of his sack...

(3)   a. John 15:18
        If the *world* hates you, know that it has hated me before it hated you.
    b. Matt. 13:35
        I will utter what has been hidden since the foundation of the *world.*
    c. 1 John 5:4
        ...this is the victory that overcometh the *world,* our faith.

(4)   a. Mark 9:42
        ...it would be better for him if a great millstone were hung round his *neck* and he were thrown into the sea.
    b. Rom. 16:4
        ...who risked their *necks* for my life...

(5)   a. 2 Tim. 4:17
          So I was rescued from the lion's *mouth.*
       b. Rev. 1:16
          ...from his *mouth* issued a sharp two-edged sword...
       c. Gen. 29:2
          The stone on the well's *mouth* was large...

B. Figurative senses, based on association

In each of the following, the italicized word is being used in a figurative sense based on another concept with which it is closely associated. Rewrite the passage using nonfigurative wording.

Example: 2 Pet. 3:12
              ...waiting for and hastening the coming of the *day* of God...
Answer: Waiting for and hastening the coming of the day when God will judge ungodly men.

(1)   Matt. 3:5
      Then went out to him *Jerusalem* and all *Judea...*

(2)   Matt. 5:13
      You are the salt of the *earth...*

(3)   Mark 3:25
      And if a *house* is divided against itself, that *house* will not be able to stand.

(4)   Luke 1:32
      ...the Lord God will give to him the *throne* of his father David...

(5)   Luke 22:14
      And when the *hour* came, he sat at table...

(6)   John 15:18
      If the *world* hates you, know that it has hated me...

C. Figurative senses, based on part-whole associations

In each of the following, the italicized word is being used in a figurative sense based on part-whole association. Rewrite the passage, using nonfigurative wording.

Example: Matt. 8:8
              Lord, I am not worthy to have you come under my *roof...*
Answer: Lord, I am not worthy to have you come into my *house.*

(1)   Matt. 27:4
      I have sinned in betraying innocent *blood.*

(2)   Luke 7:27
      Behold, I send my messenger before thy *face...*

(3)   Luke 12:19
      ...I will say to my *soul...*

(4)   John 1:19
      ...the *Jews* sent priests and Levites from Jerusalem to ask him...

(5)   Rom. 12:1
       ...present your *bodies* as a living sacrifice...

(6)   Eph. 6:22
       I have sent him...that he may encourage your *hearts.*

(7)   James 1:26
       If any one...does not bridle his tongue but deceives his *heart,* this man's religion is vain.

(8)   Rev. 10:4
       ...I heard a *voice* from heaven saying...

D. Meaning in context

The senses intended by secondary and figurative senses are determined by the context in which the word or phrase is used. State the contextual meaning of the italicized word and state what in the context determines the meaning which you assign to the word or phrase in this passage.

Example: Titus 3:13
       Do your best to speed Zenas...and Apollos on their way; *see* that they lack nothing.
Answer: "See" is used in the sense of *take care (look after).* This meaning is indicated by the context of someone going on a journey and the word "lack."

(1)   Mark 7:2–3
       ...they saw that some of his disciples ate with hands defiled, that is, *unwashed.* (For the Pharisees, and all the Jews, do not eat unless they wash their hands, observing the tradition of the elders...)

(2)   Luke 1:53
       ...he has *filled* the hungry with good things...

(3)   Acts 5:3
       ...why has Satan *filled* your heart to lie to the Holy Spirit and to keep back part of the proceeds...

(4)   Acts 13:11–12
       Immediately mist and darkness *fell* upon him and he went about seeking people to lead him by the hand. Then the proconsul believed, when he saw what had occurred...

(5)   Acts 13:22
       And when he had removed him, he *raised up* David to be their king...

E. Metonymy

Metonymy is the substitution of one term for another having an associative relationship with it. In some languages, e.g., Huixteco of Mexico, this figure of speech is not used and so the translation must restate what is meant without using the substitution.

Give the meaning of the italicized metonymies, tell what the associative relationship is between the two (temporal, spatial, or logical), and give an alternate translation which removes the figure and makes the meaning clear.

Example: Phil. 1:6
               the day of Jesus Christ

Answer: "day" stands for the event of the "coming"—time is substituted for the event that will happen at that time = temporal.

(1) Matt. 7:22
     On that day many will say to me, "Lord, Lord..."

(2) Mark 4:29
     ...he puts in the *sickle*...

(3) Luke 1:32
     ...the Lord God will give to him the *throne* of his father David, ...

(4) John 17:14
     ...the *world* has hated them because they are not of the *world*...

(5) Acts 5:28
     ...to bring this man's *blood* upon us.

(6) Acts 13:44
     ...almost the *whole city* gathered together...

(7) Acts 15:21
     ...*Moses* has had in every city those who preach *him*...

(8) Acts 22:3
     ...*at the feet of* Gamaliel...

F. Identifying metonymy

List the word(s) involved in the figures of metonymy in the following passages and give an alternate translation of the portion, removing the figure.

Example: John 3:16
               For God so loved the world...

Answer: world = people of the world

(1) Matt. 3:2
     "Repent, for the kingdom of heaven is at hand."

(2) Matt. 15:8
     This people honors me with their lips, but their heart is far from me...

(3) Matt. 17:8
     And when they lifted up their eyes, they saw no one but Jesus only.

(4)   Mark 1:2
       Behold, I send my messenger before thy face, who shall prepare thy way; ...

(5)   Mark 1:33
       And the whole city was gathered together about the door.

(6)   Mark 3:25
       And if a house is divided against itself, that house will not be able to stand.

(7)   Mark 7:6
       Well did Isaiah prophesy of you hypocrites, as it is written, 'This people honors me with their
       lips, but their heart is far from me...'

(8)   Luke 16:31
       If they do not hear Moses and the prophets, neither will they be convinced if some one should
       rise from the dead.

(9)   John 1:12
       But to all who received him, who believed in his name, he gave power to become children of
       God...

(10)   John 12:27
       Now is my soul troubled. And what shall I say? 'Father, save me from this hour'? No, for this
       purpose I have come to this hour.

(11)   John 17:1
       When Jesus had spoken these words, he lifted up his eyes to heaven and said, "Father, the
       hour has come; glorify thy Son that the Son may glorify thee..."

(12)   John 17:9
       I am praying for them; I am not praying for the world but for those whom thou hast given
       me, for they are thine...

(13)   Acts 3:6
       But Peter said, "I have no silver and gold, but I give you what I have; in the name of Jesus
       Christ of Nazareth, walk."

(14)   Rom. 3:30
       ...since God is one; and he will justify the circumcised on the ground of their faith and the
       uncircumcised through their faith.

(15)   Heb. 1:8
       But of the Son he says, "Thy throne, O God, is for ever and ever, the righteous scepter is the
       scepter of thy kingdom."

G. Synecdoche

Synecdoche is the figure of speech by which the whole of a thing is put for the part, or a part for the whole, an individual for a class or a class for an individual, or an attribute for the whole.

In the following passages the italicized words are conveying a synecdoche. Tell what specific type of synecdoche relation it is, and give an alternate translation expressing the meaning in a nonfigurative way.

(1) Luke 3:6
...and all *flesh* shall see the salvation of God.

(2) Luke 12:19
And I will say to my *soul...*

(3) Acts 2:26
...my *tongue* rejoiced...

(4) Acts 5:9
Hark, the *feet* of those that have buried your husband are at the door...

(5) Rom. 16:4
...who risked their *necks* for my life...

H. Identifying synecdoche

List the word(s) involved in the figures of synecdoche in the following passages and give an alternate translation to that portion, removing the figure.

Example: John 10:31
The Jews took up stones again to stone him.
Answer: the Jews = the Jewish religious leaders

(1) Matt. 13:16
But blessed are your eyes, for they see, and your ears, for they hear.

(2) Luke 3:6
...and all flesh shall see the salvation of God.

(3) Luke 7:27
This is he of whom it is written, 'Behold, I send my messenger before thy face, who shall prepare thy way before thee.'

(4) Luke 9:51
When the days drew near for him to be received up, he set his face to go to Jerusalem.

(5) John 19:7
The Jews answered him, "We have a law, and by that law he ought to die, because he has made himself the Son of God."

(6) Acts 2:26
...therefore my heart was glad, and my tongue rejoiced; moreover my flesh will dwell in hope.

(7) Acts 4:1
And as they were speaking to the people, the priests and the captain of the temple and the Sadducees came upon them...

(8)   Acts 7:50
       Did not my hand make all these things?

(9)   Acts 9:23
       When many days had passed, the Jews plotted to kill him...

(10)   Phil. 2:11
       ...and every tongue confess that Jesus Christ is Lord, to the glory of God the Father.

(11)   Heb. 13:9
       Do not be led away by diverse and strange teachings; for it is well that the heart be
       strengthened by grace, not by foods, which have not benefited their adherents.

(12)   James 3:6
       And the tongue is a fire. The tongue is an unrighteous world among our members, staining
       the whole body, setting on fire the cycle of nature, and set on fire by hell.

(13)   2 Pet. 2:14
       They have eyes full of adultery, insatiable for sin. They entice unsteady souls. They have
       hearts trained in greed. Accursed children!

(14)   Rev. 1:7
       Behold, he is coming with the clouds, and every eye will see him, every one who pierced
       him; and all tribes of the earth will wail on account of him. Even so. Amen.

I. Changing hyperbole

"A hyperbole is an exaggeration for effect, not meant to be taken literally" (*Webster's New
World Dictionary*). Since, in many cases, hyperboles cannot be translated literally into another
language without giving a wrong idea, one must determine the actual nonfigurative meaning. What
meaning is being conveyed by the following hyperbolic phrases?

Example: Matt. 11:18
              For John came neither eating nor drinking...
Answer: If translated literally this would not be true. Rather, the idea to be conveyed is that
              "John didn't eat at banquets or drink strong drink."

(1)   John 3:32
          ...yet *no one* receives his testimony...

(2)   John 12:19
          ...*the world* has gone after him.

(3)   John 21:25
          ...*the world itself could not contain the books...*

(4)   Mark 1:33
       And the *whole city* was gathered together about the door.

(5)   Num. 13:27
       the land...*flows with milk and honey,*...

(6)   Acts 19:27
          ...Artemis...she whom *all Asia and the world* worship.

(7)   Mark 1:5
      And there went out to him *all the country of Judea,* and *all the people of Jerusalem;* and
      they were baptized by him in the river Jordan, ...

(8)   John 10:8
      All who came before me are thieves and robbers; but the sheep did not heed them.

J. Identifying hyperbole and hypobole

In each of the following passages state the word or phrase that expresses either a hyperbole or a
hypobole. Rewrite the phrase removing the figure of speech.

Example: Job 33:14
                  Although God speaks again and again, no one pays attention to what He says. (GNB)
Answer: no one = very few people/hardly anyone

(1)   Matt. 10:22
      ...and you will be hated by all for my name's sake. But he who endures to the end will be
      saved.

(2)   Mark 14:27
      I will strike the shepherd, and the sheep will be scattered.

(3)   Mark 10:25
      It is easier for a camel to go through the eye of a needle than for a rich man to enter the
      kingdom of God.

(4)   Luke 15:24
      ...for this my son was dead, and is alive again; he was lost, and is found. And they began to
      make merry.

(5)   John 8:2
      Early in the morning he came again to the temple; all the people came to him, and he sat
      down and taught them.

(6)   John 10:8
      All who came before me are thieves and robbers; but the sheep did not heed them.

(7)   John 15:5
      I am the vine, you are the branches. He who abides in me, and I in him, he it is that bears
      much fruit, for apart from me you can do nothing.

(8)   1 Tim. 6:4
      ...he is puffed up with conceit, he knows nothing; he has a morbid craving for controversy
      and for disputes about words, which produce envy, dissension, slander, base suspicions...

(9)   Heb. 11:28
      By faith he kept the Passover and sprinkled the blood, so the Destroyer of the first-born might
      not touch them.

(10) Acts 7:24
      And seeing one of them being wronged, he defended the oppressed man and avenged him by
      striking the Egyptian.

(11) Acts 16:28
      Do not harm yourself, for we are all here.

(12) Rom. 9:13

...Jacob have I loved, but Esau have I hated. (KJV)

K. Changing euphemisms

"A euphemism is the use of a less direct word or phrase for one considered offensive" (*Webster's New World Dictionary*). Euphemisms vary from language to language. No attempt should be made to translate these literally, although some may be translated by corresponding uphemisms in the receptor language.

What is the meaning of the italicized euphemistic phrase in the following?

Example: Acts 13:36

...David...*fell asleep,* and was laid with his fathers.

Answer: The natural meaning is "David died and was buried with his ancestors."

(1) Mark 9:7

...*a voice* came out of the cloud...

(2) Luke 2:5

...Mary...was *with child.*

(3) Acts 1:25

...Judas turned aside, to *go to his own place.*

(4) Acts 7:60

And when he had said this, he *fell asleep.*

(5) Acts 22:22

Away with such a fellow *from the earth!*

L. Identifying euphemisms

In each of the following passages state the euphemistic expression(s), and give an alternate translation, removing each euphemism or modifying it.

Example: Luke 1:34

Then said Mary unto the angel, "How shall this be, seeing I know not a man?" (KJV)

Answer: "Since I know not a man" (literally) means "since I have not had sexual relations with any man," and could also be translated as "since I am a virgin."

(1) Matt. 1:19

And Joseph her husband, being a righteous man, and not wanting to disgrace her, desired to put her away secretly. (NASB)

(2) Matt. 5:19

Whoever then relaxes one of the least of these commandments and teaches men so, shall be called least in the kingdom of heaven; but he who does them and teaches them shall be called great in the kingdom of heaven.

(3) Mark 14:61

But he was silent and made no answer. Again the high priest asked him, "Are you the Christ, the Son of the Blessed?"

(4)   Luke 1:32
      He will be great, and will be called the Son of the Most High; and the Lord God will give to
      him the throne of his father David...

(5)   Luke 1:36
      And behold, your kinswoman Elizabeth in her old age has also conceived a son; and this is
      the sixth month with her who was called barren.

(6)   Luke 7:37
      And behold, a woman of the city, who was a sinner, when she learned that he was sitting at
      table in the Pharisee's house, brought an alabaster flask of ointment...

(7)   Luke 23:46
      Then Jesus, crying with a loud voice, said, "Father, into thy hands I commit my spirit!" And
      having said this he breathed his last.

(8)   Rom. 15:24
      I hope to see you in passing as I go to Spain, and to be sped on my journey there by you,
      once I have enjoyed your company for a little.

(9)   Phil. 4:10
      I rejoice in the Lord greatly that now at length you have revived your concern for me; you
      were indeed concerned for me, but you had no opportunity.

(10) 1 Tim. 5:17
      Let the elders who rule well be considered worthy of double honor, especially those who
      labor in preaching and teaching...

M. Euphemisms: Old Testament examples

In each of the following Old Testament passages there is at least one example of euphemism. For
each passage, list the euphemistic word or phrase and give a retranslation in which the meaning is
made clearer.

Example: Gen. 4:1
              Now Adam knew Eve his wife...
Answer: "knew" is a euphemism; it is translated as "had intercourse with" in TEV.

(1)   Gen. 38:26
      Then Judah acknowledged them and said, "She is more righteous than I, inasmuch as I did
      not give her to my son Shelah." And he did not lie with her again.

(2)   Gen. 49:33
      When Jacob finished charging his sons, he drew up his feet into the bed, and breathed his last,
      and was gathered to his people.

(3)   Exod. 21:10
      If he takes another wife to himself, he shall not diminish her food, her clothing, or her marital
      rights.

(4)   Lev. 15:7
      And whoever touches the body of him who has the discharge shall wash his clothes, and
      bathe himself in water, and be unclean until the evening.

(5) Deut. 21:14
Then, if you have no delight in her, you shall let her go where she will; but you shall not sell her for money, you shall not treat her as a slave, since you have humiliated her.

(6) 2 Sam. 16:21–22
Ahithophel said to Absalom, "Go in to your father's concubines, whom he has left to keep the house; and all Israel will hear that you have made yourself odious to your father, and the hands of all who are with you will be strengthened." So they pitched a tent for Absalom upon the roof; and Absalom went in to his father's concubines in the sight of all Israel.

(7) 2 Sam. 18:32
The king said to the Cushite, "Is it well with the young man Absalom?" And the Cushite answered, "May the enemies of my lord the king, and all who rise up against you for evil, be like that young man."

(8) 1 Kings 1:4
The maiden was very beautiful; and she became the king's nurse and ministered to him; but the king knew her not.

(9) 1 Kings 18:27
And at noon Elijah mocked them, saying, "Cry aloud, for he is a god; either he is musing, or he has gone aside, or he is on a journey, or perhaps he is asleep and must be awakened."

N. Source-language idioms

What are the meanings of the following source-language idioms? Study the context if necessary.

Example: Acts 18:6
               Your blood be upon your heads!
Answer: You yourselves must take the blame for it! (TEV)

(1) Matt. 5:2
...he opened his mouth and taught them...

(2) Mark 9:1
...some...will not taste death...

(3) Mark 10:5
For your hardness of heart...

(4) Mark 10:22
...his countenance fell...

(5) Luke 17:13
(They)...lifted up their voices...

(6) Acts 11:22
News of this came to the ears of the church...

(7) Acts 17:5
They...set the city in an uproar...

(8)   1 Pet. 1:13
      ...gird up your minds...

(9)   Gen. 4:6
      ...why is your face downcast?

Chapter 12
Person Reference

Additional Reading:
   Beekman and Callow 1974: Chapter 7, section 8.

A. Identifying the pronominal referent

   Sometimes in the translation it is necessary to substitute the referent for a pronoun or other general nominal word. What is the referent of the italicized word in each of the following? Study the context carefully.

Example: Acts 13:25
   I am not *he.*
Answer: Yaweyuha: I am not the *man* God promised saying he will deliver us from evil.

(1)   Mark 6:29
   When *his* disciples heard of *it,* they came and took *his* body...

(2)   Mark 16:19
   So then the Lord Jesus, after he had spoken to *them...*

(3)   Acts 3:7
   And *he* took *him* by the right hand and raised him up...

(4)   Rom. 11:7
   The elect obtained *it,* but the *rest* were hardened...

(5)   Rom. 11:11
   So I ask, have *they* stumbled so as to fall?

(6)   1 Cor. 3:19
   He catches the wise in their craftiness...

(7)   Jude 10
   But *these men* revile whatever they do not understand...

B. Inclusive/Exclusive

   In many languages there are two sets of first person plural pronouns—one including the person(s) being addressed (called INCLUSIVE) and one excluding those addressed (called EXCLUSIVE).

   Would you use the inclusive or the exclusive "we" in the following passages for the italicized words? Make your decision on the basis of the context.

Example: Luke 7:4–5
   And when they came to Jesus, they besought him earnestly, saying, "He is worthy to have you do this for him, for he loves our nation, and he built us our synagogue."
Answer: When they say "our nation", "our" is inclusive, because Jesus, who is addressed, is a member of that nation, too. But in saying "our synagogue," "our" is exclusive, because Jesus was not a member of the congregation of that synagogue.

(1)   Luke 9:49
   John answered, "Master, *we* saw a man casting out demons in your name..."

(2)   Luke 11:4
      ...forgive *us our* sins, for we ourselves forgive everyone who is indebted to *us*...

(3)   Luke 24:20
      ...and how *our* chief priests and rulers delivered him up to be condemned to death, and
      crucified him.

(4)   John 4:20
      Our fathers worshiped on this mountain...

(5)   John 18:31
      It is not lawful for *us* to put any man to death.

(6)   Acts 2:32
      This Jesus God raised up, and of that *we* all are witnesses.

(7)   1 Thess. 1:3
      ...remembering before *our* God and Father your work of faith...

(8)   Titus 1:3
      ...with which I have been entrusted by command of God *our* Savior...

(9)   Titus 3:5
      ...not because of deeds done by *us* in righteousness...

(10) 1 John 2:1
      ...*we* have an advocate with the Father, Jesus Christ...

(11) Gen. 19:2
      ...*we* will spend the night in the street...

(12) Gen. 19:13
      ...for we are about to destroy this place, because the outcry against its people has become
      great before the Lord, and the Lord has sent *us* to destroy it.

(13) Gen. 19:32
      Come, let us make our father drink wine, and we will lie with him, that we may preserve
      offspring through *our* father.

(14) Gen. 29:26
      Laban said, "It is not so done in *our* country, to give the younger before the first-born."

(15) Gen. 31:14
      Then Rachel and Leah answered him, "Is there any portion or inheritance left to us in *our*
      father's house?"

(16) Gen. 34:22
      Only on this condition will the men agree to dwell with *us,* to become one people: that every
      male among us be circumcised as they are circumcised.

(17) Gen. 37:26
      Then Judah said to his brothers, "What profit is it if *we* slay our brother and conceal his
      blood?"

(18) Gen. 39:14
      ...she called to the men of her household and said to them, "See, he has brought among us a
      Hebrew to insult *us;* he came in to me to lie with me, and I cried out with a loud voice."

(19) Gen. 41:38

And Pharaoh said to his servants, "Can *we* find such a man as this, in whom is the Spirit of God?"

(20) Gen. 42:11

We are all sons of one man, we are honest men, your servants are not spies.

C. Pronominal distinctions of number

In English we are used to distinguishing only between singular and plural. In many languages there are further distinctions such as dual (two people involved), trial (three), and then plural. The Otomí language (Mexico) is one of these. In each of the pronouns listed in the following passages, state whether you would use the dual (two persons) or plural (more than two) form in Otomí.

Example: Acts 7:26

...he appeared to *them* as *they* were quarreling...

Answer: dual

(1) Acts 8:17

...*they* began laying *their* hands on *them,* and *they* were receiving the Holy Spirit.

(2) Acts 9:39

...*they* took him to the upper room. All the widows stood...showing...garments which Dorcas made while she was with *them*...

(3) Acts 13:3

...when *they* had fasted and prayed and laid *their* hands on *them, they* sent *them* away.

D. Honorifics

In Greek and in European languages, such as Dutch and English, the third person pronoun does not present much difficulty. In Balinese the situation becomes more complicated, for one has at least four pronouns for the third person: *ida* 'a very important person,' *dane* 'an important person,' *ipun* 'a person of lower standing spoken of in a polite manner,' *ia* 'a person of lower standing spoken of in a familiar manner.' *dane*, the pronoun of the slightly less important person of the third caste, is also in use for people of lower cast who through their official position, age, or ability have a right to be respected, and for those with whom one is trying to ingratiate oneself.

Example: In the gospel stories these simple artisans and fishermen were not of such high standing. So in referring to them, the writer uses *ia* and *ipun*. In the Acts, however, the position of apostles such as Peter and John is expressed by the use of the word *dane*.

Assume you are translating into Balinese. Which of the four pronouns might you choose in the following passages? (It is impossible to know for sure without being familiar with the culture of the Balinese, so your choice will probably not equal that of a Balinese speaker, but try to decide on the basis of the position the person mentioned had in Jewish culture and the degree of respect that the individual writing about or speaking to them might have felt toward them at that time.)

ida	very important
dane	important
ipun	low standing but polite manner
ia	low standing but familiar manner

Substitute one of these for the italicized words in the following:

(1) Matt. 2:7–8
Then Herod summoned the wise men secretly...and *he* sent them to Bethlehem...

(2) Matt. 2:14
And *he* rose and took the child and *his* mother by night, and departed to Egypt.

(3) Mark 1:42
And immediately the leprosy left *him,* and *he* was made clean.

(4) Mark 3:1–5
Again *he* entered the synagogue, and a man was there who had a withered hand...and *he* said to the man, "Stretch out your hand." *He* stretched it out...

(5) Mark 12:1–2
A man planted a vineyard...and...*he* sent a servant to the tenants...

(6) Mark 14:11
And *he* sought an opportunity to betray *him.*

(7) Mark 16:9–10
...*he* appeared first to Mary Magdalene, from whom *he* had cast out seven demons. *She* went and...

(8) Luke 4:10
...for it is written, "*He* will give *his* angels charge of you..."

(9) John 19:6
When the chief priests and the officers saw *him,* they cried out, "Crucify *him,* crucify *him!*" Pilate said to them, "Take *him* yourselves and crucify *him,* for I find no crime in *him.*"

(10) Acts 9:19–20

For several days *he* was with the disciples at Damascus. And in the synagogues...*he* proclaimed Jesus, saying, "*He* is the Son of God."

E. Use of first person plural for first person singular

In some languages, especially in certain situations, writers use first person plural forms (we, us, our) when they are really only referring to themselves. This extended use of first person plural is often called the editorial we (or royal plural). But in some languages such usage could be confusing. For instance, in 1 John 1:4 "we write" would only be understood as implying joint authorship.

Study each of the following in its context to determine whether the plural person is being used in a nonliteral usage and refers to a single person or whether it is being used in a literal sense in reference to more than one person. Answer by writing either "nonliteral" or "literal." If it is not literal change it to the correct pronoun referent.

(1) Matt. 9:14

Then the disciples of John came to him, saying, "Why do *we* and the Pharisees fast?"

(2) John 16:30

Now *we* know that you know all things...

(3) Acts 20:7

On the first day of the week, when *we* were gathered together...

(4) Acts 24:4

But...I beg you in your kindness to hear *us* briefly.

(5) 2 Cor. 8:1

We want you to know, brethren, about the grace of God which has been shown...

(6) 2 Cor. 10:11

Let such people understand that what *we* say by letter when absent, we do when present.

(7) Heb. 2:5

For it was not to angels that God subjected the world to come, of which *we* are speaking.

(8) Heb. 5:11

About this *we* have much to say...

(9) Heb. 8:1

Now the point in what *we* are saying is this: *we* have such a high priest...

(10) Heb. 9:5

Of these things *we* cannot now speak in detail.

F. Use of first person singular in a generic sense

In some languages the use of a first person singular form (I, me, my) will be understood by the readers to have general application, as when Paul says, "I can do all things through Christ..." But in other cases, such a wording would be understood to mean the writer was talking about himself alone, and what he says is not true of those addressed.

For example, in Aguacateco of Guatemala the "I" had to be changed to "we" to avoid this problem in 1 Cor. 13:12: "Now I know in part; then I shall understand fully, even as I have been fully understood."

In some languages general statements that are in the singular must be changed to a form which includes the audience if they are to have universal application. Study each of the following in context to discover whether the singular person is being used in a nonliteral usage and applies in a general way or whether it is being used in a literal sense and applies to Paul only. Answer by writing "general" or "Paul only."

(1)   1 Cor. 10:29
       For why should *my* liberty be determined by another man's scruples?

(2)   1 Cor. 11:23
       For I received from the Lord what *I* also delivered to you, that the Lord Jesus...

(3)   1 Cor. 13:1
       If *I* speak in the tongues of men and of angels, but have not love...

(4)   1 Cor. 14:6
       Now, brethren, if *I* come to you speaking in tongues, how shall *I* benefit you?

(5)   1 Cor. 14:14
       For if *I* pray in a tongue, *my* spirit prays but *my* mind is unfruitful.

G. Use of third person for first or second person

In some passages the third-person noun or pronoun is used when one is referring to himself and so the referent is really first person. Jesus said, "No one has ascended into heaven but *he* who descended from heaven, the Son of Man" (John 3:13). The pronoun "he" refers to Jesus himself. In some languages the first-person pronoun would have to be used in the translation. In some instances third person is also used in referring to a real second person. In 1 Tim. 1:2, Paul begins his letter by writing, "To Timothy..." Since Timothy is the person being addressed, it may need to be translated with a second person by saying, "To you, Timothy..." In each of the following, determine to whom the italicized word actually refers and rewrite the pronoun or phrase, making a change of person so that the person is indicated by a literal rather than extended use of the pronoun. Study the context for help.

Example: John 5:26
         For as the Father has life in himself, so he has granted the *Son* also to have life in *himself*...
Answer: ...so he has granted to me, his son, to have life in myself.

Example: John 1:51
         ...you will see heaven opened, and the angels of God ascending and descending upon *the Son of Man.*
Answer: ...descending at the place where I am, the one who was born becoming man.

(1)   Luke 1:45
       And blessed is *she* who believed that there would be a fulfillment...

(2)   John 5:28
       ...for the hour is coming when all who are in the tombs will hear *his* voice...

(3)   John 10:36
       ...do you say of *him* whom the Father consecrated and sent...

(4)   John 17:2
       ...since thou hast given *him* power over all flesh...

(5)   John 20:4
       ...but the *other disciple* outran Peter and reached the tomb first...

(6)   John 20:10
       Then the *disciples* went back to *their* homes.

(7)   Rom. 1:7
       To *all* God's beloved in Rome, who are called to be saints...

(8)   3 John 1
       The *elder* to the beloved *Gaius,* whom I love in the truth.

(9)   Jude 1
       To *those* who are called, beloved in God...

(10)   Rev. 18:4–5
       Then I heard another voice from heaven saying, "Come out of her, my people, lest you take part in her sins, lest you share in her plagues; for her sins are heaped high as heaven, and *God* has remembered her iniquities."

H. Use of second or third person for first person plural

In Villa Alta Zapotec the use of the second- and third-person pronouns excludes the first person. For example, a literal translation of "they are justified by his grace" (Rom. 3:24) would exclude the writer and so the translation must read "we are justified..." In John 3:22, the clause "After this Jesus and his disciples went" would have to be translated, "After this, Jesus and we disciples went" in order to include John as one of the disciples. Note also Col. 3:1, "If then you have been raised with Christ, we should seek those things that are above."

Change the pronoun(s) in each of the following so that the speaker (writer) is not excluded.

(1)   Matt. 10:1
       And he called to him his twelve disciples and gave them authority.

(2)   Rom. 1:16
       ...it is the power of God for salvation...the Jew first and also to the Greek.

(3)   1 Cor. 3:16
       Do you not know that you are God's temple and that God's Spirit dwells in you?

(4)   1 Cor. 6:11
       ...you were washed, you were sanctified, you were justified in the name of the Lord Jesus Christ...

(5)   Eph. 2:1
      And you he made alive, when you were dead through the trespasses and sins.

(6)   Col. 2:20
      If with Christ you died to the elemental spirits of the universe, why do you live as if you still
      belonged to the world?

I. General pronouns

Where English employs *everyone, each, whoever,* and *any* the Shilluk, Anuak, and Nuer use
plural number. Instead of English *whosoever,* one must say *all who.* "Love thy neighbour
as thyself" must be translated as "Love your neighbours as yourselves" if the admonition is
to apply to all and if one is to love more than just one neighbor. (Nida 1955:58)

Rewrite the following, changing the generic word or words to plural and adjusting other words
affected by the change.

(1)   Eph. 4:32
      ...be kind to one another...

(2)   John 3:16
      ...whoever believes in him should not perish...

(3)   Acts 2:3
      And there appeared to them tongues as of fire, distributed and resting on each one of them.

(4)   Luke 6:30
      Give to every one who begs from you...

(5)   Rom. 13:10
      Love does no wrong to a neighbor...

J. Review

Identify the usage of the italicized pronoun or noun phrase in each of the following passages by
labeling it a, b, c, or d, according to the following designation:

        a. use of first plural for first singular
        b. use of first singular in a generic sense
        c. use of third person for first person
        d. literal use

(1)   John 3:14–15
      And as Moses lifted up the serpent in the wilderness, so must *the Son of man* be lifted up,
      that whoever believes in *him* may have eternal life.

(2)   John 9:27
      He answered them, "*I* have told you already, and you would not listen."

(3)   John 9:37
      Jesus said to him, "You have seen *him,* and it is *he* who speaks to you."

(4)   John 10:36
      ...do you say of *him* whom the Father consecrated and sent into the world, "You are
      blaspheming," because I said...

(5)   1 Cor. 13:2
        And if *I* have prophetic powers, and understand all mysteries...but have not love, *I* am
        nothing.

(6)   2 Cor. 1:5
        For as *we* share abundantly in Christ's sufferings, so through Christ *we* share abundantly in
        comfort too.

(7)   2 Cor. 1:13
        For *we* write you nothing but what you can read and understand...

(8)   2 Cor. 10:11
        Let such a person consider this, that what *we* are in word by letters when absent, such persons
        we are also in deed when present. (NASB)

K. Review

In the following verses change any singular pronouns or noun phrases that are used in a generic
sense to a plural form; change all abstract nouns to verb phrases; and change negatives to positives
where needed.

Example: 1 John 2:15
                If *any one* loves the world, love for the Father is not in him.
Answer: All who love the world do not truly love the Father.

(1)   John 6:35
        I am the bread of life; he who comes to me shall not hunger...

(2)   John 6:37
        ...and him who comes to me I will not cast out.

(3)   John 12:25
        He who loves his life loses it, and he who hates his life in this world will keep it for eternal
        life.

(4)   John 12:48
        He who rejects Me...has one who judges him... (NASB)

(5)   John 14:23
        If a man loves me, he will keep my word...

(6)   1 Cor. 4:1
        Let a man regard us...as servants of Christ...

(7)   1 Cor. 7:4
        For the wife does not rule over her own body, but the husband does...

(8)   1 John 4:8
        He who does not love does not know God; for God is love.

L. Review from Psalms

In each of the following passages (check the context, using the NIV, RSV, NASB, and KJV) there are one or more instances of pronominal skewing of one of the following types:

> a. A name, noun, or noun phrase is used by a writer or speaker referring to himself; i.e., third-person singular used for first-person singular.
> b. A word or phrase using a plural noun is used to refer to a group of which the writer or speaker is a member; i.e., third-person plural used for first-person plural.
> c. A third-person singular form is used when the sense is generic; i.e., it refers to anyone and everyone, not just one specific person.

For each instance of such skewing in the verses listed below, identify the type (a, b, or c) and retranslate the word or words in an unskewed form.

Example: Jer. 14:1
The word of the Lord which came to Jeremiah... (NIV)
Answer: (a) since Jeremiah is the writer, retranslate as "...to me, Jeremiah."

(1)   Ps. 1:1–2
Blessed is the man who walks not in the counsel of the wicked, nor stands in the way of sinners, nor sits in the seat of scoffers; but his delight is in the law of the Lord, and on his law he meditates day and night.

(2)   Ps. 18:50
Great triumphs he gives to his king, and shows steadfast love to his anointed, to David and his descendants for ever.

(3)   Ps. 21:1–2
In thy strength the king rejoices, O Lord; and in thy help how greatly he exults! Thou hast given him his heart's desire, and hast not withheld the request of his lips.

(4)   Ps. 25:12–13
Who is the man that fears the Lord? Him will he instruct in the way that he should choose. He himself shall abide in prosperity, and his children shall possess the land.

(5)   Ps. 25:22
Redeem Israel, O God, out of all his troubles.

(6)   Ps. 32:1
Blessed is he whose transgression is forgiven, whose sin is covered.

(7)   Ps. 34:6
This poor man cried, and the Lord heard him, and saved him out of all his troubles.

(8)   Ps. 34:8
O taste and see that the Lord is good! Happy is the man who takes refuge in him!

(9)   Ps. 53:1
The fool says in his heart, "There is no God." They are corrupt, doing abominable iniquity; there is none that does good.

(10) Ps. 73:1
Truly God is good to the upright, to those who are pure in heart.

M. Objectivization

In each of the following, the italicized word, which is an abstract noun, is being used as if it referred to an object rather than an Event or Attribute. Rewrite the passage eliminating the objectivization.

Example: Luke 1:12
        ...*fear* fell upon him (Zechariah).
Answer: Zechariah became afraid.

(1)   Mark 5:34
      ...your *faith* has made you well...

(2)   Luke 1:79
      ...to guide our feet into the way of *peace.*

(3)   Acts 2:43
      And *fear* came upon every soul...

(4)   Rom. 5:5
      ...God's *love* has been poured into our hearts...

(5)   Rom. 13:10
      Love does no wrong to a neighbor...

(6)   Phil. 1:9
      ...it is my prayer that your *love* may abound more and more...

(7)   James 1:20
      ...the *anger* of man does not work the righteousness of God.

(8)   1 John 1:4
      ...we are writing this that our *joy* may be complete.

N. Personification

Personification involves treating some abstract concept or something not human as though it were a person.

Each of the following involves a personification. Suggest a possible rewording eliminating the personification.

Example: 1 Cor. 15:55
        "O death, where is thy victory?
        O death, where is thy sting?"
Answer: Nothing will at that time cause people to die.
        People will never die again.

(1)   Matt. 2:6
      And you, O Bethlehem, in the land of Judah, are by no means least among the rulers of Judah...

(2)   Luke 13:34
      O Jerusalem, Jerusalem...How often would I have gathered your children together...

(3)   Rom. 11:11
      But through their trespass salvation has come to the Gentiles...

(4)   Rom. 13:11
      ...salvation is nearer to us now than when we first believed.

(5)   1 John 4:18
      ...perfect love casts out fear.

O. Personification and apostrophe

The passages below contain examples of personification (inanimate things or abstract concepts treated as though a person) or apostrophe (a subtype of personification in which a thing or concept is directly addressed). Identify the things or concepts in the following which illustrate this figure of speech. Then label each one as Personification or Apostrophe.

Example: Isa. 13:8
              Pangs and agony will seize them; ...
Answer: Pangs and agony, personification

Example: Isa. 14:12
              How you have fallen from heaven, O Day Star
Answer: Day Star, apostrophe

(1)   Job 27:20
      Terrors overtake him like a flood; in the night a whirlwind carries him off.

(2)   Ps. 77:16
      When the waters saw thee, O God, when the waters saw thee, they were afraid, yea, the deep trembled.

(3)   Isa. 23:1
      The oracle concerning Tyre. Wail, O ships of Tarshish, for Tyre is laid waste, without house or haven! From the land of Cyprus it is revealed to them.

(4)   Isa. 24:17
      Terror, and the pit, and the snare are upon you, O inhabitant of the earth!

(5)   Isa. 29:1
      Ho Ariel, Ariel, the city where David encamped! Add year to year; let the feasts run their round.

(6)   Jer. 47:6
      Ah, sword of the Lord! How long till you are quiet? Put yourself into your scabbard, rest and be still!

(7)   Rom. 10:6
      But the righteousness based on faith says, Do not say in your heart, "Who will ascend into heaven?" (that is, to bring Christ down)...

(8)   James 1:15
      Then desire when it has conceived gives birth to sin; and sin when it is full-grown brings forth death.

P. Changing personification and apostrophe

Rewrite each of the verses in exercise O, eliminating the figure of personification or apostrophe.

Example: Isa. 13:8
Answer: They will be extremely afraid.

Example: Isa. 14:12
Answer: You who shine like the morning star, you...

Chapter 13
Lexical Items and Situational Context

Additional Reading:
Beekman 1968:1–11.
Beekman and Callow 1974: Chapters 10–11.
Pallesen 1970:20–26.

A. Symbolic actions

Study each of the following and give a suggested translation with reasons supporting your rendition.

Example: Matt. 27:39

...those who passed by derided him, wagging their heads and saying...

Answer: In Chol (Mexico) wagging your head from side to side indicates an emphatic "No!" and wagging it up and down signifies joy. Since "wagging their heads" would give a wrong meaning, the following substitution was made: They reviled him, and showing disgust, they said...

(1) Mark 6:11

...when you leave, shake off the dust that is on your feet for a testimony against them.
Aguaruna: The action seems strange because they live in the rain forest where desert dust is unknown. The symbolic significance would be carried out through loud conversation, not by an act of shaking off of dust.

(2) Mark 7:3

...the Jews do not eat unless they wash their hands, observing the tradition of the elders...
The language helper indicated that he thought the reason they washed their hands was so they would not get sick.

(3) Mark 11:8

...others spread leafy branches which they had cut from the fields.
Many people who have had this read to them have assumed that the people who did this were trying to block Jesus' path.

(4) Mark 14:63

...the high priest tore his mantle and said...
Tewa: the language helper could see no reason why the high priest would do this.

(5) Luke 10:13

...if the mighty works done in you had been done in Tyre and Sidon, they would have repented long ago, sitting in sackcloth and ashes.
Aguaruna: The action of sitting in sackcloth and ashes is unknown.

(6) Luke 18:13

But the tax collector...would not even lift up his eyes to heaven, but beat his breast, saying...
Mesquital Otomí: This action could only mean that he was angry.

(7) Acts 13:16

...Paul stood up, and motioning with his hand...
Papago: Orators gain attention with the opening words of their address, not by motions and so the language helper wondered why Paul was motioning with his hand.

(8)   Acts 22:23
      And as they cried out and waved their garments and threw dust into the air...
      Chol: Both actions are without significance unless explained.

B. Interpersonal relations and choice of vocabulary

Study each of the passages below. Discuss the choice of vocabulary which indicates the relationship between speaker and hearer.

(1)   Matt 12:38–39
      Then some of the scribes and Pharisees said to him, "Teacher, we wish to see a sign from you." But he answered them, "An evil and adulterous generation seeks for a sign; but no sign shall be given to it except the sign of the prophet Jonah."

(2)   Luke 3:7
      He said therefore to the multitudes that came out to be baptized by him, "You brood of vipers! Who warned you to flee from the wrath to come?"

(3)   John 19:26–27
      When Jesus saw his mother, and the disciple whom he loved standing near, he said to his mother, "Woman, behold, your son!" Then he said to the disciple, "Behold, your mother!" And from that hour the disciple took her to his own home.

(4)   Acts 3:17–18
      "And now, brethren, I know that you acted in ignorance, as did also your rulers. But what God foretold by the mouth of all the prophets that his Christ should suffer, he thus fulfilled."

(5)   Rom. 7:1
      Do you not know, brethren—for I am speaking to those who know the law— that the law is binding on a person only during his life?

(6)   1 Cor. 1:10
      I appeal to you, brethren, by the name of our Lord Jesus Christ, that all of you agree and that there be no dissensions among you, but that you be united in the same mind and the same judgment.

(7)   2 Cor. 13:9–10
      For we are glad when we are weak and you are strong. What we pray for is your improvement. I write this while I am away from you, in order that when I come I may not have to be severe in my use of the authority which the Lord has given me for building up and not for tearing down.

(8)   Philem. 1–2
      Paul, a prisoner for Christ Jesus, and Timothy our brother, to Philemon our beloved fellow worker and Apphia our sister and Archippus our fellow soldier, and the church in your house...

(9)   Heb. 3:1
      Therefore, holy brethren, who share in a heavenly call, consider Jesus, the apostle and high priest of our confession.

(10) 1 John 4:1
      Beloved, do not believe every spirit, but test the spirits to see whether they are of God; for many false prophets have gone out into the world.

C. Identifying adjustments

What adjustment has been made in each of the following, probably because of the obligatory categories of the receptor language? Choose the correct letter from the following to match your answer. There may be other adjustments also, but look for ones listed here.

- a. honorifics
- b. dual person
- c. obligatory possession
- d. different use of negatives
- e. extended use of plural for singular
- f. extended use of singular for plural
- g. extended use of person
- h. different tense system
- i. different aspect system
- j. obligatory "dead" suffix

(1) Mark 5:27
She had heard the reports about Jesus...
Aguaruna: She had heard-repeatedly people saying, "Jesus truly heals many."

(2) Luke 9:37
...when they had come down from the mountain...
Balinese: when he (very important one) came down from the mountain followed by his disciples

(3) John 1:3
...without him was not anything made that was made.
Chinanteco: All things came into being because that person made all things that exist.

(4) John 3:2
...Rabbi, we know that you are a teacher come from God...
Aguaruna: Teacher, I know saying, "Surely he is one who teaches what God has said."

(5) John 3:21
...he who does what is true...
Chinanteco: all those who are engaged in right.

(6) John 4:12
Are you greater than our father Jacob...
Amuesha: Do you surpass how he used to rule, our dead grandfather Jacob...

(7) Acts 7:20
At this time Moses was born, and was beautiful before God.
Aguaruna: When they stayed like that one little child was born-remote-past, one-chosen by God, who was to be our grandfather Moses.

(8) Acts 16:24
...he put them into the inner prison...
Pame: He took them-two into the room farthest inside the jail.

(9)   Col. 4:9
       ...and with him Onesimus, the faithful and beloved brother...
       Aguaruna: Tychicus is coming with our beloved brother, Onesimus, who is an obeyer of
       Christ, with that one.

(10)   1 Tim. 1:1
       Paul, an apostle of Christ Jesus...
       Aguaruna: I am me, I am Paul. I am one chosen by Jesus Christ.

D. Elicitation

If possible, the student should find some non-English speaker and practice the elicitation
procedure suggested in Beekman and Callow 1974:167–174.

This method is to be used in identifying the area of meaning of unknown words in the receptor
language. However, in order to practice the procedure, assume you do not know the meaning of the
words which are italicized in the text below. Discover the meaning by using elicitation procedures.
Ask some person who speaks English as their first language. Write out your questions and also
record the answers you receive.

   Rev. 9:20–21
   The rest of mankind, who were not killed by these *plagues,* did not *repent* of the works of
   their hands nor give up *worshiping demons* and *idols* of gold and silver and *bronze* and stone
   and wood, which cannot either see or hear or walk; nor did they *repent* of their *murders* or
   their *sorceries* or their *immorality* or their thefts.

Chapter 14
Collocation of Lexical Items

Additional Reading:
   Beekman and Callow 1974: Chapters 10 and 11.

Concordance and meanings in context

Concordance is what results from taking a word, expression, or construction in the source text and translating each of its occurrences by the one corresponding word, expression, or construction in the receptor language. This is good practice where the context suggests that the meaning is identical and where the receptor language allows it (e.g., in what are clearly parallel passages in the Gospels), but would not be done otherwise.

A. Tongue

The word "tongue" has many senses in Greek. It is not likely that it will have all of these same senses in another language. Study each of the following to decide what the meaning of "tongue" is in the passage. If it is used in its literal or primary sense, write "literal use." If it has a figurative sense, retranslate the italicized portion in a nonfigurative way.

Example: 1 Pet. 3:10
   ...let him keep *his tongue* from evil...
Answer: Let him refrain from speaking evil.

(1)   Luke 1:64
      And immediately his mouth was opened and *his tongue* loosed...

(2)   Luke 16:24
      ...send Lazarus to dip the end of his finger in water and cool *my tongue*...

(3)   Acts 2:3
      And there appeared to them *tongues* as of fire...

(4)   Acts 2:26
      ...therefore my heart was glad, and *my tongue* rejoiced...

(5)   Rom. 14:11
      ...every knee shall bow to me, and *every tongue* shall give praise to God.

(6)   1 Cor. 12:10
      ...to another the ability to distinguish between spirits, to another various *kinds of tongues,* to another the interpretation of tongues.

(7)   James 3:6
      And *the tongue* is a fire. The tongue is an unrighteous world among our members...

(8)   1 John 3:18
      My little children, let us not love in word, neither *in tongue;* but in deed and in truth. (KJV)

(9)   Rev. 5:9
      ...thou wast slain and by thy blood didst ransom men for God from every tribe and *tongue* and people and nation...

(10)   Rev. 16:10
       ...its kingdom was in darkness; men gnawed *their tongues* in anguish.

B. House

In each of the following verses the word "house" occurs. The Greek word "house" is used in many senses. What is the sense in each of the following occurrences? After you have decided what sense is used, look the verse up in the *Living Bible* and *Today's English Version* and compare the translation of "house" with that given in the *King James Version* below.

Example: Matt. 10:6
          But go rather to the lost sheep of the house of Israel.
Answer: "House" means "people."

(1)   Matt. 10:13
       And if the *house* be worthy, let your peace come upon it...

(2)   Matt. 12:4
       ...he entered into the *house* of God, and did eat the shewbread...

(3)   Luke 1:27
       Gabriel was sent...to a virgin espoused to a man whose name was Joseph, of the *house* of David; and the virgin's name was Mary.

(4)   Acts 7:20
       In which time Moses was born...and nourished up in his father's *house* three months...

(5)   Acts 16:31
       And they said, Believe on the Lord Jesus Christ, and thou shalt be saved, and thy *house*.

C. Comparing versions

Using the RSV, TEV, and NEB, study each of the following groups of passages to see how the Greek word has been translated.

(1)   List the different ways *katargeo* 'to render useless' is rendered:

Luke 13:7	Rom. 3:3	Rom. 6:6
Rom. 7:2	1 Cor. 2:6	1 Cor. 13:8
1 Cor. 15:24	2 Cor. 3:7	2 Cor. 3:14
Gal. 5:4	2 Thess. 2:8	Heb. 2:14

(2)   List the different ways *katartizo* 'to restore' is rendered:

Matt. 4:21	1 Thess. 3:10	1 Cor. 1:10
Luke 6:40	Heb. 10:5	1 Pet. 5:10

(3)   List the different ways *parakaleo* 'to beseech' is rendered:

Matt. 2:18	Matt. 26:53	Acts 24:4
Matt. 8:31	Acts 2:40	2 Cor. 6:1

(4)   List the different ways *agon* 'contest' is rendered:

Phil. 1:30	Heb. 12:1	1 Tim. 6:12
Col. 2:1	1 Thess. 2:2	

(5)   List the different ways *akoe* 'hearing' is rendered:

      Matt. 4:24   Matt. 13:14   Matt. 24:6
      Mark 7:35   John 12:38   1 Thess. 2:13

(6)   List the different ways *achri* 'up to a point' is rendered:

      Luke 4:13   Acts 13:11   Acts 28:15
      Acts 11:5   Acts 20:6   1 Cor. 4:11

(7)   List the different ways *astheneia* 'weakness' is rendered:

      Matt. 8:17   Acts 28:9   Gal. 4:13
      Luke 5:15   Rom. 6:19   1 Tim. 5:23

D. Old and New Testament concordance

The New Testament writers were in many ways not very good examples of literal translators when they cited Old Testament passages from memory or from the Hebrew Masoretic text or even when they cite the Greek Septuagint. At times it seems that, guided by the Holy Spirit, they changed the meaning (and we as translators do not have that liberty). But often their translations, while not changing the meaning of the Old Testament passages, illustrate the same types of change covered in this volume.

Study the following and identify the changes that were made in each passage.

Example: Isa. 7:14
           Behold, a virgin shall conceive, and bear a son, and shall call his name Immanuel...
           (KJV)

           Matt. 1:23
           Behold, a virgin shall conceive and bear a son, and his name shall be called Immanuel.

Answer: Active "shall call" was changed to passive "shall be called."

(1)   Exod. 3:10a
      Come, I will send you to Pharaoh...

      Acts 7:34b
      And now come, I will send you to Egypt.

(2)   Deut. 24:1
      ...he writes her a bill of divorce and puts it in her hand and sends her out of his house, and she departs out of his house...

      Matt. 19:7
      ...to give a certificate of divorce, and put her away?

(3)   Ps. 78:2
      I will utter dark sayings from of old...

      Matt. 13:35
      I will utter what has been hidden since the foundation of the world.

(4)   Ps. 118:22
      The stone which the builders rejected has become the chief cornerstone.

      Acts 4:11
      This is the stone which was rejected by you builders but which has become the head of the
      corner.

(5)   Isa. 6:9
      Go, and say to this people...

      Acts 28:26
      Go to this people, and say...

(6)   Isa. 6:9
      'Hear and hear, but do not understand; see and see, but do not perceive.'

      Mark 4:12
      ...so that they may indeed see but not perceive, and may indeed hear but not understand...

(7)   Isa. 6:10
      ...and turn and be healed.

      Mark 4:12
      ...turn again, and be forgiven.

(8)   Joel 2:28
      And it shall come to pass afterward, that I will pour out my spirit on all flesh; your sons and
      daughters shall prophesy, your old men shall dream dreams, and your young men shall see
      visions.

      Acts 2:17
      And in the last days it shall be, God declares, that I will pour out my Spirit upon all flesh, and
      your sons and your daughters shall prophesy, and your young men shall see visions, and your
      old men shall dream dreams.

(9)   Joel 2:29
      Even upon the menservants and maidservants in those days, I will pour out my Spirit.

      Acts 2:18
      ...yea, and on my menservants and my maidservants in those days, I will pour out my Spirit;
      and they shall prophesy.

E. Identifying potential collocational clashes

In the Ifugao language the translators tried to translate John 3:16 literally by saying "God gave
his only son," but the people objected, saying "you can give animals and things, but you can't give
people." So they had to say "God *sent* his only son." Similarly in Alekano, to translate "the
educated and the uneducated" (Rom. 1:14, LB) one does not say, "the people who have gone
to/attended school..." but say "those who have spoken school and those who have not spoken
school."

Which combinations of words in the following passages are not used in their primary meaning
and therefore may set up a collocational clash if translated literally into another language?

Example: John 11:32

...Mary, when she came where Jesus was and saw him, fell at his feet, saying...

Answer: The words "fell at his feet" if taken in their primary meaning might mean she tripped over his feet and fell. (Campa, of Peru says, "She kneeled to him.")

(1) John 4:1

Now when the Lord knew that the Pharisees had heard that Jesus was making and baptizing more disciples than John...

(2) John 12:30

Jesus answered, "This voice has come for your sake, not for mine."

(3) Acts 6:7

And the word of God increased; and the number of the disciples multiplied greatly in Jerusalem, and a great many of the priests were obedient to the faith.

(4) 1 Tim. 2:8

I desire then that in every place the men should pray, lifting holy hands without anger or quarreling...

F. Basis for collocational clashes

The italicized words in the following are not being used in their primary meaning but in an extended usage. What is probably the primary meaning of the italicized word or phrase? Explain the basis of the extension of meaning as used in English, which, however, is not allowed in the language cited.

Example: John 16:6

...sorrow has *filled* your hearts.

Shipibo (of Peru) says, "in your hearts you are very sad."

Answer: The primary meaning of "fill" is to put liquid, or other nonsolid substances into a container. This has been extended to include abstracts such as "sorrow."

(1) Matt. 8:34

...all the *city* came out to *meet* Jesus...

Kui, India: everyone went out to see him.

(2) John 3:33

...sets his *seal* to this, that God is true.

Campa, Peru: They really say about God, "He is true."

(3) John 3:35

...has *given* all things *into his hand*.

Campa, Peru: Has allowed him to rule over all.

(4) John 8:51

...he will never *see* death.

Aguaruna, Peru: He will not die.

(5) John 9:16

There was a *division* among them.

Aguaruna, Peru: Arguingly they talked.

G. Basis for collocational clashes, continued

State what restriction might be the basis for changing the italicized words in the following passages. Then retranslate, removing the clash.

Example: John 16:22
...no one will *take* your joy *from* you.

Answer: "Take" might occur with concrete nouns, not abstract nouns such as joy. No one will *make* your joy *end.*

(1) Matt. 9:2
...when Jesus *saw* their faith he said...

(2) John 12:24
...unless a grain of wheat falls into the earth and *dies*...

(3) Acts 2:41
So those who *received* his word were baptized...

(4) Acts 7:31
...the voice of the Lord *came*...

(5) Acts 9:31
...the church throughout all Judea...was *built up*...

(6) Acts 9:37
...when they had washed *her*, they laid *her* in an upper room.

(7) Acts 13:22
...he *raised* up David to be their king...

(8) Acts 15:5
...and to charge them to *keep* the law of Moses.

Chapter 15
Lexical Equivalents When Concepts are Shared

Additional Reading:
  Beekman and Callow 1974: Chapter 12.

A. Semantically complex words

In the passages that follow, some of the semantically complex words have been italicized. Rewrite the passage, using a phrase or clause to replace the italicized word, thus "unpacking" the meaning components.

Example: Mark 14:70
  But again he *denied* it.
Answer: Aguaruna: Again he said, "I don't know him."

(1) Matt. 9:3
  This man is *blaspheming.*

(2) Matt. 10:4
  Judas Iscariot, who *betrayed* him.

(3) Matt. 11:16
  But to what shall I compare this *generation?*

(4) Luke 7:34
  Behold, a *glutton* and a *drunkard...*

(5) John 10:2
  ...he who enters by the door is the *shepherd* of the sheep.

(6) John 15:1
  ...my Father is the *vinedresser.*

(7) Acts 16:25
  ...Paul and Silas were *praying* and singing hymns to God...

(8) Acts 16:39
  ...so they came and *apologized* to them.

(9) Acts 27:16
  And running under the *lee* of a small *island* called Cauda, we managed with difficulty to secure the boat...

(10) Rom. 8:26
  ...the Spirit himself *intercedes* for us...

B. Semantic doublets

This figure of speech is sometimes called *hendiadys*.

Identify the doublet in each of the following passages. Note that some of these passages contain more than one doublet. Some doublets cover a whole clause or sentence.

Example: 1 John 3:18
Little children, let us not love in word or speech but in deed and in truth.
Answer: "Word or speech"; and "in deed and in truth" are both doublets.

(1) Matt. 5:12
Rejoice and be glad, for your reward is great in heaven, for so men persecuted the prophets who were before you.

(2) Matt. 23:37
O Jerusalem, Jerusalem, killing the prophets and stoning those who are sent to you! How often would I have gathered your children together as a hen gathers her brood under her wings, and you would not!

(3) Mark 14:33
And he took with him Peter and James and John, and began to be greatly distressed and troubled.

(4) Mark 15:34
And at the ninth hour Jesus cried with a loud voice..."My God, my God, why hast thou forsaken me?"

(5) Luke 1:6
And they were both righteous before God, walking in all the commandments and ordinances of the Lord blameless.

(6) Luke 2:4
And Joseph also went up from Galilee, from the city of Nazareth to Judea, to the city of David, which is called Bethlehem, because he was of the house and lineage of David...

(7) 2 Thess. 3:2
...and that we may be delivered from wicked and evil men...

(8) James 1:17
Every good endowment and every perfect gift is from above, coming down from the Father of lights with whom there is no variation or shadow due to change.

(9) James 5:11
Behold, we call those happy who were steadfast. You have heard of the steadfastness of Job, and you have seen the purpose of the Lord, how the Lord is compassionate and merciful.

C. Negating an antonym

One way of handling a positive term for which there is no literal counterpart is by negating an antonym. Rewrite the following using a negated antonym for the italicized word.

Example: Acts 11:1

Now the apostles and the brethren who were in Judea heard that the *Gentiles* also had received the word of God.

Answer: Alekano (Papua New Guinea): After that, after talk that those who were not Jews had joined on to God's word had spread, the other apostles and their Jewish brethren who were in Judea land heard it ("Those who are not Jews" = Gentiles).

(1) Matt. 10:22

...he who *endures* to the end will be saved.

(2) Matt. 13:48

(They) sorted the good into vessels but threw away the *bad*.

(3) Mark 3:25

And if a house is *divided against itself*, that house will not be able to stand.

(4) Mark 14:4

Why was the ointment thus *wasted?*

(5) Luke 16:9

...they may receive you into the *eternal* habitations.

(6) Luke 23:2

We found this man...*forbidding* us to give tribute to Caesar... (NASB)

(7) Rom. 3:28

...we hold that a man is *justified* by faith...

(8) Rom. 14:23

...he who doubts is *condemned*... (NASB)

(9) 2 Cor. 6:17

...I will *welcome* you...

(10) 2 Cor. 7:12

...it was not on account of the one who did the *wrong*...

D. Litotes

Litotes is an idiomatic means of making an affirmation by the negation or belittlement or understatement of an opposite idea. Usually it is used for emphasis. What is the natural meaning of the following?

Example: Acts 1:5

"before many days" (RSV) really means "in a few days" (TEV)

(1) Mark 9:41

...(he) will by no means lose his reward.

(2) Mark 12:34

You are not far from the kingdom of God.

(3)   Luke 1:37
      For with God nothing will be impossible.

(4)   Acts 19:23
      ...there arose no little stir concerning the Way.

(5)   Acts 20:12
      ...not a little comforted.

(6)   Acts 21:39
      ...a citizen of no mean city...

(7)   Acts 26:19
      ...not disobedient...

(8)   Rom. 4:19
      He did not weaken in faith...

(9)   2 Cor. 1:8
      ...we do not want you to be ignorant...

(10) 2 Cor. 11:5
      ...I am not in the least inferior to these superlative apostles.

(11) Eph. 1:16
      I do not cease to give thanks for you...

(12) Heb. 2:11
      ...he is not ashamed to call them brethren...

E. Reciprocal equivalent

In a reciprocal equivalent, a noun which functions as the subject assumes a different grammatical role in the reciprocal clause, and another noun becomes the subject. The verb is different in that it is the reciprocal, but it still represents the same event. Rewrite the following, using a reciprocal equivalent.

(Note that at the same time, changing from an active to a passive construction or vice versa may make the translation sound more natural in English.)

Example: 1 Cor. 11:23
              For I *received* from the Lord what I also delivered to you...
Answer: What the Lord *gave/taught* to me is what I also *gave/taught* to you.

(1)   Matt. 4:12
      Now when he *heard* that John had been arrested, he withdrew...

(2)   Matt. 24:32
      From the fig tree *learn* its lesson...

(3)   Luke 1:45
      ...blessed is she who believed...what was *spoken* to her from the Lord.

(4)   Luke 22:47
      ...and the man called Judas, one of the twelve, was *leading* them.

(5)   Acts 24:26
       ...he hoped that money would be *given* him by Paul.

F. Changing to nonfigurative expression

Each of the following contains one or more italicized figurative expressions. Rewrite the passage using a nonfigurative expression.

Example: Matt. 10:34
              I have not come to bring peace, but *a sword.*
Answer: Yaweyuha: I am not come just with peace. I have come down to cause fighting to appear too.

(1)   Luke 7:27
       Behold, I send my messenger *before thy face,* who shall prepare thy way before thee.

(2)   John 4:35
       ...*lift up your eyes,* and see how the fields are already white for harvest.

(3)   John 4:47
       ...he was *at the point of death.*

(4)   John 5:46
       If you believed *Moses,* you would believe me...

(5)   John 7:30
       ...they sought to arrest him; but no one *laid hands on him...*

(6)   John 8:37
       ...you seek to kill me, because my word *finds no place in you.*

Chapter 16
Lexical Equivalents When Concepts are Unknown

Additional Reading:
Beekman and Callow 1974: Chapter 13.

A. Form versus function

In each of the following, a word in the passage is italicized. In the comment about a word or phrase in another language, that word or phrase is also italicized. Decide (a) which type of correspondence there is between the two words as to form and function: either

      (1) same form and same function,
      (2) same form but different function,
      (3) different form but same function,
      (4) no correspondence of either form or function.

Then state (b) whether that item is being referred to in the given passage historically or didactically.

Finally, (c) give your opinion as to whether you would recommend that the translator use this particular term in this passage or not.

Example: Acts 8:28
      (He) was returning; seated in his *chariot...*
      Zapoteco: travel in *ox carts*
Answer: a. Form is different, function is the same.
      b. historical
      c. probably all right; if they saw a chariot they would probably call it an ox cart.

(1)   Matt. 3:3
      The voice of one crying in the *wilderness...*
      In Alekano there is an expression meaning *deserted land,* a place where no one lives. It might have a lot of natural vegetation, but no one would live there because it is disputed ground between two warring clans.

(2)   Mark 12:10
      The very stone which the builders rejected has become the *head of the corner...*
      In the tropical forest of Peru, houses are not made of stone but of poles with palm thatch roofs. There is one *main pole* that is the center of the whole structure in some tribes.

(3)   Mark 15:17
      ...plaiting a *crown* of thorns they put it on him. (crown being a symbol of royalty)
      Many tribes wear crowns for ornamentation when they get dressed up to go visiting or to a fiesta.

(4)   John 6:35
      Jesus said to them, "I am the *bread* of life..."
      Among the Chontal bread is made for special fiesta days only, but *tortillas* are the regular food used each day.

(5)   John 10:12
        ...the *wolf* snatches them and scatters them (the sheep).
        In the tropical forest there are no wolves, but there are *tigers* which steal domesticated
        animals.

(6)   John 11:17
        ...Lazarus had already been in the *tomb* for four days.
        Aguarunas place the dead body on a *platform* in an abandoned house. This is called
        'the-place-where-one-is-left.' The body is left there for months and food brought daily. A fire
        is kept burning at the foot. Eventually the bones are buried in a clay pot.

B. Modified with a statement of function

In the following, for the italicized word use a generic representation of form and make the
function explicit.

Example: Matt. 12:9
            synagogue
Answer: their meeting house (State of Mexico Otomí)

(1)   Mark 6:4
        A *prophet* is not without honor...

(2)   Luke 3:17
        ...and to gather the wheat into his *granary*...

(3)   John 10:1
        ...he who does not enter the *sheepfold* by the door...

(4)   John 10:2
        ...he who enters by the door is the *shepherd*...

(5)   John 11:2
        It was Mary who anointed the Lord with *ointment*...

(6)   John 15:1
        ...my Father is the *vinedresser*.

(7)   Acts 5:20
        Go and stand in the *temple* and speak...

(8)   Acts 5:21
        Now the high priest came...and called together the *council*...

(9)   Acts 21:34
        ...he ordered him to be brought into the *barracks*.

(10)   Phil. 1:1
        ...to all the saints...and *deacons*...

C. Loan word modified with a classifier

Assume that you will use a loan word for the word italicized in the following passages. What classifier would be suitable to make the meaning clear?

Example: Luke 4:1
           And Jesus...returned from the *Jordan*...
Answer: and Jesus returned from the *Jordan River*

(1)   Matt. 2:1
      Now when Jesus was born in *Bethlehem* of *Judea* in the days of Herod the king, behold, wise men from the East came to *Jerusalem*...

(2)   Matt. 3:7
      ...he saw many of the *Pharisees* and *Sadducees* coming for baptism...

(3)   Mark 10:25
      It is easier for a *camel* to go through the eye of a needle...

(4)   Luke 6:17
      ...a great multitude of people from all *Judea* and *Jerusalem* and the seacoast of *Tyre* and *Sidon*...came to hear him...

(5)   Acts 2:1
      When the day of *Pentecost* had come...

D. Cultural substitutes

In certain situations the translator may find that equivalence using a generic term or a loan word is impossible or impractical and may need to resort to the use of equivalence by cultural substitution... A cultural substitute is the use of a real-world referent from the receptor culture for an unknown referent of the original, both of the referents having the same *function*. (Beekman and Callow 1974: 201)

Study the following passages to determine if the form of the italicized item is in focus and therefore must be retained or if the function is in focus.

Example: Matt. 28:3
           ...his raiment [was] white as *snow*.
Answer: Form not in focus and may be dropped; only the intensity of the whiteness is in focus. "Snow" is only illustrative.

Example: Mark 4:3
           A sower went out to *sow*.
Answer: Though the passage is a parable, form is in focus; that is, planting the seed by scattering it on the surface is an integral part of the rest of the parable.

(1)   Matt. 10:27
      ...and what you hear whispered, proclaim upon the *housetops*.

(2)   Matt. 23:37
      ...I have gathered your children together as a *hen* gathers her brood under her wings, and you would not!

(3)   Matt. 25:1
      ...ten maidens who took their *lamps*...

(4)   Matt. 25:3
        ...they took no *oil* with them...

(5)   Matt. 26:75
        Before the *cock* crows, you will deny me three times.

(6)   Matt. 27:32
        ...this man they compelled to carry his *cross.*

(7)   Mark 4:29
        ...he puts in the *sickle,* because the harvest has come.

(8)   Mark 14:3
        ...a woman came with an alabaster *flask* of ointment of pure nard...and she broke the *flask*
        and poured it over his head.

(9)   Acts 4:27
        ...Jesus, whom thou didst *anoint...*

E. Identifying lexical equivalence

   Study the translation made of each of the following passages. What adjustment was made as to
form and function of the italicized word? Choose your answer from the following and write the
letter on your answer sheet.

        a. Same form, function made explicit
        b. Form changed to more generic, function made explicit
        c. Loan word plus classifier or descriptive phrase
        d. Form omitted and function only retained
        e. Another specific term was substituted.

Example: Matt. 8:20
           Foxes have holes, and birds of the air have nests...
           Mazahua: coyotes
Answer: e. Another specific term was substituted.

(1)   Luke 23:48
        ...returned home *beating their breasts.*
        Yaweyuha: feeling great sorrow, repeatedly beating their chests they went to their homes.

(2)   John 1:23
        I am the voice of one crying in the *wilderness.*
        Agta: where no people dwell

(3)   John 1:48
        ...under the *fig* tree, I saw you.
        Aguaruna: the tree called *ikuira* (Spanish: higuera)

(4)   Acts 8:28
        ...seated in his *chariot...*
        Sierra Otomí: cart pulled by horses

(5)   Acts 26:29
        ...except for these *chains.*
        Northern Totonaco: not have their hands bound like me

(6) Acts 27:29

...they let out four *anchors* from the stern...

Northern Totonaco: weights, and thus they were able to make the boat stand . . .

(7) Acts 27:29

...they let out four *anchors* from the stern...

Chol: that which makes a boat stay

F. Loan word modified with a specification of form or function, or both

Assume that you are going to use a loan word for the word italicized in the following passages. What additional specification of form or function, or both form and function, might be needed?

Example: Mark 1:13

...he was...tempted by *Satan*...

Answer: He was tempted by *Satan, the ruler of the demons.*

(1) John 1:41

We have found the *Messiah*...

(2) Acts 23:6

...one part were *Sadducees*...

(3) John 3:1

Now there was a man of the *Pharisees*, named Nicodemus...

(4) Acts 27:29

...they let out four *anchors* from the stern...

(5) James 3:3

...we put *bits* into the mouths of horses that they may obey us...

G. Identifying historical and didactic passages

Persons, places, animate or inanimate things, or events which are part of a historical narrative and referred to as actually being present or taking place, must be referred to as such in a translation. But items which are referred to in illustrations which are simply for didactic purposes may be changed or substituted for if their retention in a translation would result in wrong or zero meaning.

The source material to be translated may be classified as historical or didactic. Some passages consist of both types of material interwoven within the passage. Study the passage in which each of the following occur and decide if the italicized words in each example come from a historical account or a didactic (illustrative) passage.

(1) Matt. 21:19

And seeing *a fig tree* by the wayside he went to it, and found nothing on it but leaves only.

(2) Matt. 24:32

From *the fig tree* learn its lesson: as soon as its branch becomes tender and puts forth its leaves, you know that summer is near.

(3) Mark 1:6

Now John was clothed *with camel's hair,* and had a *leather girdle* around his waist...

(4) Mark 4:7

Other *seed fell among thorns* and the thorns grew up and choked it, and it yielded no grain.

(5) Mark 6:8–9
He charged them to take nothing for their journey except a *staff; no bread, no bag, no money in their belts;* but to wear *sandals* and not put on two tunics.

(6) Luke 6:44
...each tree is known by its own fruit. For *figs* are not gathered from *thorns,* nor are *grapes* picked from a *bramble bush.*

(7) Luke 6:48
...who dug deep, and *laid the foundation upon a rock;* and when a flood arose...

(8) Luke 10:34
...and went to him and bound up his wounds, *pouring on oil and wine...*

(9) Luke 13:6
A man had *a fig tree* planted in his vineyard; and he came seeking fruit on it and found none.

(10) Luke 17:2
It would be better for him if a *millstone were hung round his neck* and he were cast into the sea, than that he should cause one of these little ones to sin.

H. Evaluating faithfulness

In each of following, there is a literal translation (represented by the RSV) and two or more additional English version translations of the same passage. State for each (including the RSV) whether or not you consider the translation acceptable from the point of view of being both dynamic and also historically and culturally faithful to the original source text and culture.

Example: 1 Kings 16:24
     RSV: He bought the hill of Samaria from Shemer for *two talents of silver.*
     TEV: for six thousand pieces of silver
     LB: for $4000

Answer: RSV is culturally faithful but not dynamic since we do not use "talent" as a monetary unit.
     TEV is culturally faithful in mentioning silver, and also dynamic in that it gives a pretty good idea of a large sum of money.
     LB is dynamic but not culturally faithful in that dollars were unknown in the Old Testament times.

(1) Exod. 27:9
     RSV: a hundred cubits long for one side
     TEV: 50 yards long
     LB: will stretch for 150 feet

(2) Lev. 14:10
     RSV: an ephah of fine flour
     TEV: five pounds of flour
     LB: ten quarts of finely ground flour

(3) Hab. 2:2
     RSV: Write the vision; make it plain upon tablets...
     TEV: Write down clearly on tablets what I reveal to you...
     LB: Write my answer on a billboard, large and clear...

(4)   Mark 6:37
    RSV: two hundred denarii
    JBP: twenty pounds
    NIV: eight months of a man's wages
    LB: a fortune

(5)   Luke 13:11
    RSV: who had had a spirit of infirmity
    JBP: had been ill for some psychological cause
    LB: seriously handicapped woman who had been bent double
    TEV: had an evil spirit in her that had kept her sick

(6)   Acts 19:19
    RSV: fifty thousand pieces of silver
    JBP: five thousand pounds
    LB: $10,000
    TEV: fifty thousand dollars
    NIV: fifty thousand drachmas

(7)   2 Cor. 13:12
    RSV: Greet one another with a holy kiss.
    JBP: A handshake all around, please!
    LB: Greet each other warmly in the Lord.

Chapter 17
Special Problems in Finding Lexical Equivalents

Additional Reading:
   Barnwell 1974: Chapter 9.

A. Identifying the meaning components of some key words

For each of the following sets of words, list the generic components that they have in common that make them members of the same semantic set, and make a chart that lists the specifying or contrastive components that make the terms contrast.

Example: tabernacle, temple, synagogue
   Generic components—shelter, used by the Jews for religious purposes.
Answer: Specifying components:

tabernacle	temple	synagogue
Place where God was worshipped	Place where God was worshipped	Place where people met for religious teaching
Temporary (movable), made from skins	Permanent, made of stone	Permanent
Only one	Only one	Many in different places
People went to make sacrifices	People went to make sacrifices, pray, learn, burn incense	People went for reading of the law, teaching, prayer

(1) angel, demon, Satan
(2) prophet, angel, apostle, pastor, evangelist
(3) disciple, apostle, believer
(4) book, epistle, Scripture, Gospel
(5) soldier, centurion, commander
(6) Levite, priest, chief priest, scribe

B. Analyzing the components of meaning of key words

Each of the words listed below is followed by a number of references containing that word. The same Greek word occurs in the original text in all the references listed, but it carries various meanings. Assume each different meaning requires a different word in some Receptor Language. Group the examples according to meaning (list the letters in which the terms have the same meaning) and suggest different translations for each different meaning.

(1)   Spirit

   a. Matt. 4:1
      Then Jesus was led up by the Spirit into the wilderness...
   b. Matt. 12:43
      When the unclean spirit has gone out of a man, he passes through waterless places seeking rest, but he finds none.
   c. Matt. 26:41
      ...the spirit indeed is willing, but the flesh is weak.

     d. Mark 2:8

       And immediately Jesus, perceiving in his spirit...said to them...

     e. Mark 6:49

       But when they saw him walking upon the sea they supposed it had been a spirit... (KJV)

     f. Mark 9:25

       You dumb and deaf spirit, I command you, come out of him...

     g. Luke 4:14

       Jesus returned in the power of the Spirit into Galilee.

     h. Luke 24:37

       ...they...supposed that they saw a spirit.

(2)   Flesh

     a. Mark 10:8

       ...the two shall become one flesh.

     b. Rom. 3:20

       ...by the works of the law no flesh will be justified in His sight; ... (NASB)

     c. Rom. 8:13

       ...if you live according to the flesh you will die...

     d. Rom. 13:14

       ...make no provision for the flesh, to gratify its desires.

     e. Rom. 14:21

       .It is good neither to eat flesh, nor to drink wine... (KJV)

     f. Col. 2:5

       For though I be absent in the flesh... (KJV)

     g. 1 Pet. 1:24

       All flesh is like grass...

     h. Rev. 19:18

       ...the flesh of horses and their riders...

(3)   Glory

     a. Matt. 4:8

       ...the devil took him to a very high mountain, and showed him all the kingdoms of the world and the glory of them...

     b. Matt. 6:2

       ...do not sound a trumpet before thee, as the hypocrites do in the synagogues and in the streets, that they may have glory of men. (KJV)

     c. Matt. 6:29

       ...Solomon in all his glory was not arrayed like one of these.

     d. Matt. 16:27

       For the Son of man is to come with his angels in the glory of his Father...

     e. Matt. 24:30

       ...they will see the Son of man coming on the clouds of heaven with power and great glory...

     f. Luke 2:9

       ...the glory of the Lord shone around them...

     g. Luke 2:14

       Glory to God in the highest...

    h. John 7:18
       He who speaks on his own authority seeks his own glory; but he who seeks the glory of
       him who sent him is true...

Review of Chapters 6–17

A. Identifying translation adjustments

Identify as many translation adjustments that have been made in the following back-translation as you can. Compare with the RSV or NASB. For your answers make four columns: verse number, RSV term, Chol back-translation, and label for the type of adjustment.

John 6:1–13 (Chol back-translation)

[1]Afterwards Jesus crossed the Galilee Sea. Its name is also Tiberias. [2]Many went following Jesus because they saw the picture of his power which he showed on behalf of the sick ones. [3]Jesus went up into the mountains. There he sat with his learners. [4]It was near the day of the Pascua which the Jews celebrated. [5]Jesus looked, he saw men and women coming where he was. Jesus said to Philip, "How can we buy food for them to eat?" he said. [6]Jesus spoke these words because he wanted to see the heart of Philip how he would answer, because Jesus knew it himself (by himself) what he wanted to do. [7]Philip said, "It would not be enough, 220 denarii, in order that tortillas be purchased, in order that a little bit each eat," he said. [8]One of his learners whose name was Andrew, the younger brother of Simon Peter, said, [9]"Here is a boy. He has five units of food made of cebada (barley) and two fish. Is this enough for so many of us-inclusive?" he said. [10]Jesus said, "Tell the men and women to sit down. There is grass," he said. The men and women sat down. There were 5,000 men. [11]Jesus took the food. When he said thanks to God he tore it. He gave to his learners. The learners distributed it to the seated ones. Thus also the fish. They all ate however much they wanted. [12]When full, Jesus said to his learners, "Gather the pieces that are left so that not even a little bit will be lost." For this reason they gathered it. [13]They filled twelve baskets with he pieces of the five units of food which were left over after they had eaten.

John 6:1–13 RSV

[1]After this Jesus went to the other side of the Sea of Galilee, which is the Sea of Tiberias. [2]And a multitude followed him, because they saw the signs which he did on those who were diseased. [3]Jesus went up on the mountain, and there sat down with his disciples. [4]Now the Passover, the feast of the Jews, was at hand. [5]Lifting up his eyes, then, and seeing that a multitude was coming to him, Jesus said to Philip, "How are we to buy bread, so that these people may eat?" [6]This he said to test him, for he himself knew what he would do. [7]Philip answered him, "Two hundred denarii would not buy enough bread for each of them to get a little." [8]One of his disciples, Andrew, Simon Peter's brother, said to him, [9]"There is a lad here who has five barley loaves and two fish; but what are they among so many?" [10]Jesus said, "Make the people sit down." Now there was much grass in the place; so the men sat down, in number about five thousand. [11]Jesus then took the loaves, and when he had given thanks, he distributed them to those who were seated; so also the fish, as much as they wanted. [12]And when they had eaten their fill, he told his disciples, "Gather up the fragments left over, that nothing may be lost." [13]So they gathered them up and filled twelve baskets with fragments from the five barley loaves, left by those who had eaten.

B. Identifying translation adjustments

Identify the adjustments that have been made in the following back-translations.

Example: John 2:1

...there was a marriage...

Shipibo: a certain man got married. For him to marry they made food.

Answer: Abstract noun changed to verb phrase, and participants and events made more explicit.

(1) John 2:3

They have no wine.

Aguaruna: There is no drink.

(2) John 2:6

...each holding twenty or thirty gallons.

Chinanteco: each pot held about eight small waterpots

(3) John 2:8

Now draw some out...

Chinanteco: dip up a little of that

(4) John 2:8

...the steward of the feast.

Campa: the boss of the servants who served (the guests) at the feast

(5) John 2:12

...went down to Capernaum...

Tepehua: went to the town of Capernaum

(6) John 2:13

The Passover of the Jews was at hand...

Chinanteco: Time was approaching for the Jews to make a feast, feast of the passing by of God's angel.

(7) John 2:14

In the temple...

Aguaruna: in the house for talking to God

(8) John 2:19

Destroy this temple...

Isthmus Mixe: cause this temple to fall

(9) John 3:3

...he cannot see the kingdom of God.

Chinanteco: God cannot rule over that one

(10) John 3:4

Can he enter a second time into his mother's womb and be born?

Northern Totonac: He cannot enter into the womb of his mother to be born again.

C. Identifying translation adjustments

Identify the adjustment that has been made in each of the following translations.

Example: John 3:11
...but you do not receive our testimony.
Aguaruna: but you don't listen to what we tell

Answer: "receive"—collocational clash, words are "listened to"
"our testimony"—abstract noun changed to "what we tell"

(1) John 3:14
...Moses lifted up the serpent...
Aguaruna: Moses put up high that which had been made imitating a snake

(2) John 3:15
...have eternal life.
Campa: he will keep on living

(3) John 3:17
...but that the world might be saved through him.
Aguaruna: rather, "that he save people" saying, he sent him.

(4) John 3:19
And this is the judgment...
Northern Totonac: for this reason they will be punished

(5) John 3:23
...at Aenon near Salim...
Tepehua: in the town of Aenon near the town of Salim

(6) John 3:26
...they came to John...
Tepehua: John's disciples came to their teacher.

(7) John 3:35
...the Father loves the Son...
Aguaruna: God, our Father loves his son.

(8) John 3:36
...but the wrath of God rests upon him.
Chinanteco: for God has already become angry with him

(9) John 4:6
Jacob's well was there...
Aguaruna: There was a well which had been dug by Jacob.

III. Propositional Structure

Chapter 18
Propositions

Additional Reading:
   Barnwell 1974: Chapter 15.

A. Adjusting adjectives

Some words which are adjectives in English (or Greek) may not correspond to adjectives in other languages. In many such cases it will be necessary to translate them by a modifying phrase. "Unbelieving people" thus becomes "people who do not believe," "eternal home" becomes "home which is forever." In some cases a relative clause, a conditional clause, a verb phrase, or some other adjustment may be used.

Rewrite the following passages eliminating the adjective. Be sure the English still gives the right sense.

Example: 2 Cor. 1:12
         ...not by *earthly* wisdom...
Answer: —wisdom that is derived from those of this earth who do not know God
         —wisdom that ordinary people possess

(1)   Prov. 21:9
      ...than in a house shared with a *contentious* woman.

(2)   Prov. 22:24
      ...nor go with a *wrathful* man...

(3)   Acts 4:6
      ...all who were of the *high-priestly* family...

(4)   Acts 4:13
      ...they were *uneducated*...men...

(5)   Rom. 2:5
      ...by your...*impenitent* heart you are storing up wrath for yourself...

(6)   2 Tim. 3:8
      ...men of *corrupt* mind...

(7)   Heb. 11:25
      ...rather...than to enjoy the *fleeting* pleasures of sin... (NASB)

(8)   James 1:19
      Know this, my *beloved* brethren.

(9)   1 Pet. 2:9
      But you are a *chosen* race...

(10)   Rev. 11:7
      ...that ascends from the *bottomless* pit...

B. Adjective modifying an abstract noun

Rewrite the following, eliminating the adjective and also changing the abstract noun that it modifies to a verb phrase.

Example: Luke 1:72
                ...and to remember his *holy covenant*... ·
Answer: and to remember that God, who is perfect, covenanted...

(1)   2 Cor. 7:10
        For *godly grief* produces a repentance...

(2)   1 Thess. 5:20
        ...do not despise *prophetic utterances*. (NASB)

(3)   2 Tim. 1:9
        ...who saved us and called us with a *holy calling*...

(4)   2 Tim. 2:23
        Have nothing to do with *foolish, stupid, senseless controversies.*

(5)   Heb. 7:16
        ...but by the power of an *indestructible life.*

(6)   Heb. 10:27
        ...but a *fearful prospect* of *judgment*...

C. Eliminating abstract nouns and participles

For each of the following passages rewrite eliminating abstract nouns and participles, forming a nonparticipial expression using an active verb.

Example: 1 Cor. 15:52
                ...the dead will be raised imperishable...
Answer: Those (Christians) who have died will be raised with bodies that will never perish/never die again.

(1)   Acts 3:19
        ...that times of refreshing may come... (NASB)

(2)   Rom. 12:7
        ...he who teaches, in his teaching...

(3)   Rom. 13:6
        ...for the authorities are ministers of God, attending to this very thing.

(4)   Rom. 13:10
        ...therefore love is the fulfilling of the law.

(5)   1 Cor. 7:19
        For neither circumcision counts for anything nor uncircumcision, but keeping the commandments of God.

D. Adjectival constructions, abstract nouns, and propositions

Rewrite the following as propositions, eliminating the adjectival constructions and abstract nouns. Use only active verb constructions.

Example: 1 Pet. 2:15

For it is God's will that by doing right you should put to silence the ignorance of foolish men.

Answer: God wills. You do right. You cause men to be silent. The men are ignorant. The men act foolish.

(1) James 1:16

Do not be deceived, my beloved brethren.

(2) James 1:11

For the sun rises with its scorching heat and withers the grass...

(3) James 5:15

...the prayer of faith will save the sick man, and the Lord will raise him up; and if he has committed sins, he will be forgiven.

(4) 1 Pet. 1:8

Without having seen him you love him; though you do not now see him you believe in him and rejoice with unutterable and exalted joy.

(5) 1 Pet. 1:23

You have been born anew, not of perishable seen but of imperishable, through the living and abiding word of God...

E. Metonymy, synecdoche, and propositions

In the following passages identify the metonymy or synecdoche. Rewrite the passage in propositions, being sure to eliminate the figurative usage.

Example: Luke 1:32

...the Lord God will give to him the throne of his father David...

Answer: "Throne" and "father" both are metonymy. God is Lord. God will cause Christ to rule. David ruled. Christ is a descendant of David.

(1) Luke 1:49

...he who is mighty has done great things for me, and holy is his name.

(2) Luke 1:70–71

...he spoke by the mouth of his holy prophets from of old, that we should be saved...from the hand of all who hate us...

(3) Luke 3:6

...all flesh shall see the salvation of God.

(4) Acts 2:36

Let all the house of Israel therefore know assuredly that God has made him both Lord and Christ, this Jesus whom you crucified.

(5) Col. 4:18

I, Paul, write this greeting with my own hand. Remember my fetters.

F. Writing propositions

Rewrite the following passages in propositions.

Review the steps on page 191 and 192 of Larson 1984.

Example: Luke 24:13–14

That very day two of them were going to a village named Emmaus, about seven miles from Jerusalem, and talking with each other about all these things that had happened.

Answer: That day two disciples were going to Emmaus. Emmaus was a village. Emmaus was seven miles from Jerusalem. The two disciples were talking to each other. The two disciples were talking about all the things that had happened.

(1)   Matt. 10:1

And he called to him his twelve disciples and gave them authority over unclean spirits, to cast them out, and to heal every disease and every infirmity.

(2)   Matt. 17:2–3

And he was transfigured before them, and his face shone like the sun, and his garments became white as light. And behold, there appeared to them Moses and Elijah, talking with him.

(3)   Mark 1:35–37

And in the morning, a great while before day, he rose and went out to a lonely place, and there he prayed. And Simon and those who were with him pursued him, and they found him and said to him...

G. Writing Luke 1:76–77 as propositions

Following the four steps on pages 191–92 of the textbook, list the proposition found in this passage. First list all Events, add all participants, express as proposition with finite verb, and rewrite the passage, reordering as necessary any connecting propositions.

Luke 1:76–77

[76]And you, child, will be called the prophet of the Most High; for you will go before the Lord to prepare his ways, [77]to give knowledge of salvation to his people in the forgiveness of their sins...

H. Writing Titus 1:1–3 as propositions

Rewrite these three verses as propositions making all participants and events explicit. Follow the steps on pages 191–92 of Larson 1984.

Titus 1:1–3

[1]Paul, a servant of God and an apostle of Jesus Christ, to further the faith of God's elect and their knowledge of the truth which accords with godliness, [2] in hope of eternal life which God, who never lies, promised ages ago [3] and at the proper time manifested in his word through the preaching with which I have been entrusted by command of God our Savior;

I. Writing propositions

For each of the following passages (selection follows Barnwell 1974:164–66) apply the three steps of the procedure for analysis given in the textbook on pages 191–92. Be careful to avoid the use of passive constructions.

(1)   Luke 24:46–47
        ...[46]and said to them, "Thus it is written, that the Christ should suffer and on the third day rise from the dead, [47]and that repentance and forgiveness of sins should be preached in his name to all nations, beginning from Jerusalem."

(2)   Eph. 2:8–9
        [8]For by grace you have been saved through faith; and this is not your own doing, it is the gift of God—[9]not because of works, lest any man should boast.

(3)   Jude 16
        These are grumblers, malcontents, following their own passions, loud-mouthed boasters, flattering people to gain advantage.

(4)   1 Pet. 2:15
        For it is God's will that by doing right you should put to silence the ignorance of foolish men.

(5)   1 Thess. 1:2–3
        [2]We give thanks to God always for you all, constantly mentioning you in our prayers, [3]remembering before our God and Father your work of faith and labor of love and steadfastness of hope in our Lord Jesus Christ.

(6)   1 Pet. 1:3b–4
        [3]...By his great mercy we have been born anew to a living hope through the resurrection of Jesus Christ from the dead, [4]and to an inheritance which is imperishable, undefiled, and unfading, kept in heaven for you.

(7)   Heb. 2:2–3
        [2]For if the message declared by angels was valid and every transgression or disobedience received a just retribution, [3]how shall we escape if we neglect such a great salvation? It was declared at first by the Lord, and it was attested to us by those who heard him...

Chapter 19
Relations within Event Propositions

Additional Reading:
Beekman, Callow, and Kopesec 1981.

A. Making implied Events explicit

The following phrases indicating possession, without using "of," cannot be translated into some languages with a simple possession. Make explicit the verb that tells the relationship.

Example: Prov. 10:15
A rich man's wealth...
Answer: the wealth a rich man possesses

(1) John 4:6
Jacob's well

(2) Mark 2:18
John's disciples

(3) 1 John 1:10
his word

(4) 1 John 2:12
your sins

(5) Col. 1:24
Christ's afflictions

(6) Mark 3:27
strong man's house

(7) Mark 1:39
their synagogues

(8) Acts 16:26
every one's fetters

(9) Acts 21:11
he took Paul's girdle

B. Analyzing "work of…"

Surface structure is what may be termed "multifunctional." That is to say, a given grammatical construction may signal different meanings, depending on the context; a lexical item also can have a number of senses. Further, and more significant, a given word or expression may be fulfilling several functions simultaneously. (Beekman and Callow 1974:270–71)

All of the following contain the genitive construction "work of…" Study each passage and reword it so as to give the meaning of the construction.

Example: John 9:4
           We must work *the works of him who sent me…*
Answer: We must do what the one who sent me wants us to do.

(1)   John 6:29
     This is *the work of God*, that you believe in him whom he has sent.

(2)   John 9:3
     It was not that this man sinned, or his parents, but that *the works of God* might be manifest in him.

(3)   John 10:37
     If I am not doing *the works of my Father*, then do not believe me…

(4)   Rom. 14:20
     Do not, for the sake of food, destroy *the work of God.*

(5)   Gal. 2:16
     …yet who know that a man is not justified by *works of the law* but through faith in Jesus Christ…

(6)   Phil. 2:30
     …for he nearly died for *the work of Christ…*

(7)   2 Thess. 1:11
     …that our God may make you worthy of his call, and may fulfil every good resolve and *work of faith* by his power…

(8)   Gal. 5:19
     Now *the works of the flesh* are plain.

(9)   1 John 3:8
     The reason the Son of God appeared was to destroy *the works of the devil.*

C. Analyzing "love of…"

In each of the following, the genitive construction "love of…" occurs. Reword the passage so as to give the meaning of the genitive construction.

Example: Rom. 8:35
           Who shall separate us from *the love of Christ?*
Answer: Who shall separate us from the love which Christ has for us?

(1)   Luke 11:42
     But woe to you Pharisees! for you…neglect justice and *the love of God…*

(2)   John 5:42
       But I know that you have not *the love of God* within you.

(3)   Rom. 5:5
       and hope does not disappoint us, because *God's love* has been poured into our hearts through
       the Holy Spirit...

(4)   Rom. 15:30
       I appeal to you, brethren, by our Lord Jesus Christ and by *the love of the Spirit...*

(5)   2 Cor. 5:14
       For *the love of Christ* controls us...

(6)   2 Cor. 13:11
       ...*the God of love* and peace will be with you.

(7)   Eph. 3:19
       ...to know *the love of Christ* which surpasses knowledge...

(8)   1 John 2:5
       but whoso keepeth his word, in him verily is *the love of God* perfected... (KJV)

(9)   1 John 5:3
       For this is *the love of God...*

(10)   Jude 21
       ...keep yourselves in *the love of God...*

D. Identifying the underlying meaning of identical grammatical structures

In each of the following, two or three verses are cited in which the same grammatical
construction is used but the underlying meaning is distinct. Reword each passage so as to show the
difference in meaning.

Example: Luke 18:27
               "What is impossible *with men* is possible *with God.*"
Answer: Things which men are not able to do, God is able to do.

Example: 2 Pet. 3:8
               ...*with the Lord* one day is as a thousand years...
Answer: The Lord perceives one day and a thousand years as if they were exactly the same

(1)   Acts 21:21
       ...they have been told...that you teach all the Jews who are *among the Gentiles* to forsake
       Moses...

(2)   Rom. 2:24
       The name of God is blasphemed *among the Gentiles* because of you.

(3)   Acts 15:12
       ...they related what signs and wonders God had done through them *among the Gentiles.*

(4)   Philem. 13
       I would have been glad to keep him *with me...*

(5)   Matt. 26:23
       He who has dipped his hand in the dish *with me...*

(6)   Luke 1:59
      And *on* the eighth day they came to circumcise the child...

(7)   Luke 13:7
      I have come seeking fruit *on* this fig tree...

(8)   Matt. 14:26
      But when the disciples saw him walking *on the sea*, they were terrified...

(9)   Matt. 27:25
      And all the people answered, "His blood be *on us* and *on our children!*"

(10) Acts 4:5
      On the morrow their rulers and elders and scribes were gathered together in Jerusalem...

E. Identifying semantic roles

In each of the following examples, identify the semantic role of the italicized word as Agent, Patient, Beneficiancy, or Instrument.

Example: Mary was hit by a car.
Answer: patient

(1)   *Peter* coughed.

(2)   *The cakes* are selling well.

(3)   *The little girl* was given *a present* by *each of the guests.*

(4)   *He* was knocked out by *a flying saucer.*

(5)   *The doctor*'s *lancet* pierced *the boil.*

(6)   *The doctor*'s *assistant* pierced *the child's boil.*

F. Restructuring for naturalness

The following exercise (from Barnwell 1980:174–75) illustrates the fact that, in any language, the same surface form may represent a number of different relationships. In another language, these different relationships may be expressed by a variety of different forms.

Each of the following examples includes an italicized phrase which in Greek has the form of the preposition *en* followed by a noun or pronoun in the dative case. Into English, or any language of your choice, translate these italicized phrases into the natural form with equivalent meaning in the context. You may refer to any translations which are available to you.

Be ready to restructure the form of the passage where necessary.

(1)   Mark 2:1
      Kai eiselthōn   palin eis Kapharnaoum di'   hēmerōn ēkousthē   hoti en
      and having^entered again into Capernaum   through days   it^was^heard that *in*
          oikō   estin.
          house he^is

      RSV And when he returned to Capernaum after some days, it was reported that he
      was_____.

(2)   Acts 9:17

Iēsous ho ophtheis   soi   en tē' hodō hē   erchou
Jesus   the having^appeared to^you *XX the way*   by^which you^came

RSV the Lord Jesus who appeared to you _____by which you came

(3)   Luke 22:24

Egeneto   de kai philoneikia en autois
there^happened and also rivalry   *XX them*

RSV A dispute also arose_____.

(4)   Luke 22:49

Kurie, ei pataksomen   en   machairē
Lord   if we^shall^strike *XX sword*

RSV Lord, shall we strike_____?

(5)   Luke 22:20

Touto to potērion hē kainē diathēkē en   tō   haimati mou
this   the cup   the new covenant *XX the blood of^me*

RSV This cup…is the new covenant_____.

(6)   Rom. 1:25

Hoitines metēllaksan tēn alētheian tou   Theou en tō seudei
who   changed   the truth   of^the God *XX the lie*

RSV they exchanged the truth about God_____.

(7)   Eph. 1:20

hēn   enērgēken   en tō Christō egeiras   auton ek   nekrōn, kai
which he^accomplished *XX the Christ* having^raised him   from dead, and
    kathisas   en deksia autou   en   tois epouraniois
    having^seated *XX right   of^him XX the heavenlies*

RSV which he accomplished _____ when he raised him from the dead and made him
    sit_____.

G. One form with various meanings (from Barnwell 1974:174–75)

Imagine that you are preparing to translate into a language which has the following
characteristics:

     a. no preposition which is equivalent to the English "with"
     b. no passive form—the Agent role must always coincide with the grammatical subject

Recase each of the following passages into a form which might be more readily transferred into
such a language, and which expresses the underlying relations clearly.

Make implied Event concepts explicit where necessary. Remember that there may be more than
one proposition involved.

(1)   Acts 1:5
      …John baptized with water…

(2)   Acts 1:22
      ...one of these men must become with us a witness to his resurrection.

(3)   Acts 2:13
      They are filled with new wine.

(4)   Acts 2:22
      ...Jesus of Nazareth, a man attested to you by God with mighty works and wonders and signs which God did through him...

(5)   Acts 2:29
      ...his tomb is with us to this day.

(6)   Acts 27:10
      ...the voyage will be with injury and much loss, not only of the cargo and the ship, but also of our lives.

(7)   Acts 27:19
      ...they cast out with their own hands the tackle of the ship.

(8)   Mark 1:13
      ...he was with the wild beasts...

(9)   Mark 1:32
      ...all who were...possessed with demons.

(10) Mark 5:4
      ...for he had often been bound with fetters and chains...

(11) Mark 1:41
      Moved with pity, he stretched out his hand and touched him...

Chapter 20
Relations within State Propositions

Additional Reading:
Beekman, Callow, and Kopesec 1981: Chapter 6.

A. Genitive constructions restated as State propositions

Certain genitive constructions may be restated in the form of a State proposition. When this is the case, the two nominals usually represent Things, though there is a less common form in which an Abstraction and a Thing are represented. (Beekman and Callow 1974:251)

Restate each of the following as a State proposition, eliminating the genitive construction.

Example: Mark 14:13
    jar of water
Answer: the jar contains water

(1) Eph. 1:13
    the word of truth

(2) Mark 1:9
    Nazareth of Galilee

(3) Mark 14:3
    the house of Simon

(4) Rom. 11:22
    the kindness...of God

(5) Eph. 1:7
    the riches of his grace

(6) Matt. 26:71
    Jesus of Nazareth

(7) Acts 11:5
    the city of Joppa

(8) Mark 6:15
    prophets of old

B. Identifying State and Event propositions

A proposition is the minimal semantic unit consisting of a concept or a combination of concepts which communicates an *Event* or *Relation*.

On the basis of this definition, two different classes of propositions may be distinguished: those which have an Event central are called Event propositions, and those which have a Relation central are called State propositions... An *Event proposition* communicates an Event and consists of any other concepts related to that Event... A *State proposition* communicates a Relation, either between two concepts belonging to the same semantic class, or between an Abstraction and a Thing or Event. (Beekman and Callow 1974:273–74, emphasis added)

The following propositions are taken from the propositional display of the book of Jude presented in Blight 1970. Which of these are State propositions and which are Event propositions?

Example: Jude 1
I am Jude. I serve Christ.
Answer: State proposition; Event proposition

(1) God called you.

(2) and they are ungodly

(3) He is our only Master and Lord

(4) that God destroyed some of the people of Israel

(5) in order that God will judge them

(6) Michael is the archangel

(7) and because they rebel against (authority)

(8) these men are (dangerous to the believers)

(9) They have no fruit (at harvest time)

(10) (He was) in the seventh generation from Adam

C. Identifying implicit Events

In each of the following passages some Events have been left implicit and some Events are grammatically nouns (abstract nouns). List all the Events for each passage, including those which are only implicit. Then indicate who is the agent of each Event.

(1) Matt. 2:7
Then Herod summoned the wise men secretly and ascertained from them what time the star appeared...

(2) John 4:12
Are you greater than our father Jacob, who gave us the well, and drank from it himself, and his sons, and his cattle?

(3) Luke 2:4–5
And Joseph also went up from Galilee, from the city of Nazareth, to Judea, to the city of David, which is called Bethlehem, because he was of the house and lineage of David, to be enrolled with Mary, his betrothed, who was with child.

D. Writing State propositions

Identify the topic, relation (state role), and comment in the phrase which is italicized. Write as a State proposition in English. (See page 215 of the textbook.)

Example: Mark 15:17
...plaiting a *crown of thorns* they put it on him.
Answer: Topic: crown   Role: Substance   Comment: thorns
A crown made of thorns *or* A crown woven of thorns.

(1) John 19:17
...he went out, bearing *his own cross*...

(2) Luke 19:4
...he ran on ahead and climbed up into a *sycamore tree*...

(3) Luke 20:47
...who devour *widow's houses* and...make long prayers.

(4) Luke 21:5
And as some spoke of the temple, how it was adorned with *noble stones*...

(5) Luke 22:7
Then came the day of *Unleavened Bread*...

(6) Luke 22:39
...and went...to the *Mount of Olives*...

(7) Luke 23:2
...saying that he himself is *Christ a King.*

(8) Luke 23:27
And there followed him *a great multitude of people*...

(9) Col. 1:18
He is *the head of the body*...

(10) Rev. 5:8
...with *golden bowls full of incense*...

E. Writing Romans 1:1–7 as propositions

Rom. 1:1–7 is one sentence in the RSV. First go through and write down every abstract noun which occurs in each verse. Next list all the genitive constructions by the verse in which they occur. If there are any passive clauses, list these and indicate in which verse they are found. These lists will help you to focus on some of the main things you will want to change in order to rewrite the passage into propositions. Rewrite in propositions making explicit the subject of every verb.

Rom. 1:1–7 RSV

Paul, a servant of Jesus Christ, called to be an apostle, set apart for the gospel of God [2]which he promised beforehand through his prophets in the holy scriptures, [3] the gospel concerning his Son, who was descended from David according to the flesh [4]and designated Son of God in power according to the Spirit of holiness by his resurrection from the dead, Jesus Christ our Lord, [5]through whom we have received grace and apostleship to bring about the obedience of faith for the sake of his name among all the nations, [6]including yourselves who are called to belong to Jesus Christ; [7]To all God's beloved in Rome, who are called to be saints:

Chapter 21
Skewing between Propositional Structure and Clause Structure

Additional Reading:
   Beekman and Callow 1974: Chapter 14.

A. Identifying abstract nouns

   Which noun (or nouns) in each of the following examples is derived from a verb and therefore has a basic semantic meaning of Event or Action?

Example: 1 Cor. 16:24
             My love be with you all in Christ Jesus.
Answer: love

(1)   Rom. 1:16
      ...for salvation to every one who has faith...

(2)   Rom. 3:20
      ...through the law comes knowledge of sin.

(3)   1 Thess. 2:9
      For you remember our labor and toil, while we preached to you...

(4)   1 Thess. 3:5
      I sent that I might know your faith, for fear that somehow the tempter had tempted you and that our labor would be in vain.

(5)   James 1:15
      ...sin...brings forth death.

(6)   Rev. 20:4
      ...seated on them were those to whom judgment was committed.

B. Changing abstract nouns to verb phrases

   Assuming that the language into which you are translating does not have special nouns to express concepts such as those italicized in the following passages, how might you give the same meaning by using an active verb phrase for the noun? Do not use a participle (e.g., dying) or an infinitive (e.g., to die) in retranslating the italicized words.

Example: Rev. 21:4
             ...and *death* shall be no more...
Answer: and no one shall die any more

(1)   Matt. 9:13
      ...I came...to call *sinners.*

(2)   Matt. 21:22
      ...whatever you ask in *prayer...*

(3)   Luke 4:18
      ...to proclaim *release* to the captives...

(4)   John 3:19
       ...because their *deeds* were evil.

(5)   John 4:10
       If you knew the *gift* of God... .

(6)   Acts 4:12
       ...there is *salvation* in no one else...

(7)   Acts 16:13
       ...where we supposed there was a place of *prayer*...

(8)   Col. 1:8
       ...has made know to us your *love*...

(9)   1 John 4:21
       And this *commandment* we have from him...

C. Identifying and unskewing abstract nouns

In each of the following passages there are one or more abstract nouns, which may be derived from adjectives as well as verbs. Retranslate the passage so as to eliminate the skewing shown by these abstract nouns.

Example: Rom. 6:4
                 We were buried therefore with him by baptism into death.
Answer: When we were baptized it was as though we died and were buried with him.

(1)   Acts 2:42
       • And they devoted themselves to the apostles' teaching and fellowship, to the breaking of bread and the prayers.

(2)   Acts 5:31
       God exalted him...as Leader and Savior, to give repentance to Israel and forgiveness of sins.

(3)   Rom. 13:13
       ...let us conduct ourselves becomingly...not in reveling and drunkenness, not in debauchery and licentiousness, not in quarreling and jealousy.

(4)   Eph. 1:7–8
       In him we have redemption...the forgiveness of our trespasses, according to the riches of his grace which he lavished upon us.

(5)   2 Tim. 3:16
       All Scripture is...profitable for teaching, for reproof, for correction, and for training in righteousness...

D. Changing abstract nouns to relative clauses

Many times abstract nouns will need to be translated by relative clauses beginning with "that," "who," "which," etc. Change the abstract noun in each of the following to a relative clause. Do not use a participle.

Example: Acts 17:7
                 ...they are all acting against the decrees of Caesar...
Answer: They are all acting against that which Caesar has decreed.

(1)   Rom. 1:8
       ...your *faith* is proclaimed in all the world.

(2)   Acts 2:42
       And they devoted themselves to the apostles' *teaching*...

(3)   Prov. 21:17
       He who loves *pleasure* will be a poor man...

(4)   Matt. 5:9
       Blessed are the *peacemakers*...

(5)   Rom. 1:9
       For God is my *witness*, whom I serve...

E. Changing order within clauses

The necessity for adjustments in the order of words seems so obvious as scarcely to require mention. However, there are certain situations in which the shifts of order may not seem so vital, but in which they are nevertheless important if the translation is to be natural. (Nida 1964:235)

In Aguaruna of Peru, the word order within the clause may vary considerably. However, the most frequent order, especially in narrative material is: time, subject, object, indirect object, location, manner, and (finally) predicate. The predicate may be a compound verb. Quotations are direct objects. Rewrite the following putting the clause units into this order.

Example: John 4:7
                There came a woman of Samaria to draw water. Jesus said to her, "Give me a drink."

                Aguaruna back-translation:
                A woman of Samaria, water drawing came, Jesus "Water me give, that I drink," said.

(1)   Mark 5:1
       They came to the other side of the sea...

(2)   Mark 5:21
       Jesus had crossed again in the boat to the other side...

(3)   Mark 6:13
       And they cast out many demons, and anointed with oil many that were sick and healed them.

(4)   Mark 8:27
       And Jesus went on...to the villages of Caesarea Philippi; and on the way he asked..."Who do men say that I am?"

(5)   Mark 9:2
       After six days Jesus took with him Peter and James and John, and led them up a high mountain...

F. Placing verbal complements before the verb

In many languages the modifiers of the verb must always precede the verb. Rewrite the following, putting all verbal complements just before the verb.

Example: Luke 1:64
                   And immediately his mouth was opened...
Answer: His mouth was immediately opened.

(1)   Matt. 5:11
        ...utter all kinds of evil against you falsely...

(2)   Matt. 5:25
        Make friends quickly with your accuser...

(3)   Matt. 13:26
        ...then the weeds appeared also.

(4)   Acts 10:2–3
        who...gave alms liberally...and prayed constantly to God. About the ninth hour of the day he saw clearly in a vision...

(5)   Rev. 2:16
        ...I will come to you soon...

G. Review

In the following passages, change all passive constructions to active and all italicized abstract nouns to active verb phrases, adding implicit participants as needed.

Example: 1 Pet. 1:7
                   ...at the *revelation* of Jesus Christ.
Answer: ...at the time when Jesus Christ will reveal himself

(1)   Mark 2:5
        ...your *sins* are forgiven.

(2)   Matt. 28:18
        All *authority* has been given to me.

(3)   Mark 6:14
        John the *baptizer* has been raised from the dead...

(4)   Gal. 6:1
        ...if a man is overtaken in any *trespass*...

(5)   Rev. 20:4
        Then I saw thrones, and seated on them were those to whom *judgment* was committed.

H. Identifying passives and actives

State whether the following verb phrases are passive or active.

Example: Mark 6:14
                   John the baptizer has been raised from the dead...
Answer: passive

(1) Matt. 28:18
All authority...has been given unto me.

(2) Mark 13:13
...you will be hated by all for my name's sake.

(3) John 1:6
There was a man sent from God...

(4) John 1:29
The next day he saw Jesus coming toward him...

(5) John 1:45
Philip found Nathaniel, and said to him...

(6) John 2:12
After this he went down to Capernaum...

(7) Acts 8:10
They all gave heed to him...

(8) Acts 8:33
For his life is taken up from the earth.

(9) 2 Cor. 1:6
If we are afflicted...if we are comforted...

(10) 1 John 4:9
In this the love of God was made manifest among us...

I. Changing passives to actives

Among the many hundreds of languages in the East New Guinea Highlands stock, none has a regular construction equivalent to the passive. In some cases an intransitive verb is the semantic equivalent, but in most cases the translation must use a transitive verb, meaning that the actual agent is supplied as the subject or an unspecified "they" is supplied if the actual agent is not known.

Example: Eph. 1:13
Ye were sealed with that Holy Spirit... (KJV)

Answer: Alekano: (God) having bestowed his spirit on you, you have become accompanied with God's ownership-mark...

Example: Eph. 3:5
...it has now been revealed... (KJV)

Answer: Yaweyuha: Later God's Spirit revealed and told it to...

Suppose the language into which you are translating has no passive verb constructions. Write the following passages so that the passive is changed to active. Examine the context. If the subject is not indicated in the passage, supply one which is appropriate, or "they/people/someone" if the agent is unknown or not in focus.

Example: Mark 1:9
Jesus...was baptized by John in the Jordan.

Answer: John baptized Jesus in the Jordan.

Example: Mark 1:14
...John was arrested...

Answer: Soldiers/they arrested John.

(1)   Matt. 5:9
...for they shall be called sons of God.

(2)   Matt. 5:14
A city set on a hill cannot be hid.

(3)   Mark 2:1
...it was reported that he was at home.

(4)   Mark 2:5
...your sins are forgiven.

(5)   Mark 3:22
He is possessed by Beelzebub...

(6)   Mark 14:9
...wherever the gospel is preached...

(7)   John 19:20
...the place where Jesus was crucified...

(8)   1 Cor. 11:23
...the Lord Jesus on the night when he was betrayed...

(9)   1 Cor. 11:31
...if we judged ourselves truly, we should not be judged.

(10) Col. 1:11
      May you be strengthened with all power...

J. Making the agent explicit

In each of the passages listed below, change the passive to an active construction, inserting the agent which seems most appropriate. (Note: check the context!) In doing so, try to take into account the reason the original writer used the passive—e.g., the agent was unknown, or irrelevant, or not in focus, or (being God) was avoided euphemistically.

Example: Luke 17:34
      " ...one will be taken, and the other left."
Answer: "God will take the one and he will leave the other," because the agent, God, is probably unstated simply for euphemistic reasons.

(1) Matt. 22:14
     For many are called, but few are chosen.

(2) Mark 2:20
     The days will come, when the bridegroom is taken away from them, and then they will fast in that day.

(3) Mark 2:27
     And he said to them, "The sabbath was made for man, not man for the sabbath... "

(4) Mark 3:28
     Truly, I say to you, all sins will be forgiven the sons of men, and whatever blasphemies they utter...

(5) Mark 4:25
     For to him who has will more be given; and from him who has not, even what he has will be taken away.

(6) Mark 6:2
     And on the sabbath he began to teach in the synagogue; and many who heard him were astonished, saying, "Where did this man get all this? What is the wisdom given to him? What mighty works are wrought by his hands!"

(7) Mark 10:33
     Behold, we are going up to Jerusalem; and the Son of man will be delivered to the chief priests and the scribes, and they will condemn him to death, and deliver him to the Gentiles.

(8) 1 Cor. 1:13
     Is Christ divided? Was Paul crucified for you? Or were you baptized in the name of Paul?

(9) 1 Cor. 1:18
     For the word of the cross is folly to those who are perishing, but to us who are being saved it is the power of God.

(10) 1 Cor. 1:28
      God chose what is low and despised in the world, even things that are not, to bring to nothing things that are.

(11) 1 Cor. 3:15
      If any man's work is burned up, he will suffer loss, though he himself will be saved, but only
      as through fire.

(12) 1 Cor. 4:2
      Moreover it is required of stewards that they be found trustworthy.

K. Changing actives to passives

There are some languages that have a preference for passive constructions. In such cases a translator should try to shift from active to passive whenever possible to maintain naturalness.

Change the following active constructions to passive.

Example: Acts 1:23
             And they put forward two, Joseph...and Matthias.
Answer: Two were nominated (by them), Joseph and Matthias.

(1)   Mark 12:43
      ...this poor widow has put in more than all those who are contributing...

(2)   Mark 13:5
      Take heed that no one leads you astray.

(3)   John 9:13
      They brought to the Pharisees the man who had formerly been blind.

(4)   Acts 1:6
      Lord, will you at this time restore the kingdom to Israel?

(5)   1 Cor. 16:10
      When Timothy comes, see that you put him at ease...

L. Causative

Sometimes a writer will state an agent of an action when what he means is that the individual mentioned instigated or ordered the action, but that it was actually carried out by others. So in Mark 6:16 where Herod says "John whom I beheaded" he means "I caused John to be beheaded," and in languages where a literal translation would be understood literally the translation will have to be adjusted accordingly.

The following passages may need to be recast from active to causative action in some languages. Rewrite, making clear the relation of the actor to the action. Consult the context for names of participants and include the specific name in place of the pronoun when rewriting. The following example shows three possible ways of stating the answer.

Example: Acts 5:18
             ...they arrested the apostles and put them in...prison.
Answer: The high priest and those with him had the apostles arrested and put in prison.

             At the command of the high priest and those with him they arrested the apostles and put
             them in prison.

             The high priest and those with him ordered the soldiers to arrest the apostles and put
             them in prison.

(1)   Matt. 2:13
      ...Herod is about to search for the child, to destroy him.

(2)   Matt. 2:16
      Then Herod...killed all the male children in Bethlehem...

(3)   Matt. 14:3
      For Herod had seized John and bound him and put him in prison...

(4)   Matt. 27:1–2
      ...all the chief priests and the elders...bound him and led him away and delivered him to Pilate...

(5)   Luke 9:9
      Herod said, "John I beheaded;"

(6)   Luke 22:2
      ...the scribes were seeking how to put him to death...

(7)   Acts 2:36
      ...this Jesus whom you crucified.

(8)   Acts 3:15
      ...you...killed the Author of life...

(9)   Acts 5:25
      And some one came and told them, "The men whom you put in prison are standing in the temple and teaching the people."

(10) Acts 12:1–3
      About that time Herod the king laid violent hands upon some who belonged to the church. He killed James... and...proceeded to arrest Peter also.

M. Changing participles to relative clauses

Participles which modify a noun can often be translated using a modifying clause. Change each of the following italicized attributive participles to a relative clause, using "who," "which," or "that."

Example: John 6:51
           I am the living bread...
Answer: I am the bread that gives life.

(1)   Isa. 30:28
      ...his breath is like an *overflowing stream*...

(2)   Dan. 3:26
      ...came near to the door of the *burning fiery furnace*...

(3)   Rom. 2:15
      ...and their *conflicting thoughts* accuse or perhaps excuse them...

(4)   2 Cor. 6:16
      ...we are the temple of the *living God*...

(5)   James 1:11
      ...the sun rises with its *scorching heat*...

(6)   Jude 13
       ...*wandering stars* for whom the nether gloom of darkness has been reserved...

N. Changing participles to finite verbs

Assume that the language into which you are translating has no participles. Rewrite the following passages, using a finite verb form. You may need to make more than one sentence in order to do this. Add any implicit participants as needed.

Example: John 16:1
                I have said all this to you to keep you from *falling away.*
Answer: I have said all this so you will not fall away.

(1)   Mark 6:20
       ...Herod feared John, *knowing* that he was a righteous and holy man...

(2)   Mark 15:29
       And those who passed by derided him, *wagging* their heads, and *saying*...

(3)   John 5:18
       ...also called God his own Father, *making* himself equal with God.

(4)   Acts 2:13
       But others *mocking* said, "They are filled with new wine."

(5)   Acts 5:7
       ...his wife came in, not *knowing* what had happened.

(6)   Acts 7:56
       ...I see the heavens opened, and the Son of man *standing* at the right hand of God.

O. Changing finite verbs to participles

In Aguaruna of Peru, a verb form similar to a participle is used frequently, often in preference to a series of finite verbs, i.e., several English clauses connected by "and" may be one Aguaruna sentence with participial phrases and one finite verb.

Example: Mark 8:23
                And he took the blind man by the hand and led him out of the village; and when he had spit on his eyes and laid his hands upon him, he asked him, "Do you see anything?"
Answer: Aguaruna: Taking the blind man by the hand, leading him out of the village, spitting on his eyes, laying his hands upon him, speaking to him, he asked, "Do you see anything?"

Rewrite the following so that they consist of one sentence made up of participial phrases and one main verb at the end. Do not change the direct quotes, but keep them as separate sentences. Sometimes a compound participial verb phrase may be needed, such as "having seen." If the actions represent a chronological sequence, the last verb must state the final event in the sequence.

(1)   Mark 8:6
       And he commanded the crowd to sit down...and he took the seven loaves, and having given thanks he broke them and gave them to the disciples to set before the people...

(2)   Mark 10:16
       And he took them in his arms and blessed them, laying his hands upon them.

(3)   Mark 11:4
       And they went away, and found a colt tied at the door out in the open street; and they untied it.

(4)   John 1:43
       The next day Jesus decided to go to Galilee. And he found Philip and said to him, "Follow me."

(5)   Acts 2:6
       And when this sound occurred, the multitude came together, and were bewildered, because they were each one hearing them speak in his own language. (NASB)

(6)   Acts 7:55
       But Stephen... looked up to heaven and saw the glory of God, and Jesus standing at the right hand of God. (NIV)

P. Genitive constructions with no explicit event

The English construction which most frequently is used in literal translations of Greek genitives is two nominals linked by the preposition "of." Often receptor languages will not allow a possessive construction to represent all the semantic relationships permitted by the one construction in Greek or English.

Rewrite each of the following constructions without using "of" as a preposition and without using a possessive form; i.e., neither possessive pronouns nor "noun" + "s."

Example: Mark 14:13
              a jar of water
Answer: a jar which contains water

(1)   Matt. 26:71
       Jesus of Nazareth

(2)   Mark 1:9
       Nazareth of Galilee

(3)   Mark 1:29
       the house of Simon

(4)   Mark 6:15
       prophets of old

(5)   Acts 11:5
       the city of Joppa

(6)   Rom. 11:22
       the kindness...of God

(7)   Eph. 1:7
       the riches of his grace

(8)   Eph. 1:13
       the word of truth

Q. Genitive constructions with an explicit event

Here are some "A of B" constructions in which the "A" noun represents an Event or Experience. Rewrite each one without using "of" as a preposition, or a possessive form, and replacing the abstract nouns with a verb or adjective. Check the context in each case.

Example: Acts 9:31
...the comfort of the Holy Spirit...
Answer: as the Holy Spirit comforts them

Example: Titus 1:1
Paul, a servant of God...
Answer: I, Paul, who serves God

(1)   Luke 1:41
...the greeting of Mary...

(2)   Luke 24:49
...the promise of my Father...

(3)   John 3:36
...the wrath of God...

(4)   John 6:29
...the work of God...

(5)   Rom. 15:16
...the offering of the Gentiles...

(6)   Gal. 1:10
...the favor of men...

(7)   Col. 1:10
...the knowledge of God.

(8)   1 Tim. 6:10
...the love of money...

(9)   1 Pet. 1:11
...the sufferings of Christ...

(10) 2 Pet. 1:3
...knowledge of him...

R. Genitive constructions containing abstract nouns

Change the second noun in each of the "A of B" constructions below to a verb phrase. Do not use "of" as a preposition; instead use a relative clause beginning with a word like "who" or "which," and make explicit any participants that you need to. Generic terms such as "people" or "someone" may be as specific as the context will allow in some cases.

Example: Heb. 11:9
...the land of promise...
Answer: the land which God had promised him

(1)   Matt. 10:15
...the day of judgment...

(2)   2 Cor. 1:3
       ...God of all comfort...

(3)   2 Cor. 13:11
       ...God of love...

(4)   Gal. 2:12
       ...party of the circumcision... (NASB)

(5)   Heb. 7:2
       ...king of righteousness...

S. Genitive constructions containing implied Events

In some genitive constructions the Event is only implied and has to be supplied from the context. Reword the following, making the implied Event explicit with an appropriate verb.

Example: Luke 2:11
             ...the city of David...
Answer: the city where David was born

Example: Prov. 10:15
             A rich man's wealth...
Answer: the wealth a rich man possesses

(1)   Matt. 3:4
       ...garment of camel's hair...

(2)   Matt. 12:8
       ...lord of the sabbath.

(3)   Luke 1:11
       ...the altar of incense.

(4)   Luke 2:41
       ...the feast of the Passover.

(5)   Luke 3:2
       ...the word of God...

(6)   Luke 4:17
       ...the book of the prophet Isaiah.

(7)   John 1:29
       ...the Lamb of God...

(8)   2 Cor. 3:3
       ...tablets of stone... (KJV)

(9)   Mark 1:39
       ...their synagogues...

(10)   Mark 2:18
       ...John's disciples...

(11)   Mark 3:27
       ...strong man's house...

(12)   John 4:6
       Jacob's well...

(13)   Acts 16:26
       ...every one's fetters...

(14)   Acts 21:11
       ...he took Paul's belt... (NIV)

(15)   2 Cor. 2:17
       ...God's word...

(16)   Col. 1:24
       ...Christ's afflictions...

(17)   1 John 1:10
       ...his word...

(18)   1 John 2:12
       ...your sins...

T. Genitive constructions representing two propositions

Sometimes both nominals in an "A of B" construction represent propositions, with the "of" preposition representing an unspecified relation between them. In some cases the analyst will need to study the context to decide what relation is signaled by the preposition.

Rewrite each of these phrases as two clauses (changing abstract nouns into verbs) and link them using a word (or words) which show what relation was intended by the author, e.g., "and then," "so," "but," "that which," etc. Check the context as needed.

Example: John 5:29
                ...the resurrection of life...
Answer: (people) will rise *and then* (they) will live

(1)   Eph. 1:5
       ...the purpose of his will...

(2)   Eph. 1:7
       ...the forgiveness of our trespasses...

(3)   Eph. 2:12
       ...the covenants of promise...

(4)   Eph. 3:6
       ...partakers of the promise...

(5)   Eph. 3:12
       ...confidence of access...

(6)   Eph. 4:13
       ...unity of the faith...

(7)   Col. 1:9
       ...the knowledge of his will...

(8)   Heb. 2:15
    ...fear of death...

(9)   Heb. 10:22
    ...assurance of faith...

U. Genitive constructions using "... of God"

In each of the following genitive constructions the word "God" occurs following "of." Rewrite so as to make clear the relationship between the first word of the construction and "God," but without using a preposition or possessive construction. You may need to study the context.

Example: Eph. 1:1
    ...by the will of God...
Answer: as God willed (as God wanted)

Example: Acts 9:31
    ...in the fear of the Lord...
Answer: as we feared the Lord

(1)   Col. 1:25
    ...to make the *word of God* fully known...

(2)   2 Thess. 1:5
    This is evidence of the righteous *judgment of God,* that you may be made worthy of the *kingdom of God,* for which you are suffering...

(3)   1 Tim. 1:1
    Paul, an apostle of Christ Jesus by *command of God...*

(4) . 1 Tim. 6:11
    But as for you, *man of God,* shun all this...

(5)   2 Tim. 1:8
    But join with me in suffering for the gospel, by the *power of God...* (NIV)

(6)   2 Tim. 3:4
    ...lovers of pleasure rather than *lovers of God...*

(7)   Titus 2:10
    ...so that in everything they may adorn the *doctrine of God...*

(8)   Heb. 4:9
    ...there remains a sabbath rest for the *people of God...*

(9)   Heb. 9:24
    ...now to appear in the *presence of God* on our behalf.

V. Old Testament examples

In each of the Old Testament passages below there is a genitive ("of") phrase with an implied Event proposition. Give a restatement which removes the "of," changes any stated abstract noun into a full clause, and adds the implied Event proposition.

Example: Exod. 10:3
        ...the Lord, the *God of the Hebrews...* (NIV)
Answer: the Lord, the God whom the Hebrews *worship*

(1) Lev. 2:13
    ...the *salt of the covenant* of your God... (NIV)

(2) Lev. 8:29
    ...the *ram of ordination...* (RSV)

(3) Lev. 12:6
    When the *time of her purification* is completed... (TEV)

(4) Lev. 16:13
    ...the *smoke of the incense* will hide the lid... (TEV)

(5) Lev. 26:39
    ...survive in the *land of your enemies...* (TEV)

(6) Num. 3:10
    ...carry out the *duties of the priesthood...* (TEV)

(7) Num. 4:2
    ...take a *census of the Levite clan...* (TEV)

(8) Num. 4:5
    ...cover the *ark of the Testimony...* (NIV)

(9) Num. 14:10
    ...the *glory of the Lord* appeared... (NIV)

(10) Num. 11:30
    ...the elders of Israel returned to camp. (NIV)

W. Adjusting genitive constructions

Rewrite the following "of" phrases without using possessive words or phrases, or abstract nouns, and expressing all Event ideas by verbs. Make explicit all participants as necessary by English grammar and for clarity. Check the context if necessary.

Example: James 1:1
        ...servant of God...
Answer: a person who serves God

(1) Matt. 8:26
    ...men of little faith?

(2) Acts 13:12
    ...the teaching of the Lord.

(3)   Acts 17:22
       Men of Athens...

(4)   Acts 27:8
       ...city of Lasea.

(5)   1 Cor. 15:49
       ...the man of dust...the man of heaven.

(6)   Phil. 1:3
       ...in all my remembrance of you...

(7)   Col. 1:20
       ...the blood of his cross.

(8)   James 5:15
       ...the prayer of faith...

X. Complex genitive phrases

In each of the examples below there is a complex genitive phrase, where both of the nouns in the "A of B" phrase are expressing either events or attributes, not things. Give a retranslation of each, eliminating the skewing by using two clauses, and expressing the appropriate implied relationship between them, using parts of speech which correspond to the basic semantic function. (All passages taken from the NASB.)

Example: Rom. 8:19
              ...the *anxious longing of the creation* waits eagerly...
Answer: All the things are longing anxiously and waiting eagerly

(1)   Rom. 4:13
       ...through the *righteousness of faith*.

(2)   Rom. 5:18
       ...there resulted *justification of life* to all men.

(3)   Rom. 6:5
       ...united with Him in the *likeness of His death*...

(4)   1 Cor. 2:1
       ...I did not come with *superiority of speech*...

(5)   1 Cor. 3:20
       The Lord knows the *reasonings of the wise*...

(6)   Eph. 1:7
       ...we have...the *forgiveness of our trespasses*...

(7)   Eph. 1:14
       ...given as a *pledge of our inheritance*...

(8)   Eph. 1:14
       ...to the *redemption of* God's own *possession*...

(9)   Eph. 4:22
       ...being corrupted in accordance with the *lusts of deceit*...

(10) 1 Pet. 1:7
      ...the *proof* of your faith...

Y. Genitive constructions which do not involve an Event proposition

For the purpose of classification, the nominal which is not in the genitive case is labeled A, and the one which is, is labeled B. The typical genitive construction is thus "A of B," where "of" is used to represent the genitive case. Classify the passages given below according to these classifications, and restate in a way which makes the relation specific, without using an "of" or "'s" construction.

    a. POSSESSION—A is possessed by B
    b. PART—A is part of B, the whole
    c. DEGREE—A indicates the degree of B
    d. KINSHIP—A and B are related by kinship
    e. ROLE—A and B are related by role
    f. LOCATION—A is located in B
    g. IDENTIFICATION—A is identified by B
    h. CONTENT—A contains B
    i. MEASUREMENT—A measures B
    j. REFERENCE—A is about B
    k. SUBSTANCE—A consists of B

(1) Matt. 9:35
     ...the gospel of the kingdom...

(2) Matt. 10:2
     ...son of Zebedee...

(3) Mark 14:3
     ...jar of ointment...

(4) Luke 1:26
     ...a city of Galilee...

(5) Luke 1:40
     ...the house of Zechariah...

(6) Luke 2:4
     ...the city of Nazareth...

(7) John 19:2
     ...crown of thorns...

(8) John 19:40
     ...the body of Jesus...

(9) Rom. 15:19
     ...power of the Holy Spirit...

(10) 2 Kings 7:1
      ...a measure of fine meal...

Z. Constructions that involve an Event proposition

In the following passages, either the A or the B element of the genitive construction represents an explicit Event. Classify the passages according to the classifications given, and restate using a verb. Check the context if necessary.

> a. AGENT—B does A
> b. EXPERIENCER—A happens to B
> c. REGARD—A is done with regard to B
> d. CONTENT—B is the content of A
> e. TIME—one indicates the time of the other

Example: Acts 1:22
      ...the baptism of John...
Answer: AGENT—when John baptized people

(1)   Luke 3:6
     ...the salvation of God.

(2)   John 5:42
     ...love of God...

(3)   Acts 10:45
     ...the gift of the Holy Spirit...

(4)   Rom. 2:5
     ...day of wrath...

(5)   Rom. 3:18
     ...fear of God...

(6)   Rom. 3:20
     ...knowledge of sin.

(7)   2 Cor. 6:2
     ...day of salvation.

(8)   Eph. 1:17
     ...knowledge of him...

(9)   Rev. 2:15
     ...the teaching of the Nicolaitans.

(10) Rev. 15:3
     ...the song of Moses...

Review of Chapters 18–21

A. Identifying translation adjustments

The following passage is a back-translation into English from Aguaruna, Peru, of Col. 1:1–4. Compare this with the RSV and see how many adjustments you can find. Label these adjustments by quoting the words from the English version and stating the name of the adjustments. For example, you might write, "abstract noun changed to verb phrase," "genitive construction changed to verb phrase," etc. There will be some adjustments that you have not yet studied, but note and label as many of these as you can.

Col. 1:1–4

[1]It's me. I am Paul. I am one sent by Jesus Christ, because God said "do thus." Timothy, Jesus' follower, he also is with me. [2]I with him writing paper, that (paper) I send to you all, you who live in Colossae, you being those who say "truly God lives," you being those who follow Jesus Christ. May God, our father, being merciful to you give you all peaceful life.

[3]Jesus Christ is our big-one (Lord). Asking his father, God, I thank him (God), [4]because I heard that you believe in Jesus Christ, and I heard that you love (mutually) those who follow Jesus Christ...

Col. 1:1–4 RSV

[1]Paul, an apostle of Christ Jesus by the will of God, and Timothy our brother,

[2]To the saints and faithful brethren in Christ at Colossae: Grace to you and peace from God our Father.

[3]We always thank God, the Father of our Lord Jesus Christ, when we pray for you, [4]because we have heard of your faith in Christ Jesus and of the love which you have for all the saints...

Chapter 22
Skewing of Illocutionary Force and Grammatical Form

Additional Reading:
   Beekman and Callow 1974: Chapter 15.

A. Real versus rhetorical questions

A real question is used to elicit a genuine answer to the question asked. A rhetorical question is used for such purposes as conveying information (often with some sort of evaluation of that information), or expressing a command or feelings. In each of the following passages there is a question asked. Which ones are real questions and which ones are rhetorical questions? Consult the context if necessary.

Example: Mark 8:37
         For what can a man give in return for his life?
Answer: Rhetorical question

Example: Matt. 13:10
         Why do you speak to them in parables?
Answer: Real question

(1) Matt. 9:14
    Then the disciples of John came to him, saying, "Why do we and the Pharisees fast, but your disciples do not fast?"

(2) John 6:70
    Jesus answered them, "Did I not choose you, the twelve, and one of you is a devil?"

(3) John 9:17
    So they again said to the blind man, "What do you say about him, since he has opened your eyes?"

(4) John 18:35
    Pilate answered, "Am I a Jew?"

(5) Acts 2:7–8
    And they were amazed and wondered, saying, "Are not all these who are speaking Galileans? And how is it that we hear, each of us in his own language?"

(6) Gal. 4:16
    Have I then become your enemy by telling you the truth?

(7) 1 Tim. 3:5
    ...for if a man does not know how to manage his own household, how can he care for God's church?

(8) Heb. 12:7
    God is treating you as sons; for what son is there whom his father does not discipline?

B. Real versus rhetorical questions, continued

Each of the following verses contains at least one question. For each of the following state:

- a. Is it real or rhetorical?
- b. The reasons for your decision.

Example: 2 Sam. 19:11

...David sent this message to the...priests, "Say to the elders of Judah, 'Why should you be last to bring the king back to his house?'..."

Answer: (a) This is considered a rhetorical question, (b) because there is no answer and because David did not want them to give an answer to that question: he wanted to shame them into action.

(1)   2 Sam. 19:22

But David said, "What have I to do with you, you sons of Zeruiah, that you should this day be as an adversary to me? Shall any one be put to death in Israel this day? For do I not know that I am this day king over Israel?"

(2)   2 Sam. 19:34

But Barzillai said to the king, "How many years have I still to live, that I should go up with the king to Jerusalem?"

(3)   2 Sam. 19:42

All the men of Judah answered the men of Israel, "Because the king is near of kin to us. Why then are you angry over this matter? Have we eaten at all at the king's expense? Or has he given us any gift?"

(4)   2 Sam. 19:43

And the men of Israel answered the men of Judah, "We have ten shares in the king, and in David also we have more than you. Why then did you despise us? Were we not the first to speak of bringing back our king?"

(5)   2 Kings 9:11

When Jehu came out to the servants of his master, they said to him, "Is all well? Why did this mad fellow come to you?"

(6)   Job 38:4a

Where were you when I laid the foundation of the earth?

(7)   Ps. 27:1

The Lord is my light and my salvation; whom shall I fear?

(8)   Isa. 55:2

Why do you spend your money for that which is not bread, and your labour for that which does not satisfy?

C. Changing rhetorical questions to statements

Often a literal translation of a rhetorical question will leave the reader confused and unable to supply the right answer. This may be because the question does not fit their patterns of questions, or because they think it is a real question, or for some other linguistic or cultural reason. In Huixteco the readers interpreted the question in John 8:46 "Which of you convicts me of sin?" to mean that Christ had sinned, but that no one had found out about it yet, and thus no one was able to reveal it. So the translation was changed to read "You cannot find my sin."

In some cases the best solution to translating a rhetorical question is to make it a statement.

Change the following questions to statements that will convey the meaning of the rhetorical question and add something else to capture the emphasis of the rhetorical question. You will need to change the positive question to a negative statement.

Example: John 18:35
Pilate answered, "Am I a Jew?"
Answer: Pilate answered, "I'm certainly not a Jew."

(1)   Matt. 5:13
...if salt has lost its taste, how shall its saltiness be restored?

(2)   Matt. 5:46
For if you love those who love you, what reward have you?

(3)   Rom. 3:9
Are we Jews any better off?

(4)   Rom. 6:15
Are we to sin because we are not under the law but under grace?

(5)   Heb. 1:5
For to what angel did God ever say, "Thou art my Son...?"

D. Real versus rhetorical questions, continued

In the following passages, change all rhetorical questions to statements. Real questions should be left as questions. See sections 1–3 above.

(1)   Matt. 7:9
Or what man of you, if his son asks him for a loaf, will give him a stone?

(2)   Matt. 11:3
...and said to him, "Are you he who is to come, or shall we look for another?"

(3)   John 6:30
So they said to him, "Then what sign do you do, that we may see, and believe you?"

(4)   1 Cor. 2:16
For who has known the mind of the Lord so as to instruct him?

(5)   1 Cor. 4:7
For who sees anything different in you? What have you that you did not receive? If then you received it, why do you boast as if it were not a gift?

(6)   2 Cor. 1:17
      Was I vacillating when I wanted to do this? Do I make my plans like a worldly man, ready to
      say Yes and No at once?

(7)   2 Cor. 2:16–17
      Who is sufficient for these things? For we are not...peddlers of God's word...

(8)   Heb. 2:3
      ...how shall we escape if we neglect such a great salvation?

E. Rewriting rhetorical questions

Rewrite John 7:45–52, so that clauses which contain rhetorical questions express the underlying
meaning. Questions for information should be kept as questions and others should be adjusted.

> [45]The officers then went back to the chief priests and Pharisees, who said to them, "Why
> did you not bring him?" [46]The officers answered, "No man ever spoke like this man!" [47]The
> Pharisees answered them, "Are you led astray, you also? [48]Have any of the authorities or of
> the Pharisees believed in him? [49]But this crowd, who do not know the law, are accursed."
> [50]Nicodemus, who had gone to him before, and who was one of them, said to them, [51]"Does
> our law judge a man without first giving him a hearing and learning what he does?" [52]They
> replied, "Are you fromGalilee too? Search and you will see that no prophet is to rise from
> Galilee."

F. Supplying the answer to a rhetorical question

Assume you are translating into a language in which the following may be translated by a
rhetorical question but in which the answer to the question must be given. Give the answer for the
question in each of the following passages.

Example: John 2:20
      ...will you raise it up in three days?
Answer: There is no way you can do that.

(1)   Luke 5:21
      Who can forgive sins but God only?

(2)   John 6:9
      There is a lad here who has five barley loaves and two fish; but what are they among so
      many?

(3)   John 8:57
      You are not yet fifty years old, and have you seen Abraham?

(4)   John 14:2
      ...if it were not so, would I have told you that I go to prepare a place for you?

(5)   2 Cor. 6:15
      Or what has a believer in common with an unbeliever?

G. Functions of rhetorical questions

Rhetorical questions have different functions. After studying the passage given in its context, decide which of the following functions applies to the passage. Answer with the correct letter from the following list (some may have more than one possible answer) and suggest an alternative translation.

 a. to emphasize the negative or affirmative aspect of a statement
 b. to make a statement of incertitude, contingency, doubt, or deliberation
 c. to make an evaluation or appraisive statement, usually accompanied with favorable or unfavorable emotional attitudes supplied by the context, or to make a command (entreaty, exhortation, or injunction)
 d. to introduce a new subject or new aspect of the same subject

Example: Matt. 8:26
 ..."Why are you afraid, O men of little faith?"
Answer: c or d; "You men of little faith, I'm disappointed that you are afraid."

(1) Matt. 7:3
Why do you see the speck that is in your brother's eye, but do not notice the log that is in your own eye?

(2) Mark 14:6
But Jesus said..."why do you trouble her?"

(3) Luke 12:6
Are not five sparrows sold for two pennies?

(4) Luke 12:14
But he said to him, "Man, who made me a judge or divider over you?"

(5) Luke 13:20
And again he said, "To what shall I compare the kingdom of God?"

(6) Luke 19:23
Why then did you not put my money into the bank, and at my coming I should have collected it with interest?

(7) John 4:29
Come, see a man who told me all that I ever did. Can this be the Christ?

(8) Rom. 14:10
Why do you pass judgment on your brother?

H. Adjusting to a rhetorical question

There may be places where it seems best to remove rhetorical questions, but there are other places where it may be appropriate in the receptor language to change a statement in the original to a rhetorical question. Each of the following verses presented such an opportunity in one language in Guatemala. See if you can determine what was adjusted into a question, and give an English paraphrase expressing what you think that question form was.

Example: Acts 5:28
           "We gave you strict orders..." (NIV)
Answer: "Didn't we give you strict orders...?"/"We gave you strict orders..., so how come you
           have filled...?"

(1)   Luke 19:46
      "It is written, 'My house shall be house of prayer'; but you have made it a den of robbers."

(2)   Luke 22:33
      And he said to him, "Lord, I am ready to go with you to prison and to death."

(3)   Luke 22:53
      When I was with you day after day in the temple, you did not lay hands on me. But this is
      your hour, and the power of darkness.

(4)   Luke 23:14
      "You brought me this man as one who was perverting the people; and after examining him
      before you, behold, I did not find this man guilty of any of your charges against him..."

(5)   Luke 23:37
      "If you are the King of the Jews, save yourself!"

(6)   Acts 4:19
      But Peter and John answered them, "Whether it is right in the sight of God to listen to you
      rather than to God, you must judge..."

(7)   Acts 12:15
      They said to her, "You are mad." But she insisted that it was so. They said, "It is his angel!"

I. Adjusting forms of questions

Each of the following passages contains a rhetorical question. Give a revised English translation which still asks a question but in which the form of the question is changed (e.g., change a yes/no question to a 'who' or 'why' question, change a 'who' question to a 'why' or yes/no question).

Example: 1 Cor. 9:7
           "Who serves as a soldier at his own expense?"
Answer: "Does anyone serve as a soldier at his own expense?"

(1)   Gal. 2:14
      But when I saw that they were not straightforward about the truth of the gospel, I said to
      Cephas before them all, "If you, though a Jew, live like a Gentile and not like a Jew, how can
      you compel the Gentiles to live like Jews?"

(2) Gal. 3:1–3
O foolish Galatians! Who has bewitched you, before whose eyes Jesus Christ was publicly portrayed as crucified? Let me ask you only this: Did you receive the Spirit by works of the law, or by hearing with faith? Are you so foolish? Having begun with the Spirit, are you now ending with the flesh?

(3) Gal. 4:15
What has become of the satisfaction you felt? For I bear you witness that, if possible, you would have plucked out your eyes and given them to me.

(4) Gal. 4:21
Tell me, you who desire to be under law, do you not hear the law?

(5) Gal. 5:7
You were running well; who hindered you from obeying the truth?

(6) 1 Cor. 2:11
For what person knows a man's thoughts except the spirit of the man which is in him?

(7) 1 Cor. 3:5a
What then is Apollos? What is Paul?

(8) 1 Cor. 6:1
When one of you has a grievance against a brother, does he dare go to law before the unrighteous instead of the saints?

(9) 1 Cor. 6:7
To have lawsuits at all with one another is defeat for you. Why not rather suffer wrong? Why not rather be defrauded?

(10) 1 Cor. 7:16
Wife, how do you know whether you will save your husband? Husband, how do you know whether you will save your wife?

J. Adjusting rhetorical questions

English versions exhibit some of the ways rhetorical questions can be adjusted in translation. In each of the following verses there is given a fairly literal translation from the Greek, followed by examples of how the question has been rendered. State for each translation cited whether the adjustment is (a) literal, (b) a revised question, (c) an answer supplied for the question, or (d) a change to a statement.

Example: Luke 6:39

	Original:	Can a blind (man) guide a blind (man)?
	RSV:	Can a blind man lead a blind man?
	LB:	What good is it for one blind man to lead another?
	TEV:	One blind man cannot lead another one...

Answer:

	RSV:	(a) literal
	LB:	(b) different kind of question
	TEV:	(d) changed to a statement

(1) Matt. 9:15

	Original:	Can the sons of the bride chamber mourn...?
	NEB:	Can you expect the bridegroom's friends to go mourning...?
	JB:	Surely the bridegroom's attendants would never think of mourning...
	NIV:	How can the guests of the bridegroom mourn...?

(2) Matt. 12:11

	Original:	What man of you will there be...who will not lay hold of it...?
	RSV:	What man of you...will not lay hold of it...?
	NEB:	...is there one of you who would not catch hold of it...?
	LB:	...would you work to rescue it...? Of course you would.

(3) Mark 8:4

	Original:	From where will anyone be able to satisfy these people...?
	RSV:	How can one feed these men...?
	LB:	Are we supposed to find food for them...?
	TEV:	Where...can anyone find enough food to feed all these people?

(4) Mark 8:36

	Original:	What profits a man to gain the whole world...?
	RSV:	...what does it profit a man, to gain the whole world...?
	LB:	And how does a man benefit if he gains the whole world...?
	TEV:	Does a man gain anything if he wins the whole world...? Of course not!

(5) Mark 8:37

	Original:	What might a man give as an exchange (for) his soul?
	RSV:	...what can a man give in return for his life?
	LB:	...is anything worth more than his soul?
	TEV:	There is nothing a man can give to regain his life.

(6) Mark 12:24

	Original:	Do you not err therefore...?
	NEB:	You are mistaken...
	NIV:	Are you not in error because...?
	LB:	Your trouble is that...

(7)   Luke 17:7
    Original: Who of you having a slave...will say to him...?
    RSV: Will any one of you, who has a servant...say to him...?
    JB: Which of you, with a servant...would say to him...?
    LB: When a servant...he doesn't just sit down...
    TEV: Suppose one of you has a servant...do you say to him...? Of course not!

(8)   Luke 17:18
    Original: Were there not found...only this stranger?
    RSV: Was no one found...except this foreigner?
    TEV: Why is this foreigner the only one...?
    JB: It seems that no one...except this foreigner.

K. Double negatives

Languages handle negatives in many different ways. A negative in the source language will not always be translated by a negative in the receptor language. Double negatives may need to be translated by a positive statement in some languages. Restate the following, eliminating the negatives.

Example: John 1:3
    ...*without* him was *not* anything made that was made.
Answer: Chinanteco: All things came into being because that person made all that exists.

(1)   Matt. 10:29
And *not* one of them will fall to the ground *without* your Father's will.

(2)   Matt. 10:38
...and he who does *not* take his cross and follow me is *not* worthy of me.

(3)   Mark 4:34
...he did *not* speak to them *without* a parable...

(4)   Luke 18:29–30
...there is *no* man who has left house or wife or brothers or parents or children, for the sake of the kingdom of God, who will *not* receive manifold more...

(5)   1 Cor. 9:21
To those outside the law I became as one outside the law—*not* being *without* law toward God but under the law of Christ...

L. Restating as a positive statement

Other negatives occur with words such as "till," "until," and "except." These may sometimes need to be translated with a positive statement. Restate the following, using a positive statement rather than a negative one to convey the same meaning. Often it may be necessary to use the word "only" in the translation.

Example: Mark 4:22
For there is *nothing* hid, *except* to be made manifest...

Answer: Cuicateco: Everything that is hidden will have to be exhibited (shown).
Yaweyuha: God's secret things will not disappear. They only exist in order to be revealed later.

(1) Matt. 13:57
A prophet is *not without* honor *except* in his own country...

(2) Luke 13:35
...you will *not* see me *until* you say...

(3) Luke 21:32
...this generation will *not* pass away *till* all has taken place.

(4) John 13:10
...does *not* need to wash, *except* for his feet...

(5) John 13:38
...the cock will *not* crow, *till* you have denied me three times.

(6) John 20:25
Unless I see in his hands the print of the nails...I will *not* believe.

M. Negatives in statements of exception

In some languages there is no way to say "there is no A except B" because if you say "there is no A" you have already eliminated the possibility of exceptions. In such cases one has to reverse the order of the clauses and say "only *B*, there is no other A." Change the following to fit that pattern.

Example: John 14:6
...no one comes to the Father, but by me.

Answer: I am the only way people can come to (my) father, there is no other way.

(1) Mark 6:5
And he could do *no mighty work* there, *except* that he laid his hands upon a few sick...

(2) Mark 6:8
He charged them to take *nothing* for their journey *except* a staff...

(3) John 19:15
We have *no king but* Caesar.

(4) Rom. 13:8
Owe *no one* anything, *except* to love one another...

(5) 1 Cor. 1:14
...I baptized *none of you except* Crispus and Gaius...

N. Placement of negatives

Sometimes a negative which occurs with a verb in a clause semantically only negates one element within the clause or the verb of the subordinate clause which follows. In many translations the order will have to be changed so that the negative element occurs with what it really negates. Rewrite the following clauses so that the negative occurs where it belongs semantically.

Example: Matt. 5:17
I have not come to abolish them but to fulfill them. (NIV)
Answer: I came, not to abolish them but...

(1)   Matt. 4:4
Man shall not live by bread alone...

(2)   Matt. 10:34
I have not come to bring peace...

(3)   Matt. 20:28
...the Son of Man did not come to be served...

(4)   John 3:17
...God did not send his Son into the world to condemn the world... (NIV)

(5)   John 6:27
Do not labor for the food which perishes, but for the food which endures...

O. Changing negatives to "only" clauses

In some languages the negatives are eliminated in certain constructions and "only" is used to carry the meaning. Change the following by using "only" and eliminating the negative.

Example: Matt. 5:13
It is *no longer* good for anything except to be thrown out...
Answer: It is now good *only* to be thrown out.

(1)   Gen. 44:23
Unless your youngest brother comes down with you, you shall see my face no more.

(2)   Matt. 17:21
But this kind *never* comes out *except* by prayer and fasting.

(3)   Matt. 18:3
...*unless* you turn and become like children, you will *never* enter the kingdom of heaven.

(4)   John 3:3
...*unless* one is born anew, he can*not* see the kingdom of God.

(5)   Rev. 14:3
No one could learn that song *except* the hundred and forty-four thousand who had been redeemed from the earth.

P. Negative-positive sets

In each of the following passages there is a negative-positive set. Assuming you are translating in a language which requires the positive element to come first, revise the wording of these passages accordingly.

Example: John 12:49
For I have not spoken on my own authority; the Father who sent me has himself given me commandment what to say...

Answer: For the Father himself...what to speak; I did not speak on my own authority.

(1) John 5:30
I can do nothing on my own authority; as I hear, I judge; and my judgment is just, because I seek not my own will but the will of him who sent me.

(2) John 5:45
Do not think that I shall accuse you to the Father; it is Moses who accuses you, on whom you set your hope.

(3) John 6:26
Truly, truly, I say to you, you seek me, not because you saw signs, but because you ate your fill of the loaves.

(4) John 6:27
Do not labour for the food which perishes, but for the food which endures to eternal life, which the Son of man will give to you; for on him has God the Father set his seal.

(5) John 7:24
Do not judge by appearances, but judge with right judgment.

(6) John 8:42
If God were your Father, you would love me, for I proceeded and came forth from God; I came not of my own accord, but he sent me.

(7) John 10:18
No one takes it from me, but I lay it down of my own accord. I have power to lay it down, and I have power to take it again; this charge I have received from my Father.

(8) John 10:33
We stone you for no good work but for blasphemy; because you, being a man, make yourself God.

(9) John 10:37–38
If I am not doing the works of my Father, then do not believe me; but if I do them, even though you do not believe me, believe the works, that you may know and understand that the Father is in me and I am in the Father.

Q. Positive-negative sets

In each of the following passages there is a positive-negative set. Assume you are translating into a language which prefers the negative element to come first. Revise the wording accordingly.

Example: Mark 6:8
> He charged them to take nothing for their journey except a staff; no bread, no bag, no money in their belts...

Answer: He instructed them...take no bread or bag or...for their journey; they should take only a staff.

(1) John 2:16
Take these things away; you shall not make my Father's house a house of trade.

(2) John 7:27
Yet we know where this man comes from; and when the Christ appears, no one will know where he comes from.

(3) John 8:14
Even if I do bear witness to myself, my testimony is true, for I know whence I have come and whither I am going, but you do not know whence I come or whither I am going.

(4) John 8:29
And he who sent me is with me; he has not left me alone, for I always do what is pleasing to him.

(5) John 8:33
We are descendants of Abraham, and have never been in bondage to anyone. How is it that you say, 'You will be made free'?

(6) John 9:29
We know that God has spoken to Moses, but as for this man, we do not know where he comes from.

(7) John 10:12
He who is a hireling and not a shepherd, whose own the sheep are not, sees the wolf coming and leaves the sheep and flees; and the wolf snatches them and scatters them.

(8) John 10:13
He flees because he is a hireling and cares nothing for the sheep.

(9) John 16:29
Ah, now you are speaking plainly, not in any figure!

(10) John 18:20
I have spoken openly to the world; I have always taught in synagogues and in the temple, where all Jews come together; I have said nothing secretly.

R. Changing rhetorical questions with a negative particle to positive statements

Many times rhetorical questions are asked in a negative construction. As you change the following questions to statements, change to a positive construction as well.

Example: John 7:19
Did not Moses give you the law?
Answer: Moses gave you the law.

(1) Matt. 5:46
Do not even the tax collectors do the same?

(2) Matt. 12:5
Or have you not read in the law how on the sabbath the priests in the temple profane the sabbath, and are guiltless?

(3) Matt. 13:55
Is not this the carpenter's son? Is not his mother called Mary?

(4) John 4:35
Do you not say, "There are four months, then comes the harvest"?

(5) Acts 5:4
While it remained unsold, did it not remain your own? And after it was sold, was it not at your disposal?

S. Irony

Irony is a figure of speech in which the communicator says just the opposite of what he really means, sometimes to ridicule the receiver of the message. Each passage below contains irony. Retranslate the passage to either remove the irony or make it obvious to the reader. (Eliminate any rhetorical questions as well.)

Example: Matt. 26:68
Prophesy to us, you Christ! Who is it that struck you?
Answer: They said, "If *you were* the Messiah, *you could* prophecy to us and tell us who was the one who hit you."

(1) 1 Sam. 17:43
And the Philistine said to David, "Am I a dog, that you come to me with sticks?"

(2) 1 Kings 18:27
And at noon Elijah mocked them, saying, "Cry aloud, for he is a god; either he is musing, or he has gone aside, or he is on a journey, or perhaps he is asleep and must be awakened."

(3) 1 Kings 22:15
And when he had come to the king, the king said to him, "Micaiah, shall we go to Ramoth-gilead to battle, or shall we forbear?"

(4) Job 12:1–2
Then Job answered: "No doubt you are the people, and wisdom will die with you. But I have understanding as well as you; I am not inferior to you. Who does not know such things as these?"

(5)   Job 15:2–3
Should a wise man answer with windy knowledge, and fill himself with the east wind? Should he argue in unprofitable talk, or in words with which he can do no good?

(6)   Job 26:2–3
How you have helped him who has no power! How you have saved the arm that has no strength! How you have counseled him who has no wisdom, and plentifully declared sound knowledge!

(7)   Mark 2:17
Those who are well have no need of a physician, but those who are sick; I came not to call the righteous, but sinners.

(8)   Mark 15:32
Let the Christ, the King of Israel, come down now from the cross, that we may see and believe.

T. Review

In each of the following rhetorical questions there is an additional potential translation adjustment. (a) State what this potential adjustment is and (b) change the rhetorical question into a statement, adjusting the item identified in letter a.

Example: Col. 2:20
If with Christ you died to the elemental spirits of the universe, why do you live as if you still belonged to the world?

Answer: a. Conditional clause
b. With Christ you died to the elemental spirits of the universe, therefore don't live as if you still belonged to the world.

(1)   Mark 1:24
...and he cried out, "What have you to do with us, Jesus of Nazareth?"

(2)   Mark 8:4
And his disciples answered him, "How can one feed these men with bread here in the desert?"

(3)   Mark 8:36
For what does it profit a man, to gain the whole world and forfeit his life?

(4)   Mark 12:26
And as for the dead being raised, have you not read in the book of Moses, in the passage about the bush, how God said to him...?

(5)   John 5:47
But if you do not believe his writings, how will you believe my words?

(6)   Luke 8:25
He said to them, "Where is your faith?"

(7)   Luke 18:7
And will not God vindicate his elect...?

(8)   **Rev. 6:17**
...the great day of their wrath has come, and who can stand before it?

(9) John 8:53
     Are you greater than our father Abraham, who died?

(10) John 11:40
     Jesus said to her, "Did I not tell you that if you would believe you would see the glory of
     God?"

U. Review

For each of the following passages look for two adjustments that might need to be made in
translation and identify the item you are referring to. These will include passive constructions,
abstract nouns, genitive constructions, participles, certain negatives, and obligatory possession, etc.

Example: Acts 15:7
            And after there had been much debate, Peter rose and said to them, "Brethren, you
            know that..."
Answer: debate—abstract noun
            brethren—obligatory possession

(1) Acts 3:19
     Repent therefore, and turn again, that your sins may be blotted out, that times of refreshing
     may come from the presence of the Lord...

(2) Acts 6:4
     But we will devote ourselves to prayer and to the ministry of the word.

(3) Acts 7:55
     ...gazed into heaven and saw the glory of God, and Jesus standing at the right hand of God...

(4) Acts 7:60
     And he knelt down and cried with a loud voice, "Lord, do not hold this sin against them."

(5) Acts 8:1
     And Saul was consenting to his death. And on that day a great persecution arose against the
     church...

(6) Acts 9:1
     But Saul, still breathing threats and murder against the disciples of the Lord, went to the high
     priest...

(7) Acts 10:23
     So he called them in to be his guests. The next day he arose and went off with them, and
     some of the brethren from Joppa accompanied him.

(8) Acts 10:33
     So I sent to you at once, and you have been kind enough to come. Now therefore we are all
     here present in the sight of God, to hear all that you have been commanded by the Lord.

(9) Acts 14:8
     Now at Lystra there was a man sitting, who could not use his feet; he was a cripple from
     birth, who had never walked.

(10) Acts 22:1
     Brethren and fathers, hear the defense which I now make before you.

Chapter 23
Figurative Propositions/Metaphors and Similes

Additional Reading:
    Beekman and Callow 1974: Chapters 8 and 9.

A. Analyzing similes

A *simile* is an explicit comparison in which one item of the comparison (the "image") carries a number of components of meaning of which usually only one is contextually relevant to and shared by the second item (the "topic"). (Beekman and Callow 1974:127)

Identify the shared component (sometimes called the point of similarity) that is in focus as the basis of the simile in the following.

Example: Mark 4:31
It (the kingdom of God) is like a grain of mustard seed...
Answer: Shared component in focus: The growth of the seed, which though small, grows into a large bush, and the growth of the beginning of the kingdom of God, which though starting small, becomes large.

(1) Matt. 13:33
"The kingdom of heaven is like leaven which a woman took and hid in three measures of meal..."

(2) Matt. 17:20
...if you have faith as a grain of mustard seed...

(3) Matt. 28:3
His appearance was like lightning...

(4) Luke 7:32
They are like children sitting in the market place and calling to one another...

(5) 1 Pet. 1:19
[You were ransomed] with the precious blood of Christ, like that of a lamb without blemish or spot.

(6) Rev. 3:3
...I will come like a thief...

B. Dead versus live metaphors

A difference must be made between DEAD METAPHORS, those which are just a part of the idiomatic constructions of the lexicon of the language, and LIVE METAPHORS, those which are constructed on the spot to teach or illustrate. Study the following and decide whether you think the metaphor being used was a live metaphor or a dead metaphor at the time the book was written.

Example: Luke 1:42
  ...and blessed is the *fruit* of your womb!

Answer: An idiom (dead metaphor) which means "blessed is your child" and the metaphorical construction does not need to be kept.

Example: John 10:7
  ...I am the *door*...

Answer: A live metaphor which Jesus was using to teach. The image should be kept, making whatever adjustment is needed to carry the right meaning.

(1) Matt. 3:8
  Bear fruit that befits repentance...

(2) Matt. 4:19
  ...I will make you *fishers of men.*

(3) Matt. 7:6
  "Do not give *dogs* what is holy; and do not throw your *pearls* before *swine...*"

(4) Mark 10:39
  ...with the *baptism* with which I am baptized, you will be baptized...

(5) Mark 14:36
  ...remove this *cup* from me...

(6) John 6:51
  I am the *living bread* which came down from heaven...

(7) John 8:44
  ...and the *father* of lies.

(8) 1 Cor. 3:2
  ...I gave you *milk* to drink... (NEB)

C. Meanings of dead metaphors (idioms)

The italicized words in the following are dead metaphors, idioms of the source language. What is the actual meaning of these idioms?

Example: Mark 5:22
  ...Jairus...seeing him, he *fell at his feet*...

Answer: Seeing him, he kneeled before him.

(1) Luke 1:17
  ...to *turn the hearts* of the fathers to the children...

(2) Luke 1:66
  ...and all who heard them *laid them up in their hearts*...

(3)   John 13:18
       ...has *lifted his heel* against me.

(4)   Acts 4:32
       ...those who believed *were of one heart and soul*...

(5)   Rom. 8:23
       ...we ourselves, who have the *first fruits* of the Spirit...

(6)   Rom. 15:12
       ...*root* of Jesse...

(7)   1 Cor. 3:1
       ...address you...as *men of the flesh*...

(8)   1 Cor. 16:11
       Speed him on his way in peace...

(9)   Rev. 3:8
       ...I have set before you an *open door*...

D. Analyzing metaphors

A *metaphor* is an implicit comparison in which one item of the comparison (the "image") carries a number of components of meaning of which usually only one is contextually relevant to and shared by the second item (the "topic"). (Beekman and Callow 1974:127)

One cannot adequately translate some metaphors until he has determined the component of meaning that is in focus in the metaphor. Identify and explain the shared component that is the basis of the metaphor in the following.

Example: James 3:6
             ...the tongue is a *fire.*
Answer: Component of destruction—fire can ruin things, and what we say can ruin people.

(1)   Mark 8:15
       ...beware of the *leaven* of the Pharisees...

(2)   John 1:29
       Behold, the *Lamb* of God, who takes away the sin of the world!

(3)   Acts 15:10
       Now therefore why do you make trial of God by putting a *yoke upon the neck* of the disciples...

(4)   Rom. 6:2
       How can we who *died* to sin still live in it?

E. Identifying topic, image, and point of similarity

Every simile and metaphor consists of three parts: the topic, the image, and the point of similarity (the shared component of meaning). Identify these three parts in each of the following.

Example: Isa. 53:6
                     All we like sheep have gone astray...
Answer: topic—we
                     image—sheep
                     point of similarity—gone astray

(1)   Mark 1:17
        ...I will make you become fishers of men.

(2)   Mark 6:34
        ...they were like sheep without a shepherd...

(3)   John 5:35
        ...[John] was a burning and shining lamp...

(4)   John 6:35
        I am the bread of life...

(5)   John 10:9
        I am the door...

(6)   Heb. 4:12
        ...the word of God is...sharper than any two-edged sword...

(7)   Heb. 6:19
        We have this as a sure and steadfast anchor of the soul...

(8)   James 4:14
        ...you are a mist that appears for a little time and then vanishes.

F. Changing metaphors to similes

In Alekano one cannot say "God's word is a two-edged sword" (Heb. 4:12) but one can say "it is like a knife that is sharp at its mouth and at its back," thus making the figure into a simile. The following are live metaphors, and the image of each preferably should be retained in the translation. Change each of them to a simile without adding the grounds of the comparison.

Example: Acts 2:20
                     ...the moon [shall be turned] into blood...
Answer: The moon shall become like blood.

(1)   Matt. 5:13
        You are the *salt of the earth*...

(2)   Matt. 5:14
        You are the *light of the world.*

(3)   John 1:29
        Behold, the *Lamb of God,* who takes away the sin of the world!

(4)   John 5:35
        He was a *burning and shining lamp*...

(5) John 6:35
     Jesus said to them, "I am the *bread of life...*"

(6) John 10:11
     I am the *good shepherd.*

(7) John 14:6
     Jesus said to him, "I am the *way,*"

(8) John 15:1
     I am the true vine, and my Father is the *vinedresser.*

G. Changing to a nonfigurative form

Sometimes it may be necessary, or preferable, to use a nonfigurative form to translate a metaphor or simile. Dead metaphors should always be rendered nonfiguratively. Rewrite each of the following in a nonfigurative manner.

Example: Mark 1:17
          ...I will make you become fishers of men.
Answer: Now I will give you a new work making disciples for me.

(1) Matt. 17:20
     ...if you have faith as a grain of mustard...

(2) Luke 2:35
     (...a sword will pierce through your own soul also)...

(3) Philem. 2
     ...Archippus our fellow soldier...

(4) Heb. 2:7
     ...thou hast crowned him with glory and honor...

(5) Heb. 6:19
     We have this as a sure and steadfast anchor of the soul...

H. Old Testament metaphors

The following Old Testament passages each contain a metaphor. For each one, give three translations in English:

    a. one making it a simile
    b. one adding the topic and point of similarity
    c. one making it nonmetaphorical.

Check the context if necessary.

Example: Jer. 8:17
"...I am sending among you serpents, adders, which will not be charmed; and they shall bite you..."

Answer: a. I will send among you people who will be like snakes...who will be like snakes which bite you.
    b. I will send among you your enemies who will attack and destroy you like poisonous snakes do; and like snakes which cannot be charmed their cruel actions you will not be able to hinder.
    c. I will send among you your enemies who will attack and destroy you; nothing you do will be able to hinder their plundering you.

(1) Gen. 15:1
...I am your shield...

(2) Gen. 49:17
Dan shall be a serpent...

(3) Exod. 15:3
The Lord is a man of war...

(4) Num. 14:9
...they are bread for us...

(5) 2 Sam. 5:2
You shall be shepherd of my people Israel...

(6) 2 Sam. 14:7
Thus they would quench my coal which is left, ...

(7) Job 6:4
...the arrows of the Almighty are within me...

(8) Jer. 3:1
You have played the harlot with many lovers...

(9) Jer. 4:7
A lion is has gone up from his thicket, a destroyer of nations has set out...

(10) Jer. 5:14
I am making my words in your mouth a fire, and this people wood.

I. Adjusting metaphors

In each of the following verses, suggest at least one alternate translation for the metaphor(s) making clear the topic and point of similarity of the passage as a whole in an appropriate way. Remember that you should not attempt to retain the image in a dead metaphor, but you may in some cases be able to substitute a different receptor language idiom.

Example: Matt. 26:42
...if this cannot pass away unless I drink it...

Answer: (Yaweyuha): If this heavy thing cannot by-pass me...
(Ome): If you really want heaviness and trouble to come my way...
(Guarayu): If I must endure this pain...

(1) Matt. 23:24
You blind guides, straining out a gnat and swallowing a camel!

(2) Matt. 23:25
"Woe to you, scribes and Pharisees, hypocrites! for you cleanse the outside of the cup and of the plate, but inside they are full of extortion and rapacity.

(3) Matt. 23:31
Thus you witness against yourselves, that you are sons of those who murdered the prophets.

(4) Matt. 23:33
You serpents, you brood of vipers, how are you to escape being sentenced to hell?

(5) Matt. 25:1–13
[1]Then the kingdom of heaven shall be compared to ten maidens who took their lamps and went to meet the bridegroom. [2]Five of them were foolish, and five were wise. [3]For when the foolish took their lamps, they took no oil with them; [4]but the wise took flasks of oil with their lamps. [5]As the bridegroom was delayed, they all slumbered and slept. [6]But at midnight there was a cry, 'Behold, the bridegroom! Come out to meet him.' [7]Then all those maidens rose and trimmed their lamps. [8]And the foolish said to the wise, 'Give us some of your oil, for our lamps are going out.' [9]But the wise replied, 'Perhaps there will not be enough for us and for you; go rather to the dealers and buy for yourselves.' [10]And while they went to buy, the bridegroom came, and those who were ready went in with him to the marriage feast; and the door was shut. [11]Afterward the other maidens came also, saying, 'Lord, lord, open to us.' [12]But he replied, 'Truly, I say to you, I do not know you.' [13]Watch therefore, for you know neither the day nor the hour.

(6) Matt. 25:14–30
[14]For it will be as when a man going on a journey called his servants and entrusted to them his property; [15]to one he gave five talents, to another two, to another one, to each according to his ability. Then he went away. [16] He who had received the five talents went at once and traded with them; and he made five talents more. [17]So also, he who had the two talents made two talents more. [18]But he who had received the one talent went and dug in the ground and hid his master's money. [19]Now after a long time the master of those servants came and settled accounts with them. [20]And he who had received the five talents came forward, bringing five talents more, saying, 'Master, you delivered to me five talents; here I have made five talents more.' [21]His master said to him, 'Well done, good and faithful servant; you have been faithful over a little, I will set you over much; enter into the joy of your master.' [22]And he also who had the two talents came forward, saying, 'Master, you delivered to me two talents; here I have made two talents more.' [23]His master said to him, 'Well done,

good and faithful servant; you have been faithful over a little, I will set you over much; enter into the joy of your master.' 24He also who had received the one talent came forward, saying, 'Master, I knew you to be a hard man, reaping where you did not sow, and gathering where you did not winnow; 25so I was afraid, and I went and hid your talent in the ground. Here you have what is yours.' 26But his master answered him, 'You wicked and slothful servant! You knew that I reap where I have not sowed, and gather where I have not winnowed? 27Then you ought to have invested my money with the bankers, and at my coming I should have received what was my own with interest. 28So take the talent from him, and give it to him who has the ten talents. 29For to every one who has will more be given, and he will have abundance; but from him who has not, even what he has will be taken away. 30And cast the worthless servant into the outer darkness; there men will weep and gnash their teeth.'

J. Review of figures of speech

List the word(s) expressing the figure(s) of speech that occur in each of the following and tell what kind it is. (Includes similes, metaphors, metonymy, personification, apostrophe, synecdoche, irony, euphemism). There may be more than one figure in each verse.

Example: 1 Cor. 3:9
            For we are fellow workmen for God; you are God's...building.
Answer: Building is a metaphor.

(1)   Matt. 2:6
      And you, O Bethlehem, in the land of Judah, are by no means least among the rulers of Judah...

(2)   Mark 6:11
      If any place will not receive you and they refuse to hear you...

(3)   John 6:33
      For the bread of God is that which comes down from heaven, and gives life to the world.

(4)   Acts 6:15
      And gazing at him, all who sat in the council saw that his face was like the face of an angel.

(5)   1 Cor. 4:8a
      Already you are filled! Already you have become rich! Without us you have become kings!

(6)   Eph. 6:17
      And take the helmet of salvation, and the sword of the Spirit, which is the word of God.

(7)   Col. 1:20
      ...through him to reconcile to himself all things, whether on earth or in heaven, making peace by the blood of his cross.

(8)   James 1:15
      Then, after desire has conceived, it gives birth to sin... (NIV)

Chapter 24
More on Propositional Analysis

A. Identifying the underlying meaning of identical grammatical structures

In each of the following, two or three verses are cited in which the same grammatical construction is used but the underlying meaning is distinct. Reword each passage so as to show the difference in meaning.

Example: Luke 18:27

The things which are impossible *with men* are possible *with God.* (KJV)

Answer: Things which men are not able to do, God is able to do.

Example: 2 Pet. 3:8

...*with the Lord* one day is as a thousand years...

Answer: The Lord perceives one day and a thousand years as if they were exactly the same.

(1) Acts 21:21

...they have been told...that you teach all the Jews who are *among the Gentiles* to forsake Moses...

Rom. 2:24

The name of God is blasphemed *among the Gentiles* because of you.

Acts 15:12

...they related what signs and wonders God had done through them *among the Gentiles.*

(2) Philem. 13

I would have been glad to keep him *with me...*

Matt. 26:23

"...He who has dipped his hand in the dish *with me...*"

(3) Luke 1:59

And *on* the eighth day they came to circumcise the child...

Luke 13:7

I have come seeking fruit *on* this fig tree...

(4) Matt. 14:26

But when the disciples saw him walking *on the sea,* they were terrified...

Matt. 27:25

And all the people answered, "His blood be *on us* and *on our children!*"

Acts 4:5

On the morrow their rulers and elders and scribes were gathered together in Jerusalem...

B. Identifying Event words

Identify the Event words in each of the following passages.

Example: Philem. 5
...because I hear of your love and of the faith which you have toward the Lord Jesus and all the saints...

Answer: Events are: hear, love, have faith

(1)   Matt. 16:28
Truly, I say to you, there are some standing here who will not taste death before they see the Son of man coming in his kingdom.

(2)   Matt. 18:14
So it is not the will of my Father who is in heaven that one of these little ones should perish.

(3)   John 7:38
He who believes in me, as the scripture has said, 'Out of his heart shall flow rivers of living water.'

(4)   Acts 3:14
But you denied the Holy and Righteous One, and asked for a murderer to be granted to you...

(5)   Rom. 7:8
But sin, finding opportunity in the commandment, wrought in me all kinds of covetousness. Apart from the law sin lies dead.

(6)   Col. 1:23
provided that you continue in the faith, stable and steadfast, not shifting from the hope of the gospel which you heard, which has been preached to every creature under heaven, and of which I, Paul, became a minister.

(7)   2 Thess. 2:16–17
Now may our Lord Jesus Christ himself, and God our Father, who loved us and gave us eternal comfort and good hope through grace, comfort your hearts and establish them in every good work and word.

(8)   Heb. 3:16
Who were they that heard and yet were rebellious? Was it not all those who left Egypt under the leadership of Moses?

(9)   Heb. 5:7–8
In the days of his flesh, Jesus offered up prayers and supplications, with loud cries and tears, to him who was able to save him from death, and he was heard for his godly fear. Although he was a Son, he learned obedience through what he suffered...

(10) 1 Pet. 5:1–2
So I exhort the elders among you, as a fellow elder and a witness of the sufferings of Christ as well as a partaker in the glory that is to be revealed. Tend the flock of God that is your charge, not by constraint but willingly, not for shameful gain but eagerly...

C. Using verbs to express Events

Many events are expressed grammatically by means of abstract nouns. All of these must be expressed as verbs in the semantic structure. Restate each of the following passages, using an active verb to express the Event ideas.

Example: Phil. 4:17
Not that I seek the gift...
Answer: I do not say that because I seek that you give to me

(1) 1 John 4:21
...this commandment we have from him...

(2) Rev. 21:4
...death shall be no more...

(3) Luke 12:58
...go with your accuser...

(4) Philem. 21
Confident of your obedience...

(5) Luke 2:47
...all who heard him were amazed at his understanding and his answers.

(6) Acts 4:12
...there is salvation in no one else...

(7) Luke 4:18
...to proclaim release to the captives...

(8) Matt. 24:31
...they will gather his elect...

(9) Col. 1:8
He...has made known to us your love...

(10) Luke 8:48
...your faith has made you well...

D. Figures of speech and propositions

In each of the following passages there is at least one figure of speech. Identify the figures of speech and then write them as propositions, eliminating the figurative usage. You may, however, use a simile in your proposition.

Example: Mark 5:34
And he said to her, "Daughter, your faith has made you well..."
Answer: "Faith" is a personification.
Jesus spoke to the woman. You believed. God healed you.

(1) Luke 3:22
...the Holy Spirit descended upon him in bodily form, as a dove, and a voice came from heaven, "Thou are my beloved Son; with thee I am well pleased."

(2)   Luke 4:20
       And he closed the book, and gave it back to the attendant, and sat down; and the eyes of all in
       the synagogue were fixed on him.

(3)   Acts 15:21
       For from early generations Moses has had in every city those who preach him, for he is read
       every sabbath in the synagogues.

(4)   Col. 2:9
       For in him the whole fullness of deity dwells bodily...

E. Metaphors, genitive constructions, and propositions

   The following metaphors occur in a genitive construction. Change the construction to a
proposition without changing the metaphor.

Example: Amos 6:12
               ...*fruit of righteousness...*
Answer: righteousness produces fruit

(1)   John 1:29
       "Behold, the *Lamb of God,* who takes away the sin of the world!"

(2)   Eph. 2:20
       ...build upon the *foundation of the apostles and prophets...*

(3)   Eph. 6:11
       Put on the whole *armor of God...*

(4)   Phil. 1:11
       ...filled with the *fruits of righteousness...*

(5)   James 1:12
       ...he will receive the *crown of life...*

Review of Chapters 18–24

A. Writing propositions

Rewrite the following passage in propositions. Notice that there are a number of metaphors in the passage. Change the metaphors to similes or nonfigurative expressions.

James 1:12–15

[12]Blessed is the man who endures trial, for when he has stood the test he will receive the crown of life which God has promised to those who love him. [13]Let no one say when he is tempted, "I am tempted by God"; for God cannot be tempted with evil and he himself tempts no one; [14]but each person is tempted when he is lured and enticed by his own desire. [15]Then desire when it has conceived gives birth to sin; and sin when it is full-grown brings forth death.

B. Stating propositions

Restate each of the following passages in the form of propositions.

(1)   John 4:7
There came a woman of Samaria to draw water. Jesus said to her, "Give me a drink."

(2)   Rev. 2:9
"'I know your tribulation and your poverty (but you are rich) and the slander of those who say that they are Jews and are not, but are a synagogue of Satan.

(3)   Acts 7:11–13
[11]Now there came a famine throughout all Egypt and Canaan, and great affliction, and our fathers could find no food. [12]But when Jacob heard that there was grain in Egypt, he sent forth our fathers the first time. [13]And at the second visit Joseph made himself known to his brothers, and Joseph's family became known to Pharaoh.

(4)   Mark 8:22–26
[22]And they came to Bethsaida. And some people brought to him a blind man, and begged him to touch him. [23]And he took the blind man by the hand, and led him out of the village; and when he had spit on his eyes and laid his hands upon him, he asked him, "Do you see anything?" [24]And he looked up and said, "I see men; but they look like trees, walking." [25]Then again he laid his hands upon his eyes; and he looked intently and was restored, and saw everything clearly. [26]And he sent him away to his home, saying, "Do not even enter the village."

(5)   Acts 5:1–6
[1]But a man named Ananias with his wife Sapphira, sold a piece of property, [2]and with his wife's knowledge he kept back some of the proceeds, and brought only a part and laid it at the apostles' feet. [3]But Peter said, "Ananias, why has Satan filled your heart to lie to the Holy Spirit and to keep back part of the proceeds of the land? [4]While it remained unsold, did it not remain your own? And after it was sold, was it not at your disposal? How is it that you have contrived this deed in your heart? You have not lied to men but to God." [5]When Ananias heard these words, he feel down and died. And great fear came upon all who heard of it. [6]The young men rose and wrapped him up and carried him out and buried him.

(6)   Mark 15:42–47
42And when evening had come, since it was the day of Preparation, that is, the day before
the sabbath, 43Joseph of Arimathea, a respected member of the council, who was also himself
looking for the kingdom of God, took courage and went to Pilate, and asked for the body of
Jesus. 44And Pilate wondered if he were already dead; and summoning the centurion, he
asked him whether he was already dead. 45And when he learned from the centurion that he
was dead, he granted the body to Joseph. 46And he brought a linen shroud, and taking him
down, wrapped him in the linen shroud, and laid him in a tomb which had been hewn out of
the rock; and he rolled a stone against the door of the tomb. 47Mary Magdalene and Mary the
mother of Joses saw where he was laid.

(7)   1 John 5:13–17
13I write this to you who believe in the name of the Son of God, that you may know that
you have eternal life. 14And this the confidence which we have in him, that if we ask
anything according to his will he hears us. 15And if we know that he hears us in whatever we
ask, we know that we have obtained the requests made of him. 16If any one sees his brother
committing what is not a mortal sin, he will ask, and God will give him life for those whose
sin is not mortal. There is sin which is mortal; I do not say that one is to pray for that. 17All
wrongdoing is sin, but there is sin which is not mortal.

(8)   Rev. 22:1–5
1Then he showed me the river of the water of life, bright as crystal, flowing from the
throne of God and of the Lamb 2through the middle of the street of the city; also, on either
side of the river, the tree of life with its twelve kinds of fruit, yielding its fruit each month;
and the leaves of the tree were for the healing of the nations. 3There shall no more be
anything accursed, but the throne of God and of the Lamb shall be in it, and his servants shall
worship him; 4they shall see his face, and his name shall be on their foreheads. 5And night
shall be no more; they need no light of lamp or sun, for the Lord God will be their light, and
they shall reign for ever and ever.

IV. Communications Relations

Chapter 25
Addition and Support Relations

A. Identifying larger units related to concepts

In each of the following passages, the italicized proposition(s) is in either Identification or Description relation to the Thing which it qualifies. Identify the relation in each example. (from Barnwell 1974:209)

(1)   The exercise *the students are doing today* is not difficult.

(2)   The drivers, *who all drove fast on the twisting mountain road,* caused their passengers some anxiety.

(3)   The *rising* sun, *which has been hidden behind a bank of cloud,* suddenly broke through.

(4)   Do you know that man *who is giving the lecture today?*

(5)   Bring me the coat *on the end hook.*

(6)   Matt. 5:4
Blessed are those *who mourn,* for they shall be comforted.

(7)   Luke 2:4
And Joseph also went up...to the city *of David, which is called Bethlehem...*

(8)   Luke 2:12
you will find a babe *wrapped in swaddling cloths* and *lying in a manger.*

(9)   Acts 7:32
"I am the God *of your fathers..."*

(10) Col. 1:15
He is the image of the *invisible* God...

(11) Col. 1:21
And you, *who once were estranged* and *hostile in mind, doing evil deeds,* he has now reconciled...

(12) Rom. 2:21a
...you then *who teach others,* will you not teach yourself?

(13) Phil. 1:1
Paul and Timothy, *servants of Christ Jesus...*

(14) James 1:16
Do not be deceived, my *beloved* brethren.

(15) 1 Pet. 5:8
Your adversary the devil prowls around like a *roaring* lion...

B. Propositions that are related to concepts within the proposition

In accounting for the relations of all the propositions in a paragraph, it is sometimes necessary to use one of the four relations which link a whole proposition with a concept.

These four relations are identification, description, comment, and parenthesis. Identify propositions that have these relations to some concept in the proposition they support.

Example: John 6:50
This is the bread which comes down from heaven...
Answer: The proposition "comes down from heaven" is used to identify the bread and so the relation is one of identification.

(1)   Rev. 12:9
...the great dragon was thrown down...the deceiver of the whole world...

(2)   Acts 8:26
"Rise and go toward the south to the road that goes down from Jerusalem to Gaza. This is a desert road."

(3)   Phil. 4:21
The brethren who are with me greet you.

(4)   Col. 2:12
...you were also raised with him through faith in the working of God, who raised him from the dead.

(5)   Acts 16:1
A disciple was there, named Timothy, the son of a Jewish woman who was a believer...

(6)   John 18:26
One of the servants of the high priest, a kinsman of the man whose ear Peter had cut off, asked...

(7)   Acts 9:39
...showing tunics and other garments which Dorcas made...

(8)   John 17:17
Consecrate them by the truth; thy word is truth.

C. Chronological sequence versus simultaneity

The type of ADDITION that occurs between developmental propositions is controlled to a considerable extent by the type of discourse in which they occur. In narrative material, many of the propositions are related by one of the two time relations, sequence or simultaneity. (Beekman and Callow 1974:289)

The label of Chronological sequence identifies the type of ADDITION in which one proposition follows another in time in the referential world. [p. 291] Two events are regarded as simultaneous if they overlap with one another in time in the referential world of the discourse. Events in sequence do *not* overlap at all; simultaneous Events always overlap to some extent, either partially or completely. (p. 292)

Study each of the following passages and then restate in propositional form. Is the relation between the two propositions in the passage that of sequence or simultaneity?

Example: Mark 1:31
And he...took her by the hand and lifted her up...
Answer: He took hold of her hand. He lifted her up.
Chronological sequence

(1)   Mark 1:31
...the fever left her; and she served them.

(2)   Mark 1:35
...he rose and went out to a lonely place, and there he prayed.

(3)   Mark 3:5
He stretched it out, and his hand was restored.

(4)   Mark 3:7
Jesus withdrew with his disciples to the sea, and a great multitude from Galilee followed.

(5)   Mark 3:13
And he went up into the hills, and called to him those whom he desired; and they came to him.

(6)   Mark 3:31
...his mother and his brothers came; and standing outside they sent to him...

(7)   Mark 5:13
So he gave them leave. And the unclean spirits came out, and entered into the swine; and the herd...rushed down the steep bank into the sea, and were drowned in the sea.

D. Other types of Addition

Addition may consist of listing alternatives as in Rom. 14:21, "...anything whereby thy brother stumbleth, or is offended, or is made weak." Addition is also the relation between the two halves of a conversation in sequence. It may be a simple conjoining of two propositions with no chronological relationship.

Study the following passages to identify the type of addition which occurs. This passage is first quoted from the RSV and then the propositions for the same material are given. Which of these four types occurs in each of the passages that follow?

     a. sequence
     b. simultaneity
     c. alternation
     d. conjoining

Example: Mark 4:28
...first the blade, then the ear, then the full grain in the ear.
Answer: First the blade appears. Then the ear appears. Then the grain appears in the ear.
a. sequence

(1)   Mark 4:4
...some seed fell along the path, and the birds came and devoured it.

Some seed fell on the path. Birds came. The birds ate the seed.

(2)   Luke 22:38
       And they said, "Look, Lord, here are two swords." And he said to them, "It is enough."

       They said to him...He said to them...

(3)   1 Thess. 5:10
       ...so that whether we wake or sleep we might live with him.

       whether we are awake or whether we are asleep

(4)   Mark 4:7
       Other seed fell among thorns and the thorns grew up and choked it...

       Other seed fell among thorns/the thorns grew up/they choked it.

(5)   Col. 2:13
       ...dead in trespasses and the uncircumcision of your flesh...

       spiritually dead/because you had sinned/and because you were not people who followed God

(6)   Phil. 1:27
       ...so that whether I come and see you or am absent...

       whether I come to see you/or whether I remain absent

(7)   Acts 21:31
       ...as they were trying to kill him, word came to the tribune...that...

       while they tried to kill him, someone came to the tribune and told them "..."

E. Identifying relationships

In Mark 4:37–41 identify as many of the relationships listed above as you can. There will be some propositions related by certain relations that you have not yet studied. You may skip these.

> [37]And a great storm of wind arose, and the waves beat into the boat, so that the boat was already filling. [38]But he was in the stern, asleep on the cushion; and they woke him and said to him, "Teacher, do you not care if we perish?" [39]And he awoke and rebuked the wind, and said to the sea, "Peace be still!" And the wind ceased, and there was a great calm. [40]He said to them, "Why are you afraid? Have you no faith?" [41]And they...said to one another, "Who then is this, that even wind and sea obey him?"

F. Omitted chronological sequences

In reporting any happening which involves a sequence of events, it is unlikely that all of the events will be told in detail. Some will be left implicit. When translating from one language to another, the events selected by the original author for specific mention may be too few. (Beekman 1968:7)

For example, in John 1:43—"The next day Jesus decided to go to Galilee. And he found Philip..."—Aguaruna had to add the information that Jesus went. "The next day Jesus, wanting to, he went to Galilee. Having done so, he saw Philip..."

Study the following to see what implied action would probably need to be added in some translation to make the sequence of the story clear. Assume the receptor language is like Aguaruna and rewrite the passage, making explicit this implied action.

Example: Acts 14:19–20
...they stoned Paul and dragged him out of the city, supposing that he was dead. But when the disciples gathered about him...

Answer: They stoned Paul and dragged him out of the city. Supposing that he was dead, they left him. But when the disciples arrived, they gathered about him...

(1)   Matt. 2:7
Then Herod summoned the wise men secretly and ascertained from them what time the star appeared...

(2)   John 2:9–10
...the steward of the feast called the bridegroom and said to him...

(3)   John 4:28
So the woman left her water jar, and went away into the city, and said to the people...

(4)   John 6:10
Jesus said, "Make the people sit down." Now there was much grass in the place; so the men sat down, in number about five thousand.

(5)   Acts 5:10
When the young men came in they found her dead, and they carried her out and buried her beside her husband.

(6)   Acts 9:1–2
...Saul...went to the high priest and asked him for letters to the synagogues at Damascus, so that...he might bring them bound to Jerusalem.

(7)   Acts 20:1–2
Paul...took leave of them and departed for Macedonia. When he had gone through these parts...he came to Greece.

(8)   Acts 20:5
These went on and were waiting for us at Troas...

G. Identifying Addition and Support propositions

Propositions may be classified according to their function within discourse. They may serve either to develop, i.e., to add to or to support another semantic unit. There are thus Addition propositions and Supporting propositions.

The following is a section of the semantic display of propositions occurring in the first chapter of Colossians. No indentation is included since this would show the relationships of a Supporting proposition. Classify each proposition as either Addition or Support.

Addition propositions always develop the main event line and are related to one another by addition. Supporting propositions are always related by Association.

> Col. 1:1–2
>> I, who am Paul
>> who is an apostle
>> who represents Jesus Christ
>> because God chose me
>> who is accompanied by Timothy
>> who is our brother
>> we greet you
>> who are saints
>> and who are our brothers in Christ
>> who live in Colossae
>> may God act in grace toward you
>> He is our Father
>> may God impart peace to you

H. Chronological order

In some languages it is essential to relate events in the sequence in which they occurred. What adjustments in ordering would be necessary in translating the following passages?

Example: Mark 7:17
And when he had entered the house, and left the people, his disciples asked him about the parable.

Answer: And when he had left the people, he entered the house...

(1) John 1:32–33
And John bore witness, "I saw the Spirit descend as a dove from heaven, and it remained on him. I myself did not know him; but he who sent me to baptize with water said to me, 'He on whom you see the Spirit descend and remain, this is he who baptizes with the Holy Spirit.'"

(2) John 4:1–2
Now when the Lord knew that the Pharisees had heard that Jesus was making and baptizing more disciples than John (although Jesus himself did not baptize, but only his disciples), he left Judea and departed again to Galilee.

(3) John 4:39
Many Samaritans from that city believed in him because of the woman's testimony, "He told me all that I ever did."

(4) John 12:39–41
     Therefore they could not believe. For Isaiah again said, "He has blinded their eyes and hardened their heart, lest they should see with their eyes and perceive with their heart, and turn for me to heal them."

(5) Acts 5:30–31
     The God of our fathers raised Jesus whom you killed by hanging him on a tree. God exalted him at his right hand as Leader and Saviour, to give repentance to Israel and forgiveness of sins.

(6) 1 Cor. 15:24–26
     Then comes the end, when he delivers the kingdom to God the Father after destroying every rule and every authority and power. For he must reign until he has put all his enemies under his feet. The last enemy to be destroyed is death.

(7) Acts 1:1–3
     In the first book, O Theophilus, I have dealt with all that Jesus began to do and teach, until the day when he was taken up, after he had given commandment through the Holy Spirit to the apostles whom he had chosen. To them he presented himself alive after his passion by many proofs, appearing to them during forty days, and speaking of the kingdom of God.

I. Chiasmus

Chiasmus is a rhetorical device in which there is an inversion of order of syntactically parallel elements to result in a structure in which the first and last are semantically related, the second and next to last are related, etc. Show diagrammatically, and then give a nonchiastic rendering of the chiastic structures in the following passages.

Example: Philem. 5
       ...I hear of your love and of the faith which you have toward the Lord Jesus and all the saints...
Answer: a I hear of your love
          b   and your faith
          b'   toward the Lord Jesus
       a' toward all the saints

       "I hear of how you believe in the Lord Jesus and how you love all the saints."

(1) Ruth 2:1–3
     Now Naomi had a kinsman of her husband's, a man of wealth, of the family of Elimelech, whose name was Boaz. And Ruth the Moabitess said to Naomi, "Let me go to the field, and glean among the ears of grain after him in whose sight I shall find favour." And she said to her, "Go, my daughter." So she set forth and went and gleaned in the field after the reapers; and she happened to come to the part of the field belonging to Boaz, who was of the family of Elimelech.

(2) Ps. 135:15–18
     The idols of the nations are silver and gold, the work of men's hands. They have mouths, but they speak not, they have eyes, but they see not, they have ears, but they hear not, nor is there any breath in their mouths. Like them be those who make them!—yea, every one who trusts in them!

(3)   Prov. 23:15–16
      My son, if your heart is wise, my heart too will be glad. My soul will rejoice when your lips
      speak what is right.

(4)   Hos. 13:14
      Shall I ransom them from the power of Sheol? Shall I redeem them from Death? O Death,
      where are your plagues? O Sheol, where is your destruction? Compassion is hid from my eyes.

(5)   Amos 5:4–6
      For thus says the LORD to the house of Israel: "Seek me and live; but do not seek Bethel, and
      do not enter into Gilgal or cross over to Beer-sheba; for Gilgal shall surely go into exile, and
      Bethel shall come to nought." Seek the LORD and live, lest he break out like fire in the house
      of Joseph, and it devour, with none to quench it for Bethel,

Chapter 26
Orientation and Clarification Relations

Additional Reading:
   Barnwell 1974:193–198.

A. Support propositions that orient

Classify the following support propositions that orient as to whether the orientation is that of (a) time, (b) location, or (c) circumstance.

Example: Matt. 13:25
   ...but while men were sleeping, his enemy came and sowed weeds...
Answer: a. time—While men were sleeping

(1)   John 12:36
   While you have the light, believe in the light...

(2)   John 4:5
   He came to a town in Samaria...which was not far from the field that Jacob had given...Joseph. (TEV)

(3)   Acts 9:10
   Now there was a disciple at Damascus named Ananias. The Lord said to him in a vision...

(4)   Acts 8:25
   Now when they had testified and spoken the word of the Lord, they returned to Jerusalem...

(5)   Luke 11:1
   ...when he ceased (praying), one of his disciples said to him...

(6)   Luke 9:37
   On the next day, when they had come down from the mountain, a great crowd met him.

(7)   Luke 2:25
   Now there was a man in Jerusalem, whose name was Simeon...

B. Support propositions that clarify and are distinct in meaning

There are support propositions that are distinct in meaning from the propositions they support and that serve to clarify. In each of the following there is a support proposition that functions to clarify another proposition. Identify this support proposition and state whether the relation is (a) manner, (b) comparison, or (c) contrast.

You may want to write out the propositions before stating the relation.

Example: Matt. 12:13
   ...and it was restored, whole like the other.
Answer: "It is like the other" is a support proposition. Comparison.

(1)   Acts 25:18–19
   ...they brought no charge...of such evils as I supposed; but they had certain points of dispute...about...Jesus...

(2)   Col. 3:13
      ...forgiving each other; as the Lord has forgiven you...

(3)   Jude 10
      ...they know by instinct as irrational animals do...

(4)   Jude 20
      ...pray in the Holy Spirit...

      (You must pray/let the Holy Spirit guide you)

(5)   Jude 23
      ...hating even the garment spotted by the flesh.

      (hate what evil he does, like one hates a filthy garment)

(6)   Rev. 17:8
      The beast you saw was once alive, but lives no longer... (TEV)

(7)   Acts 11:16
      John baptized with water, but you shall be baptized with the Holy Spirit.

C. Support propositions that clarify and are similar in meaning

This group of relations includes equivalence, generic-specific, and amplification-contraction. For the purpose of this drill classify the relation between the two propositions in each of the following by the three main categories. If the passage contains more than two propositions, select two propositions that may be included under one of these three main categories.

> a. HEAD-equivalence
> b. GENERIC-specific
> c. HEAD-amplification

Example: Luke 9:36
        And they kept silence and told no one...
Answer: HEAD-equivalence

(1)   Matt. 16:6
      Take heed and beware of the leaven of the Pharisees and Sadducees.

(2)   Rom. 3:1–2
      Then what advantage has the Jew? Or what is the value of circumcision? Much in every way.

(3)   Acts 2:23
      ...this Jesus, delivered up according to the definite plan and foreknowledge of God, you crucified and killed by the hands of lawless men.

(4)   Rom. 3:27
      On what principle? On the principle of works? No, but on the principle of faith.

(5)   Acts 10:34
      And Peter opened his mouth and said...

(6)   Acts 25:11
      If then I am a wrongdoer, and have committed anything for which I deserve to die...

D. Identifying clarification relations

Identify the relations between the propositions in the following. (from Barnwell 1980:199)

Example: Hurry up! Don't waste time.
Answer: HEAD-equivalence

(1) He decided to go into business and to open a fish and chip shop.

(2) He cleaned his teeth like a monkey seeing toothpaste for the first time.

(3) The new management countermanded, or canceled, all previous orders.

(4) John talks more than Jill.

(5) They chattered like a flock of twittering sparrows.

(6) The postman was badly hurt; the large black dog had bitten a large piece out of his left leg.

(7) It rained all day, drizzling ceaselessly.

(8) The child walked away, dragging his feet reluctantly.

(9) I shall buy the blue dress but not the green coat.

(10) The boys are always late for the math lesson, but they are always on time for the football game.

(11) He consented to go, I firmly refused.

(12) He taught regularly at the college, giving lectures in biochemistry at least three times a week throughout the academic year.

E. Identifying clarification relations

Identify the Clarification Relations between propositions in each of the following examples.

(1) Matt. 23:37
How often would I have gathered your children together as a hen gathers her brood under her wings...

(2) Mark 14:61
But he was silent and made no answer.

(3) Luke 18:16
"Let the children come to me, and do not hinder them..."

(4) John 3:14
...as Moses lifted up the serpent in the wilderness, so must the Son of man be lifted up...

(5) John 3:30
"He must increase, but I must decrease."

(6) Phil. 1:15
Some indeed preach Christ from envy and rivalry, but others from good will.

(7) Col. 1:29
For this I toil, striving with all the energy that he mightily inspires within me.

(8)   2 Thess. 2:15
      So then, brethren, stand firm and hold to the traditions which you were taught by us...

(9)   James 1:4
      ...that you may be perfect and complete, lacking in nothing.

(10) 1 Pet. 3:10
      ...let him keep his tongue from evil and his lips from speaking guile...

(11) 1 Pet. 5:10
      ...the God of all grace...will himself restore, establish, and strengthen you.

Chapter 27
Logical Relations

Additional Reading:
   Greenlee 1962:39–43.

A. Propositions that argue

The following drill has to do with support propositions that argue.

> Each pair of propositions in this group is associated by the general relation of cause and effect. That is to say, one of the two propositions represents a cause, and the other the consequent effect. It is in this sense that one argues for the other by giving its causal antecedent or subsequent. (Beekman and Callow 1974:300)

Classify the relationship between propositions in the following passages as one of the following. (The order may be reversed between the propositions.)

   a. reason-RESULT
   b. means-RESULT
   c. purpose-MEANS
   d. condition-CONSEQUENCE
   e. concession-CONTRAEXPECTATION
   f. grounds-CONCLUSION
   g. grounds-EXHORTATION

Example: James 4:2
         You do not have, because you do not ask.
Answer: a. RESULT-reason

(1)   Mark 3:25
      ...if a house is divided against itself, that house will not be able to stand.

(2)   Rom. 7:20
      Now if I do what I do not want, it is no longer I that do it, but sin which dwells within me.

(3)   Matt. 9:13
      I am...come to call...sinners to repentance. (KJV)

(4)   1 Thess. 5:9
      For God has not destined us for wrath, but to obtain salvation through our Lord Jesus Christ...

(5)   Rev. 5:9
      ...and by thy blood didst ransom men for God...

(6)   John 9:39
      ...I came into this world, that those who do not see may see...

(7)   1 Thess. 3:5
      ...I sent that I might know your faith...

(8)   Matt. 9:4
      But Jesus, knowing their thoughts, said...

(9)   Col. 3:2–3
      Set your minds on things that are above, not on things that are on earth. For you have died, and your life is hid with Christ in God.

(10) Luke 17:3
      ...if your brother sins, rebuke him...

(11) Col. 3:9
      Do not lie to one another, seeing that you have put off the old nature with its practices...

(12) Mark 5:26
      [She] had spent all that she had, and was no better...

(13) 1 Tim. 3:5
      ...if a man does not know how to manage his own household, how can he care for God's church?

B. Condition of fact versus contrary-to-fact

The word "if" cannot usually be translated by a single form into another language. A condition which is probably true or thought to be so by the speaker (condition of fact) is often translated differently than a condition which is probably not true (condition contrary-to-fact). The first will often be translated by a declarative clause rather than a conditional clause.

For example, when Jesus says, "And if I cast out demons by Beelzebub..." (Matt. 12:27), Jesus is hardly intending to imply that he does in fact cast out demons by Beelzebub... On the other hand, Jesus' statement in John 14:3, "And if I go and prepare a place for you..." is anything but uncertain and undependable... (Greenlee 1962:39)

Study each of the following condition sentences and decide if they are condition of fact or condition contrary-to-fact. Matt. 12:27 above is contrary-to-fact and John 14:3 is fact.

(1)   Matt. 22:45
      If David thus calls him Lord, how is he his son?

(2)   John 5:46
      If you believed Moses, you would believe me...

(3)   John 11:32
      Lord, if you had been here, my brother would not have died.

(4)   John 13:32
      ...if God is glorified in him, God will also glorify him in himself...

(5)   John 3:12
      If I have told you earthly things and you do not believe...

(6)   John 15:19
      If you were of the world, the world would love its own...

(7)   Acts 4:9–10
      ...if we are being examined today concerning a good deed done to a cripple,...be it known to you all...

(8)   1 John 2:19
        ...for if they had been of us, they would have continued with us...

C. Identifying types of conditional clauses

Both of the two previous types of clauses deal with definite events... The third type of conditional clause which commonly occurs in the N.T. ...deals...with, either (1) a general condition which may occur at various times (e.g., "if it falls into a pit on the sabbath," Matt. 12:11), or (2) a future possibility (e.g., "If I only touch his garment...," Matt. 9:21). (Greenlee 1962:41)

This third class is called CONDITION OF CONTINGENCY or POTENTIAL FACT. Study the following to see which refer to definite events and are therefore either fact or contrary-to-fact and which do not refer to a definite event but are potential fact.

Example: Matt. 4:9
        All these I will give you, if you will fall down and worship me.
Answer: Potential fact

Example: Matt. 4:3
        If you are the Son of God, command these stones to become loaves of bread.
Answer: Fact

Example: 1 Cor. 2:8
        None of the rulers of this age understood this; for if they had, they would not have crucified the Lord of glory.
Answer: Contrary-to-fact

(1)   Mark 3:25
        And if a house is divided against itself, that house will not be able to stand.

(2)   Mark 13:22
        False Christs and false prophets will arise...to lead astray, if possible, the elect.

(3)   Luke 17:3
        Take heed to yourselves; if your brother sins, rebuke him, and if he repents, forgive him.

(4)   1 Cor. 14:37
        If any one thinks that he is a prophet, or spiritual, he should acknowledge that what I am writing to you is a command of the Lord.

(5)   1 Cor. 15:16
        For if the dead are not raised, then Christ has not been raised.

(6)   2 Cor. 5:1
        For we know that if the earthly tent we live in is destroyed, we have a building from God...

D. "Unless" clauses or conditionals

A sentence of two clauses, one of which contains "unless" and the other a negative (at least implied), must often be translated as a conditional sentence.

Rewrite the following, using a conditional clause.

Example: Acts 27:31
Unless these men stay in the ship, you cannot be saved.
Answer: If these men flee, you cannot be rescued.

(1)   John 3:2
...no one can do these signs that you do, unless God is with him.

(2)   John 4:48
Unless you see signs and wonders you will not believe.

(3)   John 6:53
...unless you eat the flesh of the Son of man and drink his blood, you have no life in you...

(4)   John 6:65
...no one can come to me unless it is granted him by the Father.

(5)   John 15:4
As the branch cannot bear fruit by itself, unless it abides in the vine, neither can you, unless you abide in me.

(6)   John 19:11
You would have no power over me unless it had been given you from above...

(7)   John 20:25
Unless I see in his hands the print of the nails...I will not believe.

(8)   Rom. 10:15
And how can men preach unless they are sent?

(9)   1 Cor. 15:36
What you sow does not come to life unless it dies.

E. Omitted main clause with reason clauses

In a number of passages the reason clause is stated but the main clause is only implied, often being carried by the word "for." For example, Matt. 2:2 states, "Where is he who has been born king of the Jews? For we have seen his star." The word "for" here implies the main clause, "we know that he has been born." In Aguaruna this verse is translated "Where is the one who has been born, the one who will rule the people of Judea? We know he has been born because we saw the star."

Rewrite the following, making explicit the main clause, which is only implied in the source language. You will need to study the context.

(1)   Matt. 16:7
And they discussed it among themselves, saying, "[For] we brought no bread."

(2)   Matt. 2:20
"Rise, take the child and his mother, and go to the land of Israel, for those who sought the child's life are dead."

(3) Matt. 4:6
     If you are the Son of God, throw yourself down; for it is written, 'He shall give his angels charge of you.'

(4) Mark 3:29–30
     [He said to them,] "...whoever blasphemes against the Holy Spirit never has forgiveness, but is guilty of an eternal sin"—for they had said, "He has an unclean spirit."

(5) Acts 21:13
     Then Paul answered, "What are you doing, weeping and breaking my heart? For I am ready not only to be imprisoned but even to die at Jerusalem for the name of the Lord Jesus."

(6) Acts 23:5
     "I did not know, brethren, that he was the high priest; for it is written, 'You shall not speak evil of a ruler of your people.'"

(7) John 4:9
     The Samaritan woman said to him, "How is it that you, a Jew, ask a drink of me, a woman of Samaria?" For Jews have no dealings with Samaritans.

F. Making information explicit

In the following the item that is to be made explicit is given in parentheses following the passage. Rewrite adding this information.

Example: James 2:24
         You see that a man is justified by works and not by faith alone.
         (contrast implied by "alone")
Answer: You see that a man is justified by faith shown by his works and he is not justified by faith alone.

(1) Mark 5:41
     ...he said to her, "Talitha cumi"; which means, "Little girl, I say to you, arise." (source or language of the foreign words)

(2) James 1:5
     If any of you lacks wisdom, let him ask God, who gives to all men generously and without reproaching, and it will be given him. (condition clause to go with final main clause)

(3) Acts 6:6
     These they set before the apostles, and they prayed and laid their hands upon them. (purpose of this action)

(4) Mark 7:32
     ...they besought him to lay his hands upon him. (purpose of this action)

(5) Acts 13:47
     For so the Lord has commanded us... (result that goes with this reason clause)

G. Identifying logical relations

Write as two propositions. Use English relation forms. Write in logical order.

Example: I went to the clinic because I was sick.
Answer: I was sick so I went to the clinic.
               Reason-RESULT

(1)   We gave him money to buy food.

(2)   He came late so I did not pay him.

(3)   The children had measles because they were covered with spots.

(4)   Through standing in the rain she caught a cold.

(5)   Searching in my handbag, I found my coin purse.

(6)   She gained her knowledge through much reading.

(If you feel that examples (5) and (6) could be interpreted in two alternative ways, give both alternatives.)

(7)   I studied hard lest I fail the exams.

(8)   He doesn't like spinach, but he ate it anyway.

(9)   Don't hesitate because you won't have an offer like that again.

(10)   If he has malaria (and he certainly has) he must have been in the tropics.

(11)   His light is on so he must be still there.

(12)   The children had stomach-aches because they had eaten too many sweets.

(13)   By climbing over the wall he escaped.

(14)   That dog bites, so don't open the gate.

(15)   Even though he disliked the medicine, he took it regularly.

H. Logical order

Many languages require a reason clause to precede the main clause. Rewrite the passages below assuming you are translating into such a language. Adjust any other problems of skewing and figures of speech.

Example: Acts 8:21
               "You have neither part nor lot in this matter, for your heart is not right before God."
Answer: "Since your thoughts are wrong as God considers it, you cannot share with us at all in this ministry."

(1)   Acts 8:22–23
       "...Repent therefore of this wickedness of yours, and pray to the Lord that, if possible, the intent of your heart may be forgiven you. For I see that you are in the gall of bitterness and in the bond of iniquity."

(2)   Acts 10:45–46
       And the believers from among the circumcised who came with Peter were amazed, because the gift of the Holy Spirit had been poured out even on the Gentiles. For they heard them speaking in tongues and extolling God.

(3)   Acts 20:26–27
       Therefore I testify to you this day that I am innocent of the blood of all of you, for I did not
       shrink from declaring to you the whole counsel of God.

(4)   Acts 21:28–29
       "Men of Israel, help! This is the man who is teaching men everywhere against the people and
       the law and this place; moreover he also brought Greeks into the temple, and he has defiled
       this holy place." For they had previously seen Trophimus the Ephesian with him in the city,
       and they supposed that Paul had brought him into the temple.

(5)   Acts 21:35–36
       And when he came to the steps, he was actually carried by the soldiers because of the
       violence of the crowd; for the mob of the people followed, crying, "Away with him!"

(6)   1 John 3:22
       ...and we receive from him whatever we ask, because we keep his commandments and do
       what pleases him.

(7)   1 John 4:8
       He who does not love does not know God; for God is love.

(8)   1 John 4:13
       By this we know that we abide in him and he in us, because he has given us of his own Spirit.

I.   Order of clauses within sentences

In some languages of New Guinea, the independent clause must come last in the sentence. All
purpose, reason, conditional, and other dependent clauses precede the main clause. Rewrite the
following according to this rule.

Example: Mark 1:22
             And they were astonished at his teaching, for he taught them as one who had authority,
             and not as the scribes.
Answer: Because he taught them as one who had authority and not as the scribes, they were
             astonished at his teaching.

(1)   Matt. 9:36
       When he saw the crowds, he had compassion for them, because they were harassed and
       helpless, like sheep without a shepherd.

(2)   Matt. 10:26
       So have no fear of them; for nothing is covered that will not be revealed, or hidden that will
       not be known.

(3)   Mark 1:38
       Let us go on to the next towns, that I may preach there also; for that is why I came out.

(4)   Mark 3:2
       And they watched him, to see whether he would heal him on the sabbath, so that they might
       accuse him.

(5)   Mark 3:9–10
       And he told his disciples to have a boat ready for him because of the crowd, lest they should
       crush him; for he had healed many, so that all who had diseases pressed upon him to touch
       him.

J. More practice in identifying logical relations

Identify the relationship in each of the following. Write as two propositions. Use English relation forms. Write in logical order.

(1)   Since the paper was finished they stopped printing.

(2)   He was too tired to finish the job.

(3)   She broke her leg through wearing high-heeled shoes.

(4)   She lives in the same road, so she must know his house.

(5)   She lives in a small flat to save money.

(6)   He's an Englishman, but quite pleasant.

(7)   There's not much time so hurry up.

(8)   The school was built in spite of the opposition of the town council.

(9)   The school was built to serve the children of the area.

(10)   The school was built in response to public demand.

(11)   The school was built through the gifts of many people.

(12)   Matt. 25:13
       Watch therefore, for you know neither the day nor the hour.

(13)   Acts 2:15
       ...these men are not drunk...since it is only the third hour of the day...

(14)   Acts 3:19
       Repent, ...that your sins may be blotted out...

(15)   1 Cor. 6:20
       ...you were bought with a price. So glorify God in your body.

(16)   Heb. 6:10
       ...God is not so unjust as to overlook your work...

(17)   1 John 4:19
       We love, because he first loved us.

Chapter 28
Stimulus-RESPONSE Roles

Additional Reading:
   Larson 1978: Chapters III and IV.

A. Changing indirect speech to direct speech in Navajo

In the Navajo language indirect discourse is invariably turned into direct discourse, even to the expression of thoughts and opinions (Edgerton 1965:228). Assume that you are translating into a language such as Navajo. How might you make direct quotations from the following indirect speech, substituting "say" or "said" for the word which is italicized?

Example: Mark 3:9
            And he *told* his disciples to have a boat ready for him.
Answer: And he said to his disciples, "Get a boat ready for me."

(1)   Matt. 19:7
      Why then did Moses *command* one to give a certificate of divorce...

(2)   Mark 5:18
      ...the man who had been possessed with demons *begged* him that he might be with him.

(3)   Mark 5:43
      And he strictly *charged* them that no one should know this, and told them to give her something to eat.

(4)   Mark 7:26
      ...she *begged* him to cast the demon out of her daughter.

(5)   Mark 10:48
      And many *rebuked* him, *telling* him to be silent...

(6)   Luke 4:3
      "If you are the Son of God, *command* this stone to become bread."

B. Using "said" plus direct speech in Waiwai

Hawkins makes the following statement about the Waiwai language of British Guiana:

> We also began to realize that there was no proper word in Waiwai for various types of statements such as "to promise," "to praise," "to deny," etc. The promise or praise was merely quoted and so with the denial, and in each case this direct discourse was followed by the above-mentioned stem (*ka* meaning 'to say' or 'to do'). We heard such forms as these: *Kmokyasi men, mika harare:* 'I will certainly come, you said'; meaning 'You promised to come.' *Kanawa yenpotho okre, nikay:* 'It is a wonderful canoe, he said'; meaning 'He praised the canoe.' *Arihararo maki weesi, kekne:* 'I didn't take it, he said'; meaning 'He denied that he took it'. (Hawkins 1962:164)

Assume that you are translating into Waiwai and must use the word said with a direct quotation to translate "promise," "praise (commend)," and "deny." These words may not be used inside the quote but the context of the quote must carry the idea. How might you translate the following?

(1)   Luke 8:45
       And Jesus said, "Who was it that touched me?" When all *denied* it, Peter said...

(2)   Luke 12:9
       ...he who *denies* me before men will be *denied* before the angels of God.

(3)   Acts 3:9
       And all the people saw him walking and *praising* God...

(4)   Acts 4:16
       ...a notable sign has been performed...and we cannot *deny* it.

(5)   1 Cor. 11:2
       I *commend* you because you remember me in everything.

(6)   1 Cor. 11:22
       What shall I say to you? Shall I *commend* you in this?

(7)   Titus 1:2
       ...eternal life which God, who never lies, *promised* ages ago...

C. Using "said" plus direct speech in Chontal

In Navajo and Chontal (of Mexico) command, beg, beseech, ask, tell, proclaim, publish, question, discuss, marvel, be amazed, deny, permit, desire, and other ideas are often expressed by a direct quote following a form of a verb "say." Assume that you are translating into a language that uses a quotation with a verb say to translate the italicized words in the following, how might you state the direct quotation?

Example: Mark 1:5
               ...*confessing* their sins.
Answer: Chontal: They said, "It's true, we've done evil."

Example: Mark 8:32
               Peter...began to *rebuke* him.
Answer: Chontal: He said to Jesus, "Don't talk like that."

(1)   Matt. 8:34
       ...all the city came out to meet Jesus...they *begged* him to leave their neighborhood.

(2) Matt. 27:58
He went to Pilate and *asked* for the body of Jesus.

(3) Mark 3:12
And he strictly *ordered* them not to make him known.

(4) Mark 5:10
And he *begged* him eagerly not to send them out of the country.

(5) Mark 6:6
And he *marveled* because of their unbelief.

(6) Mark 9:18
...I *asked* your disciples to cast it out, and they were not able.

(7) Acts 9:27
...*declared* to them how on the road he had seen the Lord...

(8) Mark 10:13
And they were bringing children to him, that he might touch them; and the disciples *rebuked* them.

(9) Mark 11:16
...he *would not allow* any one to carry anything through the temple.

(10) Mark 15:11
But the chief priests *stirred up* the crowd to have him release for them Barabbas instead.

D. Using "said" plus direct speech in Auca

In Auca, of Ecuador indirect quotations must almost always be rendered by direct quotations... There are unsuspected complications in that the person and number of the direct quotations have to be decided from the context, this complexity being heightened by the fact that such renderings may produce quotes within quotes within quotes. This is an especially common problem because any expression of *desire* is also treated as direct discourse, the verb of *desire* being simply the verb *to say*. (Peeke 1965:50)

Assuming you are translating into Auca, rewrite the following passages, using direct quotations. You will not necessarily need quotes within quotes.

Example: Mark 3:12
And he strictly ordered them not to make him known.

Auca back-translation:
Jesus spoke like a chief, "'You all keep quiet!' I say. Don't be telling who I am."

(1) Luke 7:36
One of the Pharisees *asked* him to eat with him...

(2) Luke 22:31
...Satan *demanded* to have you, that he might sift you like wheat...

(3) Acts 3:14
But you *denied* the Holy and Righteous One, and asked for a murderer to be granted to you...

(4)   Acts 7:46
       ...David...found favor in the sight of God and *asked* leave to find a habitation for the God of
       Jacob.

(5)   Acts 9:1–2
       But Saul...*asked* him for letters to the synagogues at Damascus, so that if he found any
       belonging to the Way...he might bring them bound to Jerusalem.

(6)   Col. 1:9
       ...we have not ceased to pray for you, *asking* that you may be filled with the knowledge of
       his will...

(7)   Rev. 9:6
       And in those days men...will *long to* die and death will fly from them.

E. Using direct speech for purpose clauses in Aguaruna

In Aguaruna, of Peru, not only are all indirect quotes and all expressions of thought handled by
direct quotes, but all purpose clauses are made into direct quotes. A direct quote plus "saying"
indicates purpose. How might you express the following purpose clauses in direct quotations in
Aguaruna?

Example: Titus 1:5
            This is why I left you in Crete, that you might amend what was defective, and appoint
            elders in every town as I directed you...

            Aguaruna back-translation:
            I left you in Crete, "That which we did not completely cause to become good, you
            caused it to become good," saying: "You appoint leaders, that they be in each town,"
            saying; that which I told you before, you do it like that.

(1)   John 6:6
       This he said *to test him*...

(2)   Mark 3:2
       And they watched him, *to see whether he would heal him on the sabbath*...

(3)   Mark 6:46
       ...he went into the hills *to pray*.

(4)   Mark 10:13
       And they were bringing children to him, *that he might touch them*...

(5)   Mark 12:2
       ...he sent a servant...*to get* from them some of the fruit...

F. Using direct speech for purpose clauses in Gahuku

In Gahuku of New Guinea, purpose clauses are also turned into direct quotations, but the purpose
clause must precede the main clause. Rewrite the following according to the Gahuku pattern.

Example: John 6:6
            This he said to test him...

            Gahuku back-translation:
            "I will test him," saying, he said...

(1) Mark 15:32
Let the Christ...come down...*that we may see and believe.*

(2) Mark 16:1
(They) bought spices, *so that they might go and anoint him.*

(3) Rom. 1:11
...I long to see you, *that I may impart to you some spiritual gift...*

(4) John 3:14–15
...the Son of man must be lifted up, *that whoever believes in him may have eternal life.*

(5) Luke 1:3–4
...to write an orderly account for you...*that you may know the truth concerning the things of which you have been informed.*

G. Changing direct speech to indirect in Nilotic languages

There are also languages in which indirect discourse is preferred to direct discourse, and the changes must be made in that direction. Nida mentions this in discussing the Nilotic languages of Africa.

Preference for indirect quotations. The shift from direct to indirect discourse can be made easily, but the translator has to bear such matters constantly in mind. This does not mean, of course, that all direct discourse must be changed, but one should reflect something of the percentage of usage of the indigenous language. (Nida 1955:58)

Assume that you are translating into a language with a preference for indirect discourse. How might you change the following passages?

Example: Mark 10:2
And Pharisees came up and...asked, "Is it lawful for a man to divorce his wife?"
Answer: And Pharisees came up and asked him if it were lawful for a man to divorce his wife.

(1) Mark 1:38
And he said to them, "Let us go on to the next towns..."

(2) Mark 6:25
And she came in...and asked, saying "I want you to give me at once the head of John the Baptist on a platter."

(3) John 1:22
They said to him then, "Who are you? Let us have an answer for those who sent us..."

(4) Luke 15:18
I will arise and go to my father, and I will say to him, "Father, I have sinned against heaven and before you..."

(5) Luke 4:12
And Jesus answered him, "It is said, 'You shall not tempt the Lord your God.'"

(6) Matt. 21:25
And they argued with one another, "If we say, 'From heaven,' he will say to us, 'Why then did you not believe him?'"

(7)   Matt. 2:8
       ...and he sent them to Bethlehem, saying, "Go and search diligently for the child..."

(8)   Heb. 10:9
       ...then he added, "Lo, I have come to do thy will."

(9)   Luke 17:23
       And they will say to you, "Lo, there!" or "Lo, here!" Do not go, do not follow them.

(10)   1 Cor. 15:35
       But some one will ask, "How are the dead raised? With what kind of body do they come?"

H. Identifying speech roles

What are the Stimulus-RESPONSE speech roles in the following.

Example: Acts 21:33
               He inquired who he was and what he had done. Some in the crowd shouted one thing,
               some another...
Answer: question-ANSWER

(1)   Acts 1:6–7
       [6]So when they had come together, they asked him, "Lord, will you at this time restore
       the kingdom to Israel?" [7]He said to them, "It is not for you to know times or seasons which
       the Father has fixed by his own authority.

(2)   Acts 1:11–12
       [11] ...and said, "Men of Galilee, why do you stand looking into heaven? This Jesus, who
       was taken up from you into heaven, will come in the same way as you saw him go into
       heaven." [12]Then they returned to Jerusalem from the mount called Olivet, which is near
       Jerusalem, a sabbath day's journey away...

(3)   Acts 2:37–38
       [37]Now when they heard this they were cut to the heart, and said to Peter and the rest of
       the apostles, "Brethren, what shall we do?" [38]And Peter said to them, "Repent, and be
       baptized every one of you in the name of Jesus Christ for the forgiveness of your sins; and
       you shall receive the gift of the Holy Spirit.

(4)   Acts 4:6–7
       [6] ...with Annas the high priest and Caiaphas and John and Alexander, and all who were
       of the high-priestly family. [7]And when they had set them in the midst, they inquired, "By
       what power or by what name did you do this?"

(5)   Acts 5:8–9
       [8]And Peter said to her, "Tell me whether you sold the land for so much." And she said,
       "Yes, for so much." [9]But Peter said to her, "How is it that you have agreed together to tempt
       the Spirit of the Lord? Hark, the feet of those that have buried your husband are at the door,
       and they will carry you out."

(6)   Acts 5:19–20
       [19]But at night an angel of the Lord opened the prison doors and brought them out and
       said, [20]"Go and stand in the temple and speak to the people all the words of this Life."

(7)   Acts 5:27–29

[27]And when they had brought them, they set them before the council. And the high priest questioned them, [28]saying, "We strictly charged you not to teach in this name, yet here you have filled Jerusalem with your teaching and you intend to bring this man's blood upon us." [29]But Peter and the apostles answered, "We must obey God rather than men."

I. Identifying Stimulus-RESPONSE roles

Study the following propositional display from Acts 27:39–44 and identify the Stimulus-RESPONSE roles by filling in the blank spaces on the lines.

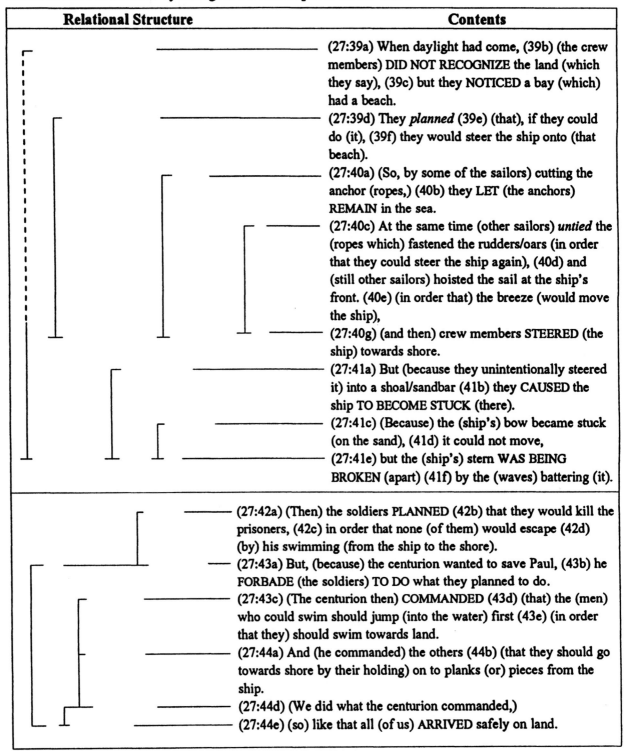

Review of Chapters 24–28

A. Labeling relations in a display

In each of the following the propositions are given. On the left, draw in a display of the relations between the propositions.

Example: Col. 1:13 (the answer is written in)

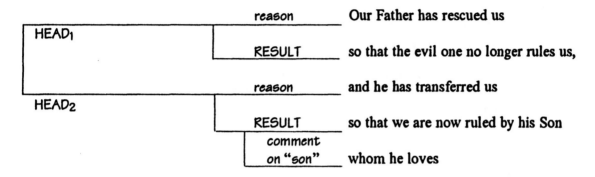

HEAD₁	reason	Our Father has rescued us
	RESULT	so that the evil one no longer rules us,
HEAD₂	reason	and he has transferred us
	RESULT	so that we are now ruled by his Son
	comment on "son"	whom he loves

(1)   Col. 1:25

I (emphatic) minister to (the Church)

because God appointed me to this office

in order that (I might help) you

in order that I might make known to all people the message

which (has been revealed) by God

(2)   Col. 1:28

I preach about Christ

I warn everyone with much wisdom

I teach everyone with much wisdom

in order that everyone will become spiritually mature (Greek: in Christ)

(3)   Col. 2:18

Do not heed anyone

who would (want to) condemn you

who advocates

that people should practice (so-called)

humility

that people should worship angels

by talking about

things which he has seen (in visions)

because he is proud without reason

because he thinks only of

things which his lower nature wants

(4)   Col. 3:5–9

Stop (Greek: put to death) yourselves

(Greek: your members on the earth) from
doing (such evil deeds as)

(Don't practice) (sexual) immorality

(Don't be) indecent

(Don't) lust

(Don't) desire (to do) evil

And (don't) covet/be greedy

inasmuch as (people) treat as gods (the things)

(which they covet)

just as (people) treat idols as gods (Greek:
which is idolatry)

(Don't do those things)

because God will certainly punish (people)

who habitually disobey (God)

because (they do) these things

You also used to behave (like that) among
them

when you lived

habitually (sinning) like that

But now you too get rid of/don't do (Greek:
put off) all (evil) things

(Don't be) angry

(Don't have) passionate outbursts

(Don't have) malice

(Don't) slander (people)

(Don't use) abusive speech

(Don't) be lying to each other

because you have gotten rid of (Greek: put off)

your evil nature (Greek: old man) and the evil

habits/evil things

which it causes you to practice

(5)   Col. 3:12–14

Acquire (Greek: put on) (these virtues)

inasmuch as you are (people)

whom God chose

whom (God) has set apart/made holy

whom (God) loves

Be compassionate

Be kind

Be humble

Be considerate

Be patient

Patiently bear with each other's (faults)

Forgive each other

whenever one of you has a complaint against another

Most important of all, love (each other)

which will enable you to practice all

these virtues (Greek: as a bond) perfectly

(6)   Titus 1:15–16

                                                People respond to all things

                                                who are clean/pure

                                                which are clean/pure

                                                Other people do not respond to (things)

                                                who are defiled/unclean

                                                who do not believe (about Christ)

                                                which are clean/pure

                                                because their minds are defiled/unclean

                                                because their consciences are corrupted

                                                (these people) say/profess

                                                that they know God

                                                but they deny

                                                that they know God

                                                by doing (evil things)

                                                because they are detestable

                                                and because they do not obey

                                                and because they are not fit/able

                                                that they do (things)

                                                which are good

B. Writing as propositions

Now work through several passages, doing a complete semantic display of the propositions. Follow the steps given below.

Step 1. Identify and list the Event words in the paragraph.
Step 2. Construct the propositions based on these explicit Events.
Step 3. Construct any additional proposition based on implicit Events.
Step 4. Relate the propositions to one another in a semantic display.

Example: Mark 1:4
John preached a baptism of repentance for the forgiveness of sins.

Step 1:   preach
          baptize
          repent
          forgive
          sin

Step 2:   John preached (something)
          (John) baptized (the people)
          (the people) repented
          (God) forgave (the people)
          (the people) sinned

Step 3:   none

Step 4:   orienter _____ John preached

                       MEANS 1 _____ that the people should repent

                       MEANS 2 _____ and that he will baptize them

          CONTENT   result _____ so that (God) will forgive them

                       comment on "people" ___ who had sinned

This semantic structure will, of course, be translated differently for every language.

Back-translated into Aguaruna: John preached to the people, saying, "You have sinned. Repent and I will baptize you so that God will forgive you."

TEV says: John...preaching his message, 'Turn away from your sins and be baptized,' he told the people, 'and God will forgive your sins.'

Now apply the four steps to each of the following passages:

(1)   Jude 16
      These are grumblers, malcontents, following their own passions, loud-mouthed boasters, flattering people to gain advantage.

(2)   Eph. 2:8-9
      For by grace you have been saved through faith; and...it is the gift of God—not because of works, lest any man should boast.

(3) 1 Pet. 2:15
For it is God's will that by doing right you should put to silence the ignorance of foolish men.

(4) 1 Thess. 1:2–3
We give thanks to God always for you all, constantly mentioning you in our prayers, remembering before our God and Father your work of faith and labour of love and steadfastness of hope in our Lord Jesus Christ.

(5) Eph. 1:7–8
In him we have redemption through his blood, the forgiveness of our trespasses, according to the riches of his grace which he lavished upon us.

C. Propositional display of Col. 1:1–5

The following are the possible propositions of Col. 1:1–5. On the far left make a display of the relations between the propositions..

Col. 1:1

(I who am)Paul

(who am) an apostle

who (represents) Christ Jesus comment on apostle

because God willed it/chose me

I and brother Timothy (greet you)

Col. 1:2

who (are) in Colossae

who are saints

and who are brothers in Christ

(May) God act in grace toward you

and (may) God (impart) peace to you

who is our Father

Col. 1:3

> We always thank God
>
> Who is the Father of our Lord Jesus Christ
>
> whenever we pray for you

Col. 1:4

> because we have heard (from Epaphras)
>
> that you believe in Christ Jesus
>
> and that you love all the saints

Col. 1:5

> because you look forward to (sharing with them)
>
> what is prepared (Greek: laid up) for you in heaven
>
> which (you came to know about)
>
> when you heard the true message
>
> which is the gospel.

D. Propositional display of Titus 1:5–16

Study Titus 1:5–16 carefully. Then write out the propositions for this passage as was done for Col. 1:1–5 above, and label the relations.

Review of Chapters 1–28

A. Identifying potential translation problems

Name at least one potential translation problem in each of the following verses. You may want to list more than one for some passages. Copy out the words that represent the problem you name.

Example: John 4:13
Jesus said to her, "Every one who drinks of this water will thirst again..."

Answer: *every one*—may need to be plural rather than singular, e.g., all who drink.

(1) John 19:13
When Pilate heard these words, he...sat down on the judgment seat...

(2) John 19:17
So they took Jesus, and he went out, bearing his own cross...

(3) John 19:19
Pilate also wrote a title and put it on the cross; it read, "Jesus of Nazareth, the King of the Jews."

(4) John 20:15
...she said to him, "Sir, if you have carried him away, tell me where you have laid him..."

(5) John 20:21
Jesus said to them again, "Peace be with you. As the Father has sent me, even so I send you."

(6) John 20:26
The doors were shut, but Jesus came and stood among them, and said...

(7) John 20:31
...these are written that you may believe that Jesus is the Christ...

(8) John 21:7
That disciple whom Jesus loved said to Peter, "It is the Lord!"

(9) John 21:22
Jesus said to him, "If it is my will that he remain until I come, what is that to you? Follow me!"

(10) John 21:24
This is the disciple who is bearing witness to these things, and who has written these things; and we know that his testimony is true.

B. Identifying potential translation problems (continued)

The following ten passages contain potential translation problems. Each passage contains a potential adjustment for one of the following:

      a. ellipsis
      b. omission of clause
      c. genitive construction
      d. rhetorical question
      e. conditional clause—fact
      f. conditional clause—contrary-to-fact
      g. conditional clause—contingence
      h. obligatory possession
      i. extended use of number
      j. extended use of person

Identify the potential adjustment from the above list. After telling what adjustment is involved, rewrite the passage, making the appropriate adjustment.

Example: John 15:4
         As the branch cannot bear fruit by itself...neither can you...
Answer: Potential adjustment concerns ellipsis.
         As the branch cannot bear fruit by itself neither can you bear fruit by yourself.

(1)   Mark 15:28
     And the Scripture was fulfilled, which saith, "And he was numbered with the transgressors." (KJV)

(2)   John 8:28
     So Jesus said, "When you have lifted up the Son of man, then you will know that I am he..."

(3)   John 18:22
     ...one of the officers standing by struck Jesus with his hand, saying, "Is that how you answer the high priest?"

(4)   John 18:23
     Jesus answered him, "If I have spoken wrongly, bear witness to the wrong; but if I have spoken rightly, why do you strike me?"

(5)   2 Cor. 1:3
     Blessed be the God and Father of our Lord Jesus Christ, the Father of mercies and God of all comfort...

(6)   Matt. 19:17–18
     "If you would enter life, keep the commandments." He said to him, "Which?"

(7)   Rom. 7:20
     Now if I do what I do not want, it is no longer I that do it, but sin which dwells within me.

(8)   John 10:30
     "I and the Father are one."

(9)   2 Thess. 1:4
     Therefore we ourselves boast of you in the churches...

C. Identifying adjustments that have been made in a translation

Identify as many translation adjustments that have been made in the following translation as you can. This is a back-translation into English of the translation into Tepehua. Compare with the RSV below. Chart your answer as follows:

RSV	Tepehua	translation principle
disciples	men	specific to generic
looked at	again saw	implicit made explicit

John 1:35–44 (Tepehua):

[35]The next day again John was standing with two of his men. [36]And he again saw Jesus where he was coming and said to them, "Look at that man who is going to be like God's lamb." [37]And those two men of John's when they heard what he said, well, immediately they followed Jesus. [38]And when Jesus turned around he saw those who were following him. He said to them. "What are you hunting for?" And they said to him, "Rabbi, where do you live?" Rabbi means teacher. [39]Well, he said to them, "Come, You will see where I live." And they went with him. They saw where he lived.

Well, that day they stayed there with him since it was about four in the afternoon. [40]And those two who heard John's words and followed Jesus, well, one was called Andrew. He was the younger brother of Simon Peter. [41]Well, Andrew immediately found his real brother who was called Simon. And he said to his brother, "We have found the Messiah." That means we have found the Christ, the one of whom it was said that God would send him here. [42]And immediately he took him to where Jesus was. When Jesus saw him he said to him, "You are Simon. You are the son of Jonas. You will be called Cephas." Cephas and Peter mean rock. [43]When the next day came, Jesus said that he was going to the land of Galilee. There he came across the one who was called Philip. And he said to him that he should follow him. [44]Philip lived in the town of Bethsaida. It was in the land of Andrew and Peter.

John 1:35–44 (RSV)

[35]The next day again John was standing with two of his disciples; [36]and he looked at Jesus as he walked, and said, "Behold the Lamb of God!" [37]The two disciples heard him say this, and they followed Jesus. [38]Jesus turned, and saw them following, and said to them, "What do you seek?" And they said to him, "Rabbi" (which means Teacher), "where are you staying?" [39]He said to them, "Come and see." They came and saw where he was staying; and they stayed with him that day, for it was about the tenth hour. [40]One of the two who heard John speak, and followed him, was Andrew, Simon Peter's brother. [41]He first found his brother Simon, and said to him, "We have found the Messiah" (which means Christ). [42]He brought him to Jesus. Jesus looked at him, and said, "So you are Simon the son of John? You shall be called Cephas" (which means Peter).

[43]The next day Jesus decided to go to Galilee. And he found Philip and said to him, "Follow me." [44]Now Philip was from Bethsaida, the city of Andrew and Peter.

D. Translation into "Glish"

Translate 1 Cor. 6:7–12 into restructured English, which we shall call "Glish." Maintain the same thematic focus and participant emphasis so that the message remains intact. The following restrictions apply to Glish.

    a. There are no abstract nouns.
    b. There are no participles.
    c. Extended usages of pronouns and kinship terms are misunderstood.
    d. Metaphors are rarely used.
    e. A literal rendition of English figures of speech will be misunderstood.
    f. Idioms and idiomatic expressions of English must be recast.
    g. Rhetorical questions are used only for self-deliberation or to scold another.
    h. "of" and ___'s mean ownership or a kinship relation.
    i. Other grammatical and lexical devices of English may be used as necessary.

1 Cor. 6:7–12 (RSV)

[7]To have lawsuits at all with one another is defeat for you. Why not rather suffer wrong? Why not rather be defrauded? [8]But you yourselves wrong and defraud, and that even your own brethren.

[9]Do you not know that the unrighteous will not inherit the kingdom of God? Do not be deceived; neither the immoral, nor idolaters, nor adulterers, nor sexual perverts, [10]nor thieves, nor the greedy, nor drunkards, nor revilers, nor robbers will inherit the kingdom of God. [11]And such were some of you. But you were washed, you were sanctified, you were justified in the name of the Lord Jesus Christ and in the Spirit of our God.

[12]"All things are lawful for me," but not all things are helpful. "All things are lawful for me," but I will not be enslaved by anything.

E. Review exercise: Identifying translation adjustments

The following passage is a back-translation of John 2:1–11 in the Ojitlan Chinantec language of Mexico. Compare this with the RSV below and see how many adjustments you can find that were made in this translation. List the adjustments and label those you can identify. For example, to the phrase "at Cana," a classifier, "town," is added.

[1]On the third day they made a wedding feast in the town of Cana which pertains to Galilee. The mother of Jesus was standing there. [2]And they called Jesus and his learners to the wedding feast. [3]The wine ran out. So the mother of Jesus spoke. She told Jesus, "They have no more wine." [4]So Jesus told his mother, "Wait, woman. I know what I am going to do about it. For my hour has not yet come." [5]So his mother said, speaking to all the servants, "Do everything he says." [6]Six large waterpots were standing there, where they put water which they said was for purifying according to the law of the Jews. Each pot held about eight small waterpots. [7]So Jesus told those servants, "Fill up those large waterpots." And they filled them. [8]After this, Jesus said, "Dip up a little of that and go and show it to the chief elder in charge of the wedding feast." So they went with it. [9]So that elder extracted the truth about the quality of the wine that had been just plain water. And he was unaware of the origin of the wine. But the servants who poured the water into the pots knew where it came from. So the elder called the groom. [10]And he told him, "All other men give first the good wine. And when they have drunk and become satisfied, they give them wine that is less than the best. But right now you have given us wine far superior to that which ran out before."

[11]There first did Jesus a miracle in the town of Cana in the land of Galilee. So that the people saw how big he was. Having seen this his learners, more than ever they believed in Him.

John 2:1–11 RSV

[1]On the third day there was a marriage at Cana in Galilee, and the mother of Jesus was there; [2]Jesus also was invited to the marriage, with his disciples. [3]When the wine failed, the mother of Jesus said to him, "They have no wine." [4]And Jesus said to her, "O woman, what have you to do with me? My hour has not yet come." [5]His mother said to the servants, "Do whatever he tells you." [6]Now six stone jars were standing there, for the Jewish rites of purification, each holding twenty or thirty gallons. [7]Jesus said to them, "Fill the jars with water." And they filled them up to the brim. [8]He said to them, "Now draw some out, and take it to the steward of the feast ." So they took it. [9]When the steward of the feast tasted the water now become wine, and did not know where it came from (though the servants who had drawn the water knew), the steward of the feast called the bridegroom [10]and said to him, "Every man serves the good wine first; and when men have drunk freely, then the poor wine; but you have kept the good wine until now." [11]This, the first of his signs, Jesus did at Cana in Galilee, and manifested his glory; and his disciples believed in him.

V. Texts

Chapter 29
Groupings

Additional Reading:
    Callow 1974: Chapter 2.

A. Dividing long sentences

In the Greek the first three verses of 1 John are one long sentence. In order to translate into clear Villa Alta Zapoteco, this passage was broken into seven sentences:

> 1 John 1:1–3 RSV
> [1]That which was from the beginning, which we have heard, which we have seen with our eyes, which we have looked upon and touched with our hands, concerning the word of life—[2]the life was made manifest, and we saw it, and testify to it, and proclaim to you the eternal life which was with the Father and was made manifest to us—[3]that which we have seen and heard we proclaim also to you, so that you may have fellowship with us; and our fellowship is with the Father and with his Son Jesus Christ.

> Villa Alta Zapoteco
>
> We proclaim to you about Jesus Christ the person who is the word, he who gives eternal life. He was already present when the world began. We heard his words, we saw him and we looked at him and we touched him. He revealed himself to us and we saw him and we say that he lives eternally. And we proclaim to you that he is with our Father God and how he revealed himself to us. The person whom we saw and heard his words, we proclaim to you what he is like, in order that our head-hearts may be one. Truly our head-hearts are one with the head-heart of our Father God and with the head-heart of his son Jesus Christ.

Assume that you are going to translate into Villa Alta Zapotec. Study the following passages to see how you might break the one long sentence down into shorter sentences and still preserve all the relationships and meaning of the original. Rewrite the passage, using three or more sentences for each passage.

(1)   John 15:16
      You did not choose me, but I chose you and appointed you that you should go and bear fruit and that your fruit should abide; so that whatever you ask the Father in my name, he may give it to you.

(2)   Mark 1:6–7
      [6]Now John was clothed with camel's hair, and had a leather girdle around his waist, and ate locusts and wild honey. [7]And he preached, saying, "After me comes he who is mightier than I, the thong of whose sandals I am not worthy to stoop down and untie.

(3)   Luke 8:1–3
      [1]Soon afterward he went on through cities and villages, preaching and bringing the good news of the kingdom of God. And the twelve were with him,[2]and also some women who had been healed of evil spirits and infirmities: Mary, called Magdalene, from whom seven demons had gone out, [3]and Joanna, the wife of Chuza, Herod's steward, and Susanna, and many others, who provided for them out of their means.

(4)   Titus 1:1–4

1Paul, a servant of God and an apostle of Jesus Christ, to further the faith of God's elect and their knowledge of the truth which accords with godliness, 2in hope of eternal life which God, who never lies, promised ages ago 3and at the proper time manifested in his word through the preaching with which I have been entrusted by command of God our Savior; 4To Titus, my true child in a common faith: Grace and peace from God the Father and Christ Jesus our Savior.

(5)   Acts 1:1–4 (Try to make six or more sentences.)

1In the first book, O Theophilus, I have dealt with all that Jesus began to do and teach, 2until the day when he was taken up, after he had given commandment through the Holy Spirit to the apostles whom he had chosen. 3To them he presented himself alive after his passion by many proofs, appearing to them during forty days, and speaking of the kingdom of God. 4And while staying with them he charged them not to depart from Jerusalem, but to wait for the promise of the Father, which he said, "you heard from me...

(6)   Acts 10:36–38

36You know the word which he sent to Israel, preaching good news of peace by Jesus Christ (he is Lord of all), 37the word which was proclaimed throughout all Judea, beginning from Galilee after the baptism which John preached: 38how God anointed Jesus of Nazareth with the Holy Spirit and with power; how he went about doing good and healing all that were oppressed by the devil, for God was with him.

(7)   Acts 17:30–31

30The times of ignorance God overlooked, but now he commands all men everywhere to repent, 31because he has fixed a day on which he will judge the world in righteousness by a man whom he has appointed, and of this he has given assurance to all men by raising him from the dead."

(8)   Rom. 1:1–7

1Paul, a servant of Jesus Christ, called to be an apostle, set apart for the gospel of God 2which he promised beforehand through his prophets in the holy scriptures, 3the gospel concerning his Son, who was descended from David according to the flesh 4and designated Son of God in power according to the Spirit of holiness by his resurrection from the dead, Jesus Christ our Lord, 5through whom we have received grace and apostleship to bring about the obedience of faith for the sake of his name among all the nations, 6including yourselves who are called to belong to Jesus Christ;

7To all God's beloved in Rome, who are called to be saints:
Grace to you and peace from God our Father and the Lord Jesus Christ.

(9)   1 Thess. 3:1–3

1Therefore when we could bear it no longer, we were willing to be left behind at Athens alone, 2and we sent Timothy, our brother and God's servant in the gospel of Christ, to establish you in your faith and to exhort you, 3that no one be moved by these afflictions. You yourselves know that this is to be our lot.

(10) 1 Tim. 1:8–11

[8]Now we know that the law is good, if any one uses it lawfully, [9]understanding this, that the law is not laid down for the just but for the lawless and disobedient, for the ungodly and sinners, for the unholy and profane, for murderers of fathers and murderers of mothers, for manslayers, [10]immoral persons, sodomites, kidnapers, liars, perjurers, and whatever else is contrary to sound doctrine, [11]in accordance with the glorious gospel of the blessed God with which I have been entrusted.

B. Combining short sentences

In Papua New Guinea there are languages that have very long sentences. The clauses are run together by using participles, temporal clauses, etc. For this reason, when one is translating into these languages, he may have to combine two or three sentences into a single sentence. In each of the following, rewrite the passage as one long sentence rather than several shorter ones. Do not connect with "and."

Example: Mark 6:1–2

He went away from there and came to his own country; and his disciples followed him. And on the sabbath he began to teach in the synagogue; and many who heard him were astonished, saying, "Where did this man get all this? What is the wisdom given to him? What mighty works are wrought by his hands!"

Answer: Going away from there, coming into his own country, his disciples following him, going into the synagogue to teach on the sabbath, many hearing him, they being astonished said, "This man having been given wisdom, doing many mighty works, from where does he receive in order to do all this?"

(1) Mark 5:14–15

[14]The herdsmen fled, and told it in the city and in the country. And people came to see what it was that had happened. [15]And they came to Jesus, and saw the demoniac sitting there, clothed and in his right mind, the man who had the legion; and they were afraid.

(2) Mark 6:45–47

[45]Immediately he made his disciples get into the boat and go before him to the other side, to Bethsaida, while he dismissed the crowd. [46]And after he had taken leave of them, he went up on the mountain to pray. [47]And when evening came, the boat was out on the sea, and he was alone on the land.

(3) Mark 6:53–55

[53]And when they had crossed over, they came to land at Gennesaret, and moored to the shore. [54]And when they got out of the boat, immediately the people recognized him, [55]and ran about the whole neighborhood and began to bring sick people on their pallets to any place where they heard he was.

(4) Mark 11:12–14

[12]On the following day, when they came from Bethany, he was hungry. [13]And seeing in the distance a fig tree in leaf, he went to see if he could find anything on it. When he came to it, he found nothing but leaves, for it was not the season for figs. [14]And he said to it, "May no one ever eat fruit from you again." And his disciples heard it.

(5)   Mark 5:16–19

>   [16]And those who had seen it told what had happened to the demoniac and to the swine. [17]And they began to beg Jesus to depart from their neighborhood. [18]And as he was getting into the boat, the man who had been possessed with demons begged him that he might be with him. [19]But he refused, and said to him, "Go home to your friends, and tell them how much the Lord has done for you, and how he has had mercy on you."

C. Reordering chronologically

In languages such as Greek and English the linguistic order does not need to match the historical order of events (the chronological or experiential order). But in some languages the linguistic order is the same as the experiential. In translating passages in which the linguistic order in the source language does not match the experiential order, the order may need to be changed. For examples, Acts 2:23 had to be changed in Chuj of Guatemala from "You killed him, putting him on the cross" to "You put him on a cross. He died because of you."

For each of the following suggest a rewording that will follow the experiential order of events.

(1)   Mark 7:17
        And when he had entered the house, and left the people, his disciples asked him about the parable.

(2)   John 4:1–3
        Now when the Lord knew that the Pharisees had heard...he left Judea and departed again to Galilee.

(3)   John 4:39
        Many Samaritans from the city believed in him because of the woman's testimony...

(4)   Acts 5:30–31
        The God of our fathers raised Jesus whom you killed by hanging him on a tree. God exalted him at his right hand...

(5)   Rev. 20:4–5
        They came to life again, and reigned with Christ a thousand years. The rest of the dead did not come to life again until the thousand years were ended. This is the first resurrection.

(6)   Luke 1:20
        And behold, you will be silent and unable to speak until the day that these things come to pass, because you did not believe my words, which will be fulfilled in their time.

(7)   Rom 4:18
        In hope he believed against hope, that he should become the father of many nations; as had been told, "So shall your descendants be."

(8)   John 1:33
        I myself did not know him; but he who sent me to baptize with water said to me, "He on whom you see the Spirit descend and remain, this is he who baptizes with the Holy Spirit."

D. Reordering for logical and chronological order

Sometimes the order within a passage has to be changed to follow the logical order of the argument. In John 1:14, "And the Word became flesh and dwelt among us, full of grace and truth; we have beheld his glory, glory as of the only Son from the Father," the parenthetical phrase, "full of grace and truth" had to be put at the end of the verse in Aguaruna. For each of the following suggest a rewording that will more closely follow the logical and/or chronological order of the argument.

Example: 1 John 2:16
...all that is in the world...is not of the Father, but is of the world.

Amuzgo back-translation:
All that is in the world is of the world, but it is not of the Father.

(1) John 1:10
He was in the world, the world was made through him, yet the world knew him not.

(2) 1 John 4:1
Beloved, do not believe every spirit, but test the spirits to see whether they are of God; for many false prophets have gone out into the world.

(3) 1 Thess. 2:13
And we also thank God constantly for this, that when you received the word of God which you heard from us, you accepted it not as the word of men but as what it really is, the word of God, which is at work in you believers.

(4) Mark 7:25–26
But immediately a woman, whose little daughter was possessed by an unclean spirit, heard of him, and came and fell down at his feet. Now the woman was a Greek, a Syrophoenician by birth. And she begged him to cast the demon out of her daughter.

(5) John 1:19–20
And this is the testimony of John, when the Jews sent priests and Levites from Jerusalem to ask him, "Who are you?" He confessed, he did not deny, but confessed, "I am not the Christ."

E. Identifying paragraph boundaries

Where do you think the following passages should be paragraphed. Explain why.

(1)   Acts 13:4–19 (KJV)
     ^{4}So they, being sent forth by the Holy Ghost, departed unto Seleucia; and from thence they sailed to Cyprus. ^{5}And when they were at Salamis, they preached the word of God in the synagogues of the Jews: and they had also John to their minister. ^{6}And when they had gone through the isle unto Paphos, they found a certain sorcerer, a false prophet, a Jew, whose name was Bar-jesus: ^{7}Which was with the deputy of the country, Sergius Paulus, a prudent man; who called for Barnabas and Saul, and desired to hear the word of God. ^{8}But Elymas the sorcerer (for so is his name by interpretation) withstood them, seeking to turn away the deputy from the faith. ^{9}Then Saul, (who also is called Paul,) filled with the Holy Ghost, set his eyes on him, ^{10}And said, O full of all subtilty and all mischief, thou child of the devil, thou enemy of all righteousness, wilt thou not cease to pervert the right ways of the Lord? ^{11}And now, behold, the hand of the Lord is upon thee, and thou shalt be blind, not seeing the sun for a season. And immediately there fell on him a mist and a darkness; and he went about seeking some to lead him by the hand. ^{12}Then the deputy, when he saw what was done, believed, being astonished at the doctrine of the Lord. ^{13}Now when Paul and his company loosed from Paphos, they came to Perga in Pamphylia: and John departing from them returned to Jerusalem. ^{14}But when they departed from Perga, they came to Antioch in Pisidia, and went into the synagogue on the sabbath day, and sat down. ^{15}And after the reading of the law and the prophets the rulers of the synagogue sent unto them, saying, Ye men and brethren, if ye have any word of exhortation for the people, say on. ^{16}Then Paul stood up, and beckoning with his hand said, Men of Israel, and ye that fear God, give audience. ^{17}The God of this people of Israel chose our fathers, and exalted the people when they dwelt as strangers in the land of Egypt, and with an high arm brought he them out of it. ^{18}And about the time of forty years suffered he their manners in the wilderness. ^{19}And when he had destroyed seven nations in the land of Chanaan, he divided their land to them by lot.

(2)   1 Cor. 11:1–22 (KJV)
     ^{1}Be ye followers of me, even as I also am of Christ. ^{2}Now I praise you, brethren, that ye remember me in all things, and keep the ordinances, as I delivered them to you. ^{3}But I would have you know, that the head of every man is Christ; and the head of the woman is the man; and the head of Christ is God. ^{4}Every man praying or prophesying, having his head covered, dishonoureth his head. ^{5}But every woman that prayeth or prophesieth with her head uncovered dishonoureth her head: for that is even all one as if she were shaven. ^{6}For if the woman be not covered, let her also be shorn: but if it be a shame for a woman to be shorn or shaven, let her be covered. ^{7}For a man indeed ought not to cover his head, forasmuch as he is the image and glory of God: but the woman is the glory of the man. ^{8}For the man is not of the woman; but the woman of the man. ^{9}Neither was the man created for the woman; but the woman for the man. ^{10}For this cause ought the woman to have power on her head because of the angels. ^{11}Nevertheless neither is the man without the woman, neither the woman without the man, in the Lord. ^{12}For as the woman is of the man, even so is the man also by the woman; but all things of God. ^{13}Judge in yourselves: is it comely that a woman pray unto God uncovered? ^{14}Doth not even nature itself teach you, that, if a man have long hair, it is a shame unto him? ^{15}But if a woman have long hair, it is a glory to her: for her hair is given her for a covering. ^{16}But if any man seem to be contentious, we have no such custom, neither the churches of God. ^{17}Now in this that I declare unto you I praise you not, that ye come together not for the better, but for the worse. ^{18}For first of all, when ye come together in the

church, I hear that there be divisions among you; and I partly believe it. [19]For there must be also heresies among you, that they which are approved may be made manifest among you. [20]When ye come together therefore into one place, this is not to eat the Lord's supper. [21]For in eating every one taketh before other his own supper: and one is hungry, and another is drunken. [22]What? have ye not houses to eat and to drink in? or despise ye the church of...

(3)   2 Cor. 4:16–5:11 (KJV)

[16]For which cause we faint not; but though our outward man perish, yet the inward man is renewed day by day. [17]For our light affliction, which is but for a moment, worketh for us a far more exceeding and eternal weight of glory; [18]While we look not at the things which are seen, but at the things which are not seen: for the things which are seen are temporal; but the things which are not seen are eternal.

5   [1]For we know that if our earthly house of this tabernacle were dissolved, we have a building of God, an house not made with hands, eternal in the heavens. [2]For in this we groan, earnestly desiring to be clothed upon with our house which is from heaven: [3]If so be that being clothed we shall not be found naked. [4]For we that are in this tabernacle do groan, being burdened: not for that we would be unclothed, but clothed upon, that mortality might be swallowed up of life. [5]Now he that hath wrought us for the selfsame thing is God, who also hath given unto us the earnest of the Spirit. [6]Therefore we are always confident, knowing that, whilst we are at home in the body, we are absent from the Lord: [7](For we walk by faith, not by sight:) [8]We are confident, I say, and willing rather to be absent from the body, and to be present with the Lord. [9]Wherefore we labour, that, whether present or absent, we may be accepted of him. [10]For we must all appear before the judgment seat of Christ; that every one may receive the things done in his body, according to that he had done, whether it be good or bad. [11]Knowing therefore the terror of the Lord, we persuade men; but we are made manifest unto God; and I trust also are made manifest in your consciences.

(4)   2 Cor. 7:5–16 (KJV)

[5]For, when we were come into Macedonia, our flesh had no rest, but we were troubled on every side; without were fightings, within were fears. [6]Nevertheless God, that comforteth those that are cast down, comforted us by the coming of Titus; [7]And not by his coming only, but by the consolation wherewith he was comforted in you, when he told us your earnest desire, your mourning, your fervent mind toward me; so that I rejoiced the more. [8]For though I made you sorry with a letter, I do not repent, though I did repent: for I perceive that the same epistle hath made you sorry, though it were but for a season. [9]Now I rejoice, not that ye were made sorry, but that ye sorrowed to repentance: for ye were made sorry after a godly manner, that ye might receive damage by us in nothing. [10]For godly sorrow worketh repentance to salvation not to be repented of: but the sorrow of the world worketh death. [11]For behold this selfsame thing, that ye sorrowed after a godly sort, what carefulness it wrought in you, yea, what clearing of yourselves, yea, what indignation, yea, what fear, yea, what vehement desire, yea, what zeal, yea, what revenge! In all things ye have approved yourselves to be clear in this matter. [12]Wherefore, though I wrote unto you, I did it not for his cause that had done the wrong, nor for his cause that suffered wrong, but that our care for you in the sight of God might appear unto you. [13]Therefore we were comforted in your comfort: yea, and exceedingly the more joyed we for the joy of Titus, because his spirit was refreshed by you all. [14]For if I have boasted any thing to him of you, I am not ashamed; but as we spake all things to you in truth, even so our boasting, which I made before Titus, is found a truth. [15]And his inward affection is more abundant toward you, whilst he remembereth the obedience of you all, how with fear and trembling ye received him. [16]I rejoice therefore that I have confidence in you in all things.

(5)   Col. 3:1–17 (KJV)

[1]If ye then be risen with Christ, seek those things which are above, where Christ sitteth on the right hand of God. [2]Set your affection on things above, not on things on the earth. [3]For ye are dead, and your life is hid with Christ in God. [4]When Christ, who is our life, shall appear, then shall ye also appear with him in glory. [5]Mortify therefore your members which are upon the earth; fornication, uncleanness, inordinate affection, evil concupiscence, and covetousness, which is idolatry: [6]For which things' sake the wrath of God cometh on the children of disobedience: [7]In the which ye also walked some time, when ye lived in them. [8]But now ye also put off all these; anger, wrath, malice, blasphemy, filthy communication out of your mouth. [9]Lie not one to another, seeing that ye have put off the old man with his deeds; [10]And have put on the new man, which is renewed in knowledge after the image of him that created him: [11]Where there is neither Greek nor Jew, circumcision nor uncircumcision, Barbarian, Scythian, bond nor free: but Christ is all, and in all. [12]Put on therefore, as the elect of God, holy and beloved, bowels of mercies, kindness, humbleness of mind, meekness, long-suffering; [13]Forbearing one another, and forgiving one another, if any man have a quarrel against any: even as Christ forgave you, so also do ye. [14]And above all these things put on charity, which is the bond of perfectness. [15]And let the peace of God rule in your hearts, to the which also ye are called in one body; and be ye thankful. [16]Let the word of Christ dwell in you richly in all wisdom; teaching and admonishing one another in psalms and hymns and spiritual songs, singing with grace in your hearts to the Lord. [17]And whatsoever ye do in word or deed, do all in the name of the Lord Jesus, giving thanks to God and the Father by him.

(6)   Col. 3:18–4:5 (KJV)

[18]Wives, submit yourselves unto your own husbands, as it is fit in the Lord. [19]Husbands, love your wives, and be not bitter against them. [20]Children, obey your parents in all things: for this is well pleasing unto the Lord. [21]Fathers, provoke not your children to anger, lest they be discouraged. [22]Servants, obey in all things your masters according to the flesh; not with eyeservice, as menpleasers; but in singleness of heart, fearing God: [23]And whatsoever ye do, do it heartily, as to the Lord, and not unto men; [24]Knowing that of the Lord ye shall receive the reward of the inheritance: for ye serve the Lord Christ. [25]But he that doeth wrong shall receive for the wrong which he hath done: and there is no respect of persons. 4   [1]Masters, give unto your servants that which is just and equal; knowing that ye also have a Master in heaven. [2]Continue in prayer, and watch in the same with thanksgiving; [3]Withal praying also for us, that God would open unto us a door of utterance, to speak the mystery of Christ, for which I am also in bonds: [4]That I may make it manifest, as I ought to speak. [5]Walk in wisdom toward them that are without, redeeming the time. [6]Let your speech be always with grace, seasoned with salt, that ye may know how ye ought to answer every man. [7]All my state shall Tychicus declare unto you, who is a beloved brother, and a faithful minister and fellowservant in the Lord: [8]Whom I have sent unto you for the same purpose, that he might know your estate, and comfort your hearts; [9]With Onesimus, a faithful and beloved brother, who is one of you. They shall make known unto you all things which are done here.

F. Identifying sections

Identify the four major sections of 1 Corinthians, which are indicated by repetition of the same Theme proposition. What is that Theme proposition?

G. Identifying larger semantic units in 3 John

Study the book of 3 John. Identify the larger semantic units of this book and indicate your reasons for grouping as you do. Make a tentative propositional display of 3 John with indentation and propositional labels.

H. Identifying larger semantic units in Luke 12

Study Luke 12. Identify the larger semantic units of this chapter and indicate your reasons for grouping as you do.

I. Topic sentences

For practice in identifying paragraph divisions in the source language, study each of the following sections of Scripture, listing any sentence that is clearly a topic sentence. How does each topic sentence function?

Example: Matt. 1:18

Now the birth of Jesus Christ took place in this way.

Answer: This topic sentence functions by giving a preview of the narrative.

(1) Matt. 1:18–3:17

[18]Now the birth of Jesus Christ took place in this way. When his mother Mary had been betrothed to Joseph, before they came together she was found to be with child of the Holy Spirit; [19]and her husband Joseph, being a just man and unwilling to put her to shame, resolved to divorce her quietly. [20]But as he considered this, behold, an angel of the Lord appeared to him in a dream, saying, "Joseph, son of David, do not fear to take Mary your wife, for that which is conceived in her is of the Holy Spirit; [21]she will bear a son, and you shall call his name Jesus, for he will save his people from their sins." [22]All this took place to fulfil what the Lord had spoken by the prophet:

[23]"Behold, a virgin shall conceive and bear a son, and his name shall be called Emmanuel" (which means, God with us). [24]When Joseph woke from sleep, he did as the angel of the Lord commanded him; he took his wife, [25]but knew her not until she had borne a son; and he called his name Jesus.

2   [1]Now when Jesus was born in Bethlehem of Judea in the days of Herod the king, behold, wise men from the East came to Jerusalem, saying, [2]"Where is he who has been born king of the Jews? For we have seen his star in the East, and have come to worship him." [3]When Herod the king heard this, he was troubled, and all Jerusalem with him; [4]and assembling all the chief priests and scribes of the people, he inquired of them where the Christ was to be born. [5]They told him, "In Bethlehem of Judea; for so it is written by the prophet: [6]'And you, O Bethlehem, in the land of Judah, are by no means least among the rulers of Judah; for from you shall come a ruler who will govern my people Israel.'"

[7]Then Herod summoned the wise men secretly and ascertained from them what time the star appeared; [8]and he sent them to Bethlehem, saying, "Go and search diligently for the child, and when you have found him bring me word, that I too may come and worship him." [9]When they had heard the king they went their way; and lo, the star which they had seen in the East went before them, till it came to rest over the place where the child was. [10]When they saw the star, they rejoiced exceedingly with great joy; [11]and going into the house they saw the child with Mary his mother, and they fell down and worshiped him. Then, opening their treasures, they offered him gifts, gold and frankincense and myrrh. [12]And being warned in a dream not to return to Herod, they departed to their own country by another way.

13Now when they had departed, behold, an angel of the Lord appeared to Joseph in a dream and said, "Rise, take the child and his mother, and flee to Egypt, and remain there till I tell you; for Herod is about to search for the child, to destroy him." 14And he rose and took the child and his mother by night, and departed to Egypt, 15and remained there until the death of Herod. This was to fulfil what the Lord had spoken by the prophet, "Out of Egypt have I called my son."

16Then Herod, when he saw that he had been tricked by the wise men, was in a furious rage, and he sent and killed all the male children in Bethlehem and in all that region who were two years old or under, according to the time which he had ascertained from the wise men. 17Then was fulfilled what was spoken by the prophet Jeremiah:

> 18 "A voice was heard in Ramah,
> wailing and loud lamentation,
> Rachel weeping for her children;
> she refused to be consoled,
> because they were no more."

19But when Herod died, behold, an angel of the Lord appeared in a dream to Joseph in Egypt, saying, 20"Rise, take the child and his mother, and go to the land of Israel, for those who sought the child's life are dead." 21And he rose and took the child and his mother, and went to the land of Israel. 22But when he heard that Archelaus reigned over Judea in place of his father Herod, he was afraid to go there, and being warned in a dream he withdrew to the district of Galilee. 23And he went and dwelt in a city called Nazareth, that what was spoken by the prophets might be fulfilled, "He shall be called a Nazarene."

3   1In those days came John the Baptist, preaching in the wilderness of Judea, 2"Repent, for the kingdom of heaven is at hand." 3For this is he who was spoken of by the prophet Isaiah when he said,

> "The voice of one crying in the wilderness:
> Prepare the way of the Lord,
> make his paths straight."

4Now John wore a garment of camel's hair, and a leather girdle around his waist; and his food was locusts and wild honey. 5Then went out to him Jerusalem and all Judea and all the region about the Jordan, 6and they were baptized by him in the river of Jordan, confessing their sins.

7But when he saw many of the Pharisees and Sadducees coming for baptism, he said to them, "You brood of vipers! Who warned you to flee from the wrath to come? 8Bear fruit that befits repentance, 9and do not presume to say to yourselves, 'We have Abraham as our father'; for I tell you, God is able from these stones to raise up children to Abraham. 10Even now the axe is laid to the root of the trees; every tree therefore that does not bear good fruit is cut down and thrown into the fire.

11"I baptize you with water for repentance, but he who is coming after me is mightier than I, whose sandals I am not worthy to carry; he will baptize you with the Holy Spirit and with fire. 12His winnowing fork is in his hand, and he will clear his threshing floor and gather his wheat into the granary, but the chaff he will burn with unquenchable fire."

13Then Jesus came from Galilee to the Jordan to John, to be baptized by him. 14John would have prevented him, saying, "I need to be baptized by you, and do you come to me?" 15But Jesus answered him, "Let it be so now; for thus it is fitting for us to fulfill all righteousness." Then he consented. 16And when Jesus was baptized, he went up immediately from the water, and behold, the heavens were opened and he saw the Spirit of God descending like a dove, and alighting on him; [17]and lo, a voice from heaven, saying, "This is my beloved Son, with whom I am well pleased."

(2)   Matt. 9

[1]And getting into a boat he crossed over and came to his own city. [2]And behold they brought to him a paralytic, lying on his bed; and when Jesus saw their faith he said to the paralytic, "Take heart, my son; your sins are forgiven." [3]And behold, some of the scribes said to themselves, "This man is blaspheming." [4]But Jesus, knowing their thoughts, said, "Why do you think evil in your hearts? [5]For which is easier, to say, 'Your sins are forgiven,' or to say, 'Rise and walk'? [6]But that you may know that the Son of man has authority on earth to forgive sins"—he then said to the paralytic—"Rise, take up your bed and go home." [7]And he rose and went home. [8]When the crowds saw it, they were afraid, and they glorified God, who had given such authority to men.

[9]As Jesus passed on from there, he saw a man called Matthew sitting at the tax office; and he said to him, "Follow me." And he rose and followed him.

[10]And as he sat at table in the house, behold, many tax collectors and sinners came and sat down with Jesus and his disciples. [11]And when the Pharisees saw this, they said to his disciples, "Why does your teacher eat with tax collectors and sinners?" [12]But when he heard it, he said, "Those who are well have no need of a physician, but those who are sick. [13]Go and learn what this means, 'I desire mercy, and not sacrifice.' For I came not to call the righteous, but sinners."

[14]Then the disciples of John came to him, saying, "Why do we and the Pharisees fast, but your disciples do not fast?" [15]And Jesus said to them, "Can the wedding guests mourn as long as the bridegroom is with them? The days will come, when the bridegroom is taken away from them, and then they will fast. [16]And no one puts a piece of unshrunk cloth on an old garment, for the patch tears away from the garment, and a worse tear is made. [17]Neither is new wine put into old wineskins; if it is, the skins burst, and the wine is spilled, and the skins are destroyed; but new wine is put into fresh wineskins, and so both are preserved."

[18]While he was thus speaking to them, behold, a ruler came in and knelt before him, saying, "My daughter has just died; but come and lay your hand on her, and she will live." [19]And Jesus rose and followed him, with his disciples. [20]And behold, a woman who had suffered from a hemorrhage for twelve years came up behind him and touched the fringe of his garment; [21]for she said to herself, "If I only touch his garment, I shall be made well." [22]Jesus turned, and seeing her he said, "Take heart, daughter; your faith has made you well." And instantly the woman was made well. [23]And when Jesus came to the ruler's house, and saw the flute players, and the crowd making a tumult, [24]he said, "Depart; for the girl is not dead but sleeping." And they laughed at him. [25]But when the crowd had been put outside, he went in and took her by the hand, and the girl arose. [26]And the report of this went through all that district.

[27]And as Jesus passed on from there, two blind men followed him, crying aloud, "Have mercy on us, Son of David." [28]When he entered the house, the blind men came to him; and Jesus said to them, "Do you believe that I am able to do this?" They said to him, "Yes, Lord." [29]Then he touched their eyes, saying, "According to your faith be it done to you." [30]And their eyes were opened. And Jesus sternly charged them, "See that no one knows it." [31]But they went away and spread his fame through all that district.

[32]As they were going away, behold, a dumb demoniac was brought to him. [33]And when the demon had been cast out, the dumb man spoke; and the crowds marveled, saying, "Never was anything like this seen in Israel." [34]But the Pharisees said, "He casts out demons by the prince of demons."

^{35}And Jesus went about all the cities and villages, teaching in their synagogues and preaching the gospel of the kingdom, and healing every disease and every infirmity. ^{36}When he saw the crowds, he had compassion for them, because they were harassed and helpless, like sheep without a shepherd. ^{37}Then he said to his disciples, "The harvest is plentiful, but the laborers are few; ^{38}pray therefore the Lord of the harvest to send out laborers into his harvest."

(3)   Matt. 13:52–15:39

^{52}And he said to them, "Therefore every scribe who has been trained for the kingdom of heaven is like a householder who brings out of his treasure what is new and what is old."

^{53}And when Jesus had finished these parables, he went away from there, ^{54}and coming to his own country he taught them in their synagogue, so that they were astonished, and said, "Where did this man get this wisdom and these mighty works? ^{55}Is not this the carpenter's son? Is not his mother called Mary? And are not his brothers James and Joseph and Simon and Judas? ^{56}And are not all his sisters with us? Where then did this man get all this?" ^{57}And they took offense at him. But Jesus said to them, "A prophet is not without honor except in his own country and in his own house." ^{58}And he did not do many mighty works there, because of their unbelief.

14   ^{1}At that time Herod the tetrarch heard about the fame of Jesus; ^{2}and he said to his servants, "This is John the Baptist, he has been raised from the dead; that is why these powers are at work in him." ^{3}For Herod had seized John and bound him and put him in prison, for the sake of Herodias, his brother Philip's wife; ^{4}because John said to him, "It is not lawful for you to have her." ^{5}And though he wanted to put him to death, he feared the people, because they held him to be a prophet. ^{6}But when Herod's birthday came, the daughter of Herodias danced before the company, and pleased Herod, ^{7}so that he promised with an oath to give her whatever she might ask. ^{8}Prompted by her mother, she said, "Give me the head of John the Baptist here on a platter." ^{9}And the king was sorry; but because of his oaths and his guests he commanded it to be given; ^{10}he sent and had John beheaded in the prison, ^{11}and his head was brought on a platter and given to the girl, and she brought it to her mother. ^{12}And his disciples came and took the body and buried it; and they went and told Jesus.

^{13}Now when Jesus heard this, he withdrew from there in a boat to a lonely place apart. But when the crowds heard it, they followed him on foot from the towns. ^{14}As he went ashore he saw a great throng; and he had compassion on them, and healed their sick. ^{15}When it was evening, the disciples came to him and said, "This is a lonely place, and the day is now over; send the crowds away to go into the villages and buy food for themselves." ^{16}Jesus said, "They need not go away; you give them something to eat." ^{17}They said to him, "We have only five loaves here and two fish." ^{18}And he said, "Bring them here to me." ^{19}Then he ordered the crowds to sit down on the grass; and taking the five loaves and the two fish he looked up to heaven, and blessed, and broke and gave the loaves to the disciples, and the disciples gave them to the crowds. ^{20}And they all ate and were satisfied. And they took up twelve baskets full of the broken pieces left over. ^{21}And those who ate were about five thousand men, besides women and children.

^{22}Then he made the disciples get into the boat and go before him to the other side, while he dismissed the crowds. ^{23}And after he had dismissed the crowds, he went up on the mountain by himself to pray. When evening came, he was there alone, ^{24}but the boat by this time was many furlongs distant from the land, beaten by the waves; for the wind was against them. ^{25}And in the fourth watch of the night he came to them, walking on the sea. ^{26}But when the disciples saw him walking on the sea, they were terrified, saying, "It is a ghost!"

and they cried out for fear. [27]But immediately he spoke to them, saying, "Take heart, it is I; have no fear."

[28]And Peter answered him, "Lord, if it is you, bid me come to you on the water." [29]He said, "Come." So Peter got out of the boat and walked on the water and came to Jesus; [30]but when he saw the wind, he was afraid, and beginning to sink he cried out, "Lord, save me." [31]Jesus immediately reached out his hand and caught him, saying to him, "O man of little faith, why did you doubt?" [32]And when they got into the boat, the wind ceased. [33]And those in the boat worshiped him, saying, "Truly you are the Son of God."

[34]And when they had crossed over, they came to land at Gennesaret. [35]And when the men of that place recognized him, they sent round to all that region and brought to him all that were sick, [36]and besought him that they might only touch the fringe of his garment; and as many as touched it were made well.

15   [1]Then Pharisees and scribes came to Jesus from Jerusalem and said, [2]"Why do your disciples transgress the tradition of the elders? For they do not wash their hands when they eat." [3]He answered them, "And why do you transgress the commandment of God for the sake of your tradition? [4]For God commanded, 'Honor your father and your mother,' and, 'He who speaks evil of father or mother, let him surely die.' [5]But you say, 'If any one tells his father or his mother, What you would have gained from me is given to God, he need not honor his father.' [6]So for the sake of your tradition, you have made void the word of God. [7]You hypocrites! Well did Isaiah prophesy of you, when he said:

[8]'This people honors me with their lips,
but their heart is far from me;
[9]in vain do they worship me,
teaching as doctrines the precepts of men.'"

[10]And he called the people to him and said to them, "Hear and understand: [11]not what goes into the mouth defiles a man, but what comes out of the mouth, this defiles a man." [12]Then the disciples came and said to him, "Do you know that the Pharisees were offended when they heard this saying?" [13]He answered, "Every plant which my heavenly Father has not planted will be rooted up. [14]Let them alone; they are blind guides. And if a blind man leads a blind man, both will fall into a pit." [15]But Peter said to him, "Explain the parable to us." [16]And he said, "Are you also still without understanding? [17]Do you not see that whatever goes into the mouth passes into the stomach, and so passes on? [18]But what comes out of the mouth proceeds from the heart, and this defiles a man. [19]For out of the heart come evil thoughts, murder, adultery, fornication, theft, false witness, slander. [20]These are what defile a man; but to eat with unwashed hands does not defile a man."

[21]And Jesus went away from there and withdrew to the district of Tyre and Sidon. [22]And behold, a Canaanite woman from that region came out and cried, "Have mercy on me, O Lord, Son of David; my daughter is severely possessed by a demon." [23]But he did not answer her a word. And his disciples came and begged him, saying, "Send her away, for she is crying after us." [24]He answered, "I was sent only to the lost sheep of the house of Israel." [25]But she came and knelt before him, saying, "Lord, help me." [26] And he answered, "It is not fair to take the children's bread and throw it to the dogs." [27]She said, "Yes, Lord, yet even the dogs eat the crumbs that fall from their masters' table," [28]Then Jesus answered her, "O woman, great is your faith! Be it done for you as you desire." And her daughter was healed instantly.

[29]And Jesus went on from there and passed along the Sea of Galilee. And he went up on the mountain, and sat down there. [30]And great crowds came to him, bringing with them the lame, the maimed, the blind, the dumb, and many others, and they put them at his feet, and he

healed them, [31]so that the throng wondered, when they saw the dumb speaking, the maimed whole, the lame walking, and the blind seeing; and they glorified the God of Israel.

[32]Then Jesus called his disciples to him and said, "I have compassion on the crowd, because they have been with me now three days, and have nothing to eat; and I am unwilling to send them away hungry, lest they faint on the way." [33]And the disciples said to him, "Where are we to get bread enough in the desert to feed so great a crowd?" [34]And Jesus said to them, "How many loaves have you?" They said, "Seven, and a few small fish." [35]And commanding the crowd to sit down on the ground, [36]he took the seven loaves and the fish, and having given thanks he broke them and gave them to the disciples, and the disciples gave them to the crowds. [37]And they all ate and were satisfied; and they took up seven baskets full of the broken pieces left over. [38]Those who ate were four thousand men, besides women and children. [39]And sending away the crowds, he got into the boat and went to the region of Magadan.

(4)   Matt. 24

[1]Jesus left the temple and was going away, when his disciples came to point out to him the buildings of the temple. [2]But he answered them, "You see all these, do you not? Truly, I say to you, there will not be left here one stone upon another, that will not be thrown down."

[3]As he sat on the Mount of Olives, the disciples came to him privately, saying, "Tell us, when will this be, and what will be the sign of your coming and of the close of the age?" [4]And Jesus answered them, "Take heed that no one leads you astray. [5]For many will come in my name, saying, 'I am the Christ,' and they will lead many astray. [6]And you will hear of wars and rumors of wars; see that you are not alarmed; for this must take place, but the end is not yet. [7]For nation will rise against nation, and kingdom against kingdom, and there will be famines and earthquakes in various places: [8]all this is but the beginning of the birth-pangs.

[9]"Then they will deliver you up to tribulation, and put you to death; and you will be hated by all nations for my name's sake. [10]And then many will fall away, and betray one another, and hate one another. [11]Any many false prophets will arise and lead many astray. [12]And because wickedness is multiplied, most men's love will grow cold. [13]But he who endures to the end will be saved. [14]And this gospel of the kingdom will be preached throughout the whole world, as a testimony to all nations; and then the end will come.

[15]"So when you see the desolating sacrilege spoken of by the prophet Daniel, standing in the holy place (let the reader understand), [16]then let those who are in Judea flee to the mountains; [17]let him who is on the housetop not go down to take what is in his house; [18]and let him who is in the field not turn back to take his mantle. [19]And alas for those who are with child and for those who give suck in those days! [20]Pray that your flight may not be in winter or on a sabbath. [21]For then there will be great tribulation, such as has not been from the beginning of the world until now, no, and never will be. [22]And if those days had not been shortened, no human being would be saved; but for the sake of the elect those days will be shortened. [23]Then if any one says to you, 'Lo, here is the Christ!' or 'There he is!' do not believe it. [24]For false Christs and false prophets will arise and show great signs and wonders, so as to lead astray, if possible, even the elect. [25]Lo, I have told you beforehand. [26]So, if they say to you, 'Lo, he is in the wilderness,' do not go out; if they say, 'Lo, he is in the inner rooms,' do not believe it. [27]For as the lightning comes from the east and shines as far as the west, so will be the coming of the Son of man. [28]Wherever the body is, there the eagles will be gathered together.

[29]"Immediately after the tribulation of those days the sun will be darkened, and the moon will not give its light, and the stars will fall from heaven, and the powers of the heavens will be shaken; [30]then will appear the sign of the Son of man in heaven, and then all the tribes of

the earth will mourn, and they will see the Son of man coming on the clouds of heaven with power and great glory; [31]and he will send out his angels with a loud trumpet call, and they will gather his elect from the four winds, from one end of the heaven to the other.

[32]"From the fig tree learn its lesson: as soon as its branch becomes tender and puts forth its leaves, you know that summer is near. [33]So also, when you see all these things, you know that he is near, at the very gates. [34]Truly, I say to you, this generation will not pass away till all these things take place. [35]Heaven and earth will pass away, but my words will not pass away.

[36]"But of that day and hour no one knows, not even the angels of heaven, nor the Son, but the Father only. [37]As were the days of Noah, so will be the coming of the Son of man. [38]For as in those days before the flood they were eating and drinking, marrying and giving in marriage, until the day when Noah entered the ark, [39]and they did not know until the flood came and swept them all away, so will be the coming of the Son of man. [40]Then two men will be in the field; one is taken and one is left. [41]Two women will be grinding at the mill; one is taken and one is left. [42]Watch therefore, for you do not know on what day your Lord is coming. [43]But know this, that if the householder had known in what part of the night the thief was coming, he would have watched and would not have let his house be broken into. [44]Therefore you also must be ready; for the Son of man is coming at an hour you do not expect.

[45]"Who then is the faithful and wise servant, whom his master has set over his household, to give them their food at the proper time? [46]Blessed is that servant whom his master when he comes will find so doing. [47]Truly, I say to you, he will set him over all his possessions. [48]But if that wicked servant says to himself, 'My master is delayed,' [49]and begins to beat his fellow servants, and eats and drinks with the drunken, [50]the master of that servant will come on a day when he does not expect him and at an hour he does not know, [51]and will punish him, and put him with the hypocrites; there men will weep and gnash their teeth."

(5)   1 Cor. 12

[1]Now concerning spiritual gifts, brethren, I do not want you to be uninformed. [2]You know that when you were heathen, you were led astray to dumb idols, however you may have been moved. [3]Therefore I want you to understand that no one speaking by the Spirit of God ever says "Jesus be cursed!" and no one can say "Jesus is Lord" except by the Holy Spirit.

[4]Now there are varieties of gifts, but the same Spirit; [5]and there are varieties of service, but the same Lord; [6]and there are varieties of working, but it is the same God who inspires them all in every one. [7]To each is given the manifestation of the Spirit for the common good. [8]To one is given through the Spirit the utterance of wisdom, and to another the utterance of knowledge according to the same Spirit, [9]to another faith by the same Spirit, to another gifts of healing by the one Spirit, [10]to another the working of miracles, to another prophecy, to another the ability to distinguish between spirits, to another various kinds of tongues, to another the interpretation of tongues. [11]All these are inspired by one and the same Spirit, who apportions to each one individually as he wills.

[12]For just as the body is one and has many members, all the members of the body, though many, are one body, so it is with Christ. [13]For by one Spirit we were all baptized into one body—Jews or Greeks, slaves or free—and all were made to drink of one Spirit.

[14]For the body does not consist of one member but of many. [15]If the foot should say, "Because I am not a hand, I do not belong to the body," that would not make it any less a part of the body. [16]And if the ear should say, "Because I am not an eye, I do not belong to the body," that would not make it any less a part of the body. [17]If the whole body were an

eye, where would be the hearing? If the whole body were an ear, where would be the sense of smell? [18]But as it is, God arranged the organs in the body, each one of them, as he chose. [19]If all were a single organ, where would the body be? [20]As it is, there are many parts, yet one body. [21]The eye cannot say to the hand, "I have no need of you," nor again the head to the feet, "I have no need of you." [22]On the contrary, the parts of the body which seem to be weaker are indispensable, [23]and those parts of the body which we think less honorable we invest with the greater honor, and our unpresentable parts are treated with greater modesty, [24]which our more presentable parts do not require. But God has so composed the body, giving the greater honor to the inferior part, [25]that there may be no discord in the body, but that the members may have the same care for one another. [26]If one member suffers, all suffer together; if one member is honored, all rejoice together.

[27]Now you are the body of Christ and individually members of it. [28]And God has appointed in the church first apostles, second prophets, third teachers, then workers of miracles, then healers, helpers, administrators, speakers in various kinds of tongues. [29]Are all apostles? Are all prophets? Are all teachers? Do all work miracles? [30]Do all possess gifts of healing? Do all speak with tongues? Do all interpret? [31]But earnestly desire the higher gifts.

And I will show you a still more excellent way.

J. Section or paragraph markers

Find two examples in the New Testament where each of the following devices mark the beginning of a new section or a new paragraph:

    a. conjunction
    b. change of setting
    c. rhetorical question
    d. vocative

K. Interpolations

In each of the following passages, identify inserted new material between two parts that go together. All such material will need to be carefully marked according to the receptor language rules, if confusion on the part of the readers is to be avoided. Sometimes reordering is necessary. Study each of the following and give a reordering and/or rewording that will eliminate any possible confusion on the part of the reader.

Example: Mark 15:33–39

[33]And when the sixth hour had come, there was darkness over the whole land until the ninth hour. [34]And at the ninth hour Jesus cried with a loud voice, "Eloi, Eloi, lama sabachthani?" which means, "My God, my God, why hast thou forsaken me?" [35]And some of the bystanders hearing it said, "Behold, he is calling Elijah." [36]And one ran and, filling a sponge full of vinegar, put it on a reed and gave it to him to drink, saying, "Wait, let us see whether Elijah will come to take him down. [37]And Jesus uttered a loud cry, and breathed his last. [38]And the curtain of the temple was torn in two, from top to bottom. [39]And when the centurion, who stood facing him, saw that he thus breathed his last, he said, "Truly this man was the Son of God!"

Answer: The comment about the curtain being torn in two from top to bottom interrupts the main story. In Nung of Vietnam, it was necessary to change the order of verses 38 and 39 because Nung paragraph structure observes strict unity of location and verse 38 involves a change of location. It is then necessary to show the time setting of verse 38 by saying, "When Jesus died, the veil was torn..."

(1) Gal. 2:2
     I went up by revelation; and I laid before them (but privately before those who were of
     repute) the gospel which I preach among the Gentiles, lest somehow I should be running or
     had run in vain.

(2) Acts 1:15–16
     In those days Peter stood up among the brethren (the company of persons was in all about a
     hundred and twenty), and said, "Brethren, the scripture had to be fulfilled..."

(3) John 1:38
     Jesus turned, and saw them following, and said to them, "What do you seek?" And they said
     to him, "Rabbi (which means Teacher), where are you staying?"

(4) John 7:22
     Moses gave you circumcision (not that it is from Moses, but from the fathers), and you
     circumcise a man upon the sabbath.

(5) John 9:7
     ...saying to him, "Go, wash in the pool of Siloam" (which means Sent). So he went and
     washed and came back seeing.

(6) Acts 4:36–37
     Thus Joseph who was surnamed by the apostles Barnabas (which means, Son of
     encouragement), a Levite, a native of Cyprus, sold a field...

L. Thematic groupings

Instead of considering a discourse as a purely grammatical entity, consisting of ordered patterns of sentences and paragraphs, it is possible also to consider it as a drama or plot. In this case, the units are not determined by grammatical criteria, but by their significance within the story or argument as a whole. Thus in many instances the introduction can be clearly distinguished from the main argument, while within the argument itself there is a distinction between complication/conflict (the period of problem or conflict), climax, resolution, and evaluation. Digressions within a major theme, or interwoven minor themes may also be discerned. These various elements in discourse may also be found in discourses in Scripture. (Callow 1974:26)

Study each of the passages below from the following points of view:

  a. List events on the time-line and look for any events not mentioned in chronological order.
  b. Note how participant reference is maintained. Are there instances where rules for English would suggest other forms?
  c. Does this narrative have dramatic structure of introduction, complication, climax, resolution, and evaluation?

(1)   John 2:1–10
      [1]On the third day there was a marriage at Cana in Galilee, and the mother of Jesus was there; [2]Jesus also was invited to the marriage, with his disciples. [3]When the wine gave out, the mother of Jesus said to him, "They have no wine." [4]And Jesus said to her, "O woman, what have you to do with me? My hour has not yet come." [5]His mother said to the servants, "Do whatever he tells you." [6]Now six stone jars were standing there, for the Jewish rites of purification, each holding twenty or thirty gallons. [7]Jesus said to them, "Fill the jars with water." And they filled them up to the brim. [8]He said to them, "Now draw some out, and take it to the steward of the feast." So they took it. [9]When the steward of the feast tasted the water now become wine, and did not know where it came from (though the servants who had drawn the water knew), the steward of the feast called the bridegroom [10]and said to him, "Every man serves the good wine first; and when men have drunk freely, then the poor wine; but you have kept the good wine until now."

(2)   Matt. 15:29–39
      [29]And Jesus went on from there and passed along the Sea of Galilee. And he went up on the mountain, and sat down there. [30]And great crowds came to him, bringing with them the lame, the maimed, the blind, the dumb, and many others, and they put them at his feet, and he healed them, [31]so that the throng wondered, when they saw the dumb speaking, the maimed whole, the lame walking, and the blind seeing; and they glorified the God of Israel.
      [32]Then Jesus called his disciples to him and said, "I have compassion on the crowd, because they have been with me now three days, and have nothing to eat; and I am unwilling to send them away hungry, lest they faint on the way." [33]And the disciples said to him, "Where are we to get bread enough in the desert to feed so great a crowd?" [34]And Jesus said to them, "How many loaves have you?" They said, "Seven, and a few small fish." [35]And commanding the crowd to sit down on the ground, [36]he took the seven loaves and the fish, and having given thanks he broke them and gave them to the disciples, and the disciples gave them to the crowds. [37]And they all ate and were satisfied; and they took up seven baskets full of the broken pieces left over. [38]Those who ate were four thousand men, besides women and

children. [39]And sending away the crowds, he got into the boat and went to the region of Magadan.

(3)   Matt. 26:20–30

[20]When it was evening, he sat at table with the twelve disciples; [21]and as they were eating, he said, "Truly, I say to you, one of you will betray me." [22]And they were very sorrowful, and began to say to him one after another, "Is it I, Lord?" [23]He answered, "He who has dipped his hand in the dish with me, will betray me. [24]The Son of man goes as it is written of him, but woe to that man by whom the Son of man is betrayed! It would have been better for that man if he had not been born." [25]Judas, who betrayed him, said, "Is it I, Master?" He said to him, "You have said so."

[26]Now as they were eating, Jesus took bread, and blessed, and broke it, and gave it to the disciples and said, "Take, eat; this is my body." [27]And he took a cup, and when he had given thanks he gave it to them, saying, "Drink of it, all of you; [28]for this is my blood of the covenant, which is poured out for many for the forgiveness of sins. [29]I tell you I shall not drink again of this fruit of the vine until that day when I drink it new with you in my Father's kingdom."

[30]And when they had sung a hymn, they went out to the Mount of Olives.

M. Review exercise

For each of the following passages give a translation that restores or clarifies chronological order, in an appropriate way, if possible.

(1)   Luke 3:18–22

[18]So, with many other exhortations, he preached good news to the people. [19]But Herod the tetrarch, who had been reproved by him for Herodias, his brother's wife, and for all the evil things that Herod had done, [20]added this to them all, that he shut up John in prison. [21]Now when all the people were baptized, and when Jesus also had been baptized and was praying, the heaven was opened, [22]and the Holy Spirit descended upon him in bodily form, as a dove, and a voice came from heaven, "Thou art my beloved Son; with thee I am well pleased."

(2)   Acts 8:1–2

[1]And Saul was consenting to his death. And on that day a great persecution arose against the church in Jerusalem; and they were all scattered throughout the region of Judea and Samaria, except the apostles. [2]Devout men buried Stephen, and made great lamentation over him.

(3)   Acts 28:10–11

[10]They presented many gifts to us; and when we sailed, they put on board whatever we needed. [11]After three months we set sail in a ship which had wintered in the island, a ship of Alexandria, with the Twin Brothers as figurehead.

(4)   Acts 28:24–28

[24]And some were convinced by what he said, while others disbelieved. [25]So, as they disagreed among themselves, they departed, after Paul had made one statement: "The Holy Spirit was right in saying to your fathers through Isaiah the prophet: [26]'Go to this people, and say, You shall indeed hear but never understand, and you shall indeed see but never perceive. [27]For this people's heart has grown dull, and their ears are heavy of hearing, and their eyes they have closed; lest they should perceive with their eyes, and hear with their ears, and understand with their heart, and turn for me to heal them.' [28]Let it be known to you then that this salvation of God has been sent to the Gentiles; they will listen."

Chapter 30
Discourse Genre

Additional Reading:
   Callow 1974: Chapter 1.
   Larson 1978: Chapters V and VI.

A. Identifying discourse types

> The Scriptures exhibit several different types of discourse... If a message is to come across clearly, it must be appropriately worded: It is important that the translator encode each different type of message in the appropriate way. (Callow 1974:13)

In order to do this encoding, the translator must know how to recognize different discourse types in the source. Review the following definitions of discourse types and then identify the type in each passage given. What factors affected your decision?

Narrative	discourse recounts a series of events.
Procedural	discourse gives instructions concerning the accomplishing of a task or the handling of a situation. It is normally ordered in a time-line, but it is a projected time-line, referring to the future rather than the past.
Expository	discourse attempts to prove something to the hearer; it has no time-line, but tends to exhibit frequent contrast between two opposing themes.
Descriptive	discourse gives detail about a person, situation, or activity, chronological factors having no major significance.
Hortatory	discourse attempts to influence conduct.
Drama/Repartee	differs from the other types in that more than one speaker is involved. In the New Testament this type occurs embedded in both narrative and argumentative discourse.

Example: 2 Tim. 4:1–5
Answer: Hortatory—because of the many commands to live well.

(1)   Matt. 2:1–12

(2)   Rev. 7:9–12

(3)   Titus 3:12–14

(4)   Matt. 7:1–6

(5)   Rom. 4:1–12

(6)   Luke 9:12–14

(7)   Acts 7:2–34

(8)   Luke 18:18–30

(9)   Heb. 12:12–17

(10) Acts 12:6–17

(11)   James 5:13–15

(12)   James 2:14–26

(13)   Luke 14:8–11

(14)   Matt. 22:41–46

(15)   1 Cor. 14:34–35

B. Changing third person to first

Assume that you are translating into a language where third person may not be used for first person. Rewrite the following passages, changing to first person and making all corresponding changes.

Example: John 1:51
You will see heaven opened and the angels of God ascending and descending upon the Son of man.

Aguaruna back-translation:
You will see the door of heaven opened and those sent from God descending and ascending at the place where I am, the one who was born becoming man.

(1)   John 20:1–10
[1]Now on the first day of the week Mary Magdalene came to the tomb early, while it was still dark, and saw that the stone had been taken away from the tomb. [2]So she ran, and went to Simon Peter and the other disciple, the one whom Jesus loved, and said the them, "They have taken the Lord out of the tomb, and we do not know where they have laid him." [3]Peter then came out with the other disciple, and they went toward the tomb. [4]They both ran, but the other disciple outran Peter and reached the tomb first; [5]and stooping to look in, he saw the linen cloths lying there, but he did not go in. [6]Then Simon Peter came, following him, and went into the tomb; he saw the linen cloths lying, [7]and the napkin, which had been on his head, not lying with the linen cloths but rolled up in a place by itself. [8]Then the other disciple, who reached the tomb first, also went in, and he saw and believed; [9]for as yet they did not know the scripture, that he must rise from the dead. [10]Then the disciples went back to their homes.

(2)   John 3:13–15
[13]No one has ascended into heaven but he who descended from heaven, the Son of man. [14]And as Moses lifted up the serpent in the wilderness, so must the Son of man be lifted up, [15]that whoever believes in him may have eternal life."

(3)   Matt. 25:31–46
[31]"When the Son of man comes in his glory, and all the angels with him, then he will sit on his glorious throne. [32]Before him will be gathered all the nations, and he will separate them one from another as a shepherd separates the sheep from the goats, [33]and he will place the sheep at his right hand, but the goats at the left. [34]Then the King will say to those at his right hand, 'Come, O blessed of my Father, inherit the kingdom prepared for you from the foundation of the world; [35]for I was hungry and you gave me food, I was thirsty and you gave me drink, I was a stranger and you welcomed me, [36]I was naked and you clothed me, I was sick and you visited me, I was in prison and you came to me.' [37]Then the righteous will answer him, 'Lord, when did we see thee hungry and feed thee, or thirsty and give thee drink? [38]And when did we see thee a stranger and welcome thee, or naked and clothe thee?

39And when did we see thee sick or in prison and visit thee?' 40And the King will answer them, 'Truly, I say to you, as you did it to one of the least of these my brethren, you did it to me.' 41Then he will say to those at his left hand, 'Depart from me, you cursed, into the eternal fire prepared for the devil and his angels; 42for I was hungry and you gave me no food, I was thirsty and you gave me no drink, 43I was a stranger and you did not welcome me, naked and you did not clothe me, sick and in prison and you did not visit me.' 44Then they also will answer, 'Lord, when did we see thee hungry or thirsty or a stranger or naked or sick or in prison, and did not minister to thee?' 45Then he will answer them, 'Truly, I say to you, as you did it not to one of the least of these, you did it not to me.' 46And they will go away into eternal punishment, but the righteous into eternal life."

C. Changing first to third person

There are, however, languages in which a narrator talks about himself in the third person. When this is the case, some passages that are told in the first person in the source language may need to be adjusted to third person in the translation. Rewrite Acts 22:6–16 so that Paul is talking about himself but using the third person.

D. Person in hortatory discourse

Hortatory discourse also shows divergences as to which person is used in a given language. Some use second person—"you do this"; others, a general third person—"people do this." Rewrite the following hortatory passages using a general third person.

(1) Matt. 6:5–6

"And when you pray, you must not be like the hypocrites; for they love to stand and pray in the synagogues and at the street corners, that they may be seen by men. Truly, I say to you, they have received their reward. But when you pray, go into your room and shut the door and pray to our Father who is in secret; and your Father who sees in secret will reward you."

(2) Luke 14:8–11

"When you are invited by any one to a marriage feast, do not sit down in a place of honor, lest a more eminent man than you be invited by him; and he who invited you both will come and say to you, 'Give place to this man,' and then you will begin with shame to take the lowest place. But when you are invited, go and sit in the lowest place, so that when your host comes he may say to you, 'Friend, go up higher'; then you will be honored in the presence of all who sit at table with you. For every one who exalts himself will be humbled, and he who humbles himself will be exalted."

E. Person orientation of metaphors

In many languages special subtypes of discourse, such as parables or examples, occur characteristically with a particular person orientation. For example, in Bahnar of Vietnam illustrative metaphors occur in first person singular. Rewrite the following passages, changing the third person to the first person singular.

Example: Mark 4:21
Is a lamp brought in to be put under a bushel...and not on a stand?

Bahnar back-translation:
Do I ever bring in a lamp...? Don't I put it on the lamp stand?

(1) Matt. 9:16–17
"And no one puts a piece of unshrunk cloth on an old garment, for the patch tears away from the garment, and a worse tear is made. Neither is new wine put into old wineskins; if it is, the skins burst, and the wine is spilled, and the skins are destroyed; but new wine is put into fresh wineskins, and so both are preserved."

(2) Matt. 13:24–30
Another parable he put before them, saying, "The kingdom of heaven may be compared to a man who sowed good seed in his field; but while men were sleeping, his enemy came and sowed weeds among the wheat, and went away. So when the plants came up and bore grain, then the weeds appeared also. And the servants of the householder came and said to him, 'Sir, did you not sow good seed in your field? How then has it weeds?' He said to them, 'An enemy has done this.' The servants said to him, 'Then do you want us to go and gather them?' But he said, 'No; lest in gathering the weeds you root up the wheat along with them. Let both grow together until the harvest; and at harvest time I will tell the reapers, 'Gather the weeds first and bind them in bundles to be burned, but gather the wheat into my barn.'"

F. Hortatory discourse

In Bontoc of the Philippines an exhortation is stated in second person singular when it is an exhortation to perform an activity, in first person dual when it is exhortation to better character. Which of the following are exhortations to perform an activity and which to better character? Rewrite using the form which Bontoc would use.

Example: Col. 4:16
And when this letter has been read among you, have it read also in the church of the Laodiceans...
Answer: exhortation to perform an activity (Rewrite: ...you be sure someone also reads it in the church of the Laodiceans.)

Example: Col. 2:6
As therefore you received Christ Jesus the Lord, so live in him...
Answer: exhortation to better character (Rewrite: As therefore we^DUAL received Christ Jesus the Lord, so let us^DUAL live in him.)

(1) 2 Tim. 4:13
When you come, bring the cloak that I left with Carpus at Troas, also the books, and above all the parchments.

(2) 2 Tim. 3:14
But as for you, continue in what you have learned and have firmly believed...

(3)   2 Tim. 4:9
        Do your best to come to me soon.

(4)   2 Tim. 2:23
        Have nothing to do with stupid, senseless controversies...

(5)   Col. 3:2
        Set your minds on things that are above, not on things that are on earth.

(6)   Col. 4:2–3
        Continue steadfastly in prayer, being watchful in it with thanksgiving; and pray for us also...

(7)   Col. 3:5
        Put to death therefore what is earthly in you: fornication, impurity, passion, evil desire, and covetousness, which is idolatry.

(8)   2 Tim. 4:19
        Greet Prisca and Aquila, and the household of Onesiphorus.

(9)   Philem. 22
        At the same time, prepare a guest room for me...

(10)   Eph. 6:10–11
        Finally, be strong in the Lord and in the strength of his might. Put on the whole armor of God...

Chapter 31
Cohesion

Additional Reading:
  Callow 1974: Chapter 3.

A. Lexical cohesion

Selection of vocabulary items from a common semantic area contributes greatly to discourse cohesion. Obviously, if many of the words in a paragraph come from the same semantic domain, they contribute to the unity of that paragraph. Study the following paragraphs and make a list of the words used that have a relationship to one another and so add lexical cohesion to the passage.

Example: Mark 1:16–20

[16]And passing along by the Sea of Galilee, he saw Simon and Andrew the brother of Simon casting a net in the sea; for they were fishermen. [17]And Jesus said to them, "Follow me and I will make you become fishers of men." [18]And immediately they left their nets and followed him. [19]And going on a little farther, he saw James the son of Zebedee and John his brother, who were in their boat mending the nets. [20]And immediately he called them; and they left their father Zebedee in the boat with the hired servants, and followed him.

Answer: sea, Galilee, fisherman, nets, and boat; brother, son, and father

(1)   John 10:7–16

[7]So Jesus again said to them, "Truly, truly, I say to you, I am the door of the sheep. [8]All who came before me are thieves and robbers; but the sheep did not heed them. [9]I am the door; if any one enters by me, he will be saved, and will go in and out and find pasture. [10]The thief comes only to steal and kill and destroy; I came that they may have life, and have it abundantly. [11]I am the good shepherd. The good shepherd lays down his life for the sheep. [12]He who is a hireling and not a shepherd, whose own the sheep are not, sees the wolf coming and leaves the sheep and flees; and the wolf snatches them and scatters them. [13]He flees because he is a hireling and cares nothing for the sheep. [14]I am the good shepherd; I know my own and my own know me, [15]as the Father knows me and I know the Father; and I lay down my life for the sheep. [16]And I have other sheep, that are not of this fold; I must bring them also, and they will heed my voice. So there shall be one flock, one shepherd.

(2)   Rom. 2:1–3

[1]Therefore you have no excuse, O man, whoever you are, when you judge another; for in passing judgment upon him you condemn yourself, because you, the judge, are doing the very same things. [2]We know that the judgment of God rightly falls upon those who do such things. [3]Do you suppose, O man, that when you judge those who do such things and yet do them yourself, you will escape the judgment of God?

(3)   John 4:1–15

[1]Now when the Lord knew that the Pharisees had heard that Jesus was making and baptizing more disciples than John [2](although Jesus himself did not baptize, but only his disciples), [3]he left Judea and departed again to Galilee. [4]He had to pass through Samaria. [5]So he came to a city of Samaria, called Sychar, near the field that Jacob gave to his son Joseph. [6]Jacob's well was there, and so Jesus, wearied as he was with his journey, sat down beside the well. It was about the sixth hour.

⁷There came a woman of Samaria to draw water. Jesus said to her, "Give me a drink." ⁸For his disciples had gone away into the city to buy food. ⁹The Samaritan woman said to him, "How is it that you, a Jew, ask a drink of me, a woman of Samaria?" For Jews have no dealings with Samaritans. ¹⁰Jesus answered her, "If you knew the gift of God, and who it is that is saying to you, 'Give me a drink,' you would have asked him, and he would have given you living water." ¹¹The woman said to him, "Sir, you have nothing to draw with, and the well is deep; where do you get that living water? ¹²Are you greater than our father Jacob, who gave us the well, and drank from it himself, and his sons, and his cattle?" ¹³Jesus said to her, "Every one who drinks of this water will thirst again, ¹⁴but whoever drinks of the water that I shall give himwill never thirst; the water that I shall give him will become in him a spring of water welling up to eternal life."

(4)   John 21:4–8

⁴Just as day was breaking, Jesus stood on the beach; yet the disciples did not know that it was Jesus. ⁵Jesus said to them, "Children, have you any fish?" They answered him, "No." ⁶He said to them, "Cast the net on the right side of the boat, and you will find some." So they cast it, and now they were not able to haul it in, for the quantity of fish. ⁷That disciple whom Jesus loved said to Peter, "It is the Lord!" When Simon Peter heard that it was the Lord, he put on his clothes, for he was stripped for work, and sprang into the sea. ⁸But the other disciples came in the boat, dragging the net full of fish, for they were not far from the land, but about a hundred yards off.

(5)   1 Cor. 13

¹If I speak in the tongues of men and of angels, but have not love, I am a noisy gong or a clanging cymbal. ²And if I have prophetic powers, and understand all mysteries and all knowledge, and if I have all faith, so as to remove mountains, but have not love, I am nothing. ³If I give away all I have, and if I deliver my body to be burned, but have not love, I gain nothing.

⁴Love is patient and kind; love is not jealous or boastful; ⁵it is not arrogant or rude. Love does not insist on its own way; it is not irritable or resentful; ⁶it does not rejoice at wrong, but rejoices in the right. ⁷Love bears all things, believes all things, hopes all things, endures all things.

⁸Love never ends; as for prophecies, they will pass away; as for tongues, they will cease; as for knowledge, it will pass away. ⁹For our knowledge is imperfect and our prophecy is imperfect; ¹⁰but when the perfect comes, the imperfect will pass away. ¹¹When I was a child, I spoke like a child, I thought like a child, I reasoned like a child; when I became a man, I gave up childish ways. ¹²For now we see in a mirror dimly, but then face to face. Now I know in part; then I shall understand fully, even as I have been fully understood. ¹³So faith, hope, love abide, these three; but the greatest of these is love.

B. Tracing participants through the discourse

Once a participant has been suitably introduced, it still remains to refer to him correctly thereafter, and to make sure that it is always clear who performed each event. (Callow 1974:33)

Passages from Mark chapter 2, in the RSV and GNB translations are printed below side by side. Compare the two versions carefully. For every noun or pronoun in the RSV list the corresponding translation in the GNB. In each instance where the GNB uses a noun rather than a pronoun, state why you think this change was made.

Mark 2 RSV

¹And when he returned to Capernaum after some days, it was reported that he was at home.

²And many were gathered together, so that there was no longer room for them, not even about the door; and he was preaching the word to them.

³And they came, bringing to him a paralytic carried by four men.

⁴And when they could not get near him because of the crowd, they removed the roof above him; and when they had made an opening, they let down the pallet on which the paralytic lay.

. . .

¹³He went out again beside the sea; and all the crowd gathered about him, and he taught them.

¹⁴ And as he passed on, he saw Levi the son of Alphaeus sitting at the tax office, and he said to him, "Follow me." And he rose and followed him.

¹⁵ And as he sat at table in his house, many tax collectors and sinners were sitting with Jesus and his disciples; for there were many who followed him.

. . .

Mark 2 GNB

¹A few days later Jesus went back to Capernaum, and the news spread that he was at home.

²So many people came together that there was no room left, not even out in front of the door. Jesus was preaching the message to them

³when four men arrived, carrying a paralyzed man to Jesus.

⁴Because of the crowd, however, they they could not get the man to him. So they made a hole in the roof right above the place where Jesus was. When they had made an opening, they let the man down, lying on his mat.

. . .

¹³Jesus went back again to the shore of Lake Galilee. A crowd came to him, and he started teaching them.

¹⁴ As he walked along, he saw a tax collector, Levi son of Alphaeus, sitting in his office. Jesus said to him, "Follow me." Levi got up and followed him.

¹⁵Later on Jesus was having a meal in Levi's house. A large number of tax collectors and other outcasts was following Jesus, and many of them joined him and his disciples at the table.

. . .

18 Now John's disciples and
the Pharisees were fasting;
and people came and said to
him, "Why do John's
disciples and the disciples of
the Pharisees fast, but your
disciples do not fast?'

. . .

23 One sabbath he was going
through the grainfields, and as
they made their way his
disciples began to pluck heads
of grain.

24 And the Pharisees said to
him, "Look, why are they
doing what is not lawful on
the sabbath?"

25And he said to them, "Have
you never read what David
did, when he was in need and
was hungry, he and those who
were with him..."

18On one occasion the followers of
John the Baptist and the Pharisees
were fasting. Some people came to
Jesus and asked him, "Why is it that
the disciples of John the Baptist and
the disciples of the Pharisees fast,
but yours do not?"

. . .

23Jesus was walking through some
wheat fields on a sabbath. As his
disciples walked along with him,
they began to pick the heads of
wheat.

24So the Pharisees said to Jesus,
"Look, it is against our Law for your
disciples to do that on the sabbath!"

25Jesus answered, "Have you never
read what David did that time when
he needed something to eat? He and
his men were hungry... "

C. Identifying the antecedent

Confusion often arises in analysis of the source language because it is not clear to whom or to what a particular pronoun refers. Study each of the following to determine who or what is the antecedent of the italicized pronouns. Rewrite, making the antecedent clear.

Example: 2 Kings 19:35
...the angel of the Lord...smote...an hundred fourscore and five thousand: and when *they* arose early in the morning, behold, *they* were all dead corpses. (KJV)
Answer: The first "they" refers to the Israelites; the second "they" refers to the Assyrians.

(1) Mark 2:15
And as *he* sat at table in *his* house... (Study the context of this passage and compare also Luke 5:29.)

(2) Matt. 2:21
And *he* rose and took the child and *his* mother, and went to the land of Israel. (Speakers of other languages have understood from the English that Joseph took his own mother along.)

(3) Luke 4:36
And *they* were all amazed...

(4) Luke 4:39
...and immediately *she* rose and served *them.*

(5) 1 John 2:13
I am writing to you, fathers, because *you* know *him* who is from the beginning.

(6) 1 Cor. 3:19
    He catches the wise in their craftiness...

(7) Acts 10:46
    For *they* heard *them* speaking in tongues and extolling God.

(8) Acts 10:43
    To *him* all the prophets bear witness...

(9) Acts 20:36–37
    And when *he* had spoken thus, *he* knelt down and prayed with *them* all. And *they* all wept...

(10) Acts 21:6
    Then *we* went on board the ship, and *they* returned home.

D. Pronominal reference

The referent in each of the following passages is ambiguous. Study the context until you know to whom or to what the pronoun, demonstrative, or relative clause refers.

Example: Matt. 15:2
              ...they do not wash their hands...
Answer: The closest antecedent of "they" is "elders." However, the proper antecedent is "disciples."

(1) Matt. 28:18
    And Jesus came and said to them...

(2) John 1:15
    John bore witness to him...

(3) Mark 9:20
    And they brought the boy to him...

(4) Luke 2:12
    And this will be a sign for you...

(5) Eph. 5:12
    For it is a shame even to speak of the things that they do in secret...

(6) Acts 19:28
    When they heard this they were enraged...

(7) John 8:40
    ...this is not what Abraham did.

(8) Acts 3:2
    ...whom they laid daily at that gate...

E. Use of role

In each of the following, substitute role for the noun or pronoun which is italicized in the source.

Example: Acts 21:40

And when he had given him leave, *Paul,* standing on the steps, motioned with his hand...

Answer: and when he had given him leave, *the prisoner,* standing on the steps motioned with his hand.

(1)   Luke 1:15

...for *he* will be great before the Lord...

(2)   Luke 1:63

And *he* asked for a writing tablet, and wrote, *"His* name is John."

(3)   Acts 7:21

...and when *he* was exposed, Pharoah's daughter adopted *him*...

(4)   Acts 7:9–10

And the patriarchs, jealous of Joseph, sold him into Egypt; but God was with *him,* and rescued him out of all his afflictions...

(5)   Acts 8:30

So Philip ran to *him,* and heard *him* reading Isaiah...

(6)   Acts 9:33–34

There *he* found a man named Aeneas, who had been bedridden for eight years and was paralyzed. And Peter said to *him*...

(7)   Acts 16:1–2

A disciple was there, named Timothy, the son of a Jewish woman who was a believer; but his father was a Greek. *He* was well spoken of by the brethren at Lystra and Iconium.

(8)   Acts 12:4

And when he had seized *him,* *he* put him in prison...

F. Fourth person

In Trique of Mexico, and other languages, there are fourth-person pronouns. If you are already talking about someone with a third-person pronoun and another actor comes into focus he is referred to, after he has been named, by fourth-person pronouns rather than third person.

Assume you are translating into a language in which fourth person, *nam,* is used rather than third person pronouns if the newly introduced person is the same number and gender. When would you use *nam* in the following verses. You need to look carefully at the context.

Example: Mark 5:2, 6

"And when he had come out of the boat, there met him out of the tombs a man with an unclean spirit, who...when he saw Jesus...he ran and worshiped him..."

Answer: "And when he had come out of the boat, there met him out of the tombs a man with an unclean spirit who when *nam* say Jesus...*nam* ran and worshiped him."

(1)   Mark 16:13

And they went back and told the rest, but they did not believe them.

(2)   Acts 9:17
So Ananias departed and entered the house. And laying his hands on him he said, "Brother Saul, the Lord Jesus who appeared to you..."

(3)   Mark 8:22–26
And they came to Bethsaida. And some people brought to him a blind man, and begged him to touch him. And he took the blind man by the hand, and led him out of the village; and when he had spit on his eyes and laid his hands upon him, he asked him, "Do you see anything?" And he looked up and said, "I see men; but they look like trees, walking." Then again he laid his hands upon his eyes; and he looked intently and was restored, and saw everything clearly. And he sent him away to his home, saying, "Do not even enter the village."

(4)   Acts 8:27–31
And he rose and went. And behold, an Ethiopian...had come to Jerusalem to worship and was returning; seated in his chariot, he was reading the prophet Isaiah. And the Spirit said to Philip, "Go up and join this chariot." So Philip ran to him, and heard him reading Isaiah the prophet, and asked, "Do you understand what you are reading?" And he said, "How can I, unless some one guides me?" And he invited Philip to come up and sit with him.

(5)   Luke 5:12–14
While he was in one of the cities, there came a man full of leprosy; and when he saw Jesus, he fell on his face and besought him, "Lord..." And he stretched out his hand, and touched him, saying, "I will; be clean." And immediately the leprosy left him. And he charged him to tell no one...

G. Introducing participants

Rewrite the following passage, using these rules of discourse structure: A participant is named within a paragraph by a noun the first time mentioned. After that, within the same paragraph a pronoun is used.

If the same participant occurs in a second or third paragraph he is introduced by a noun plus the attributive (this, that, these, or those) the first time mentioned and by pronouns after this introduction.

Mark 11:11–15
And he entered Jerusalem, and went into the temple; and when he had looked round at everything, as it was already late, he went out to Bethany with the twelve.
On the following day, when they came from Bethany, he was hungry. And seeing in the distance a fig tree in leaf, he went to see if he could find anything on it. When he came to it, he found nothing but leaves... And he said to it, "May no one ever eat fruit from you again." And his disciples heard it.
And they came to Jerusalem. And he entered the temple and began to drive out those who sold and those who bought in the temple...

H. Clause connectors

Rewrite the same passage, keeping the rules given in Section G and adding the following rules: The connector "and" is used only to connect coordinate nouns, noun phrases, or coordinate clauses and never to connect clauses or sentences in sequence. A clause beginning with "when," referring to time, always follows the main clause that it modifies.

I. Review through applying discourse rules

Below is the NEB translation of Mark 8:22–26. Following this translation there are rules for rewriting into the Kalaba English language. There is also a semantic chart. Using the information on the chart and the rules, rewrite these verses into Kalaba English.

Mark 8:22–26 (NEB)
They arrived at Bethsaida. There the people brought a blind man to Jesus and begged him to touch him. He took the blind man by the hand and led him away out of the village. Then he spat on his eyes, laid his hands upon him, and asked whether he could see anything.
The man's sight began to come back, and he said, "I see men; they look like trees, but they are walking about." Jesus laid his hands on his eyes again; he looked hard, and now he was cured so that he saw everything clearly.
Then Jesus sent him home, saying, "Do not tell anyone in the village."

a.   Clauses have this structure:
    (Manner) Pred (DO) (IO) (Loc) (Subj) (Time)

b.   Sentences have from one to five clauses.

c.   A quotation fills the object slot, but does not take the object clitic.

d.   All fillers of the location slot have an obligatory location-marking enclitic *-ta*.

e.   All fillers of the direct object (DO) slot have an obligatory object-marking enclitic *-no*.

f.   All fillers of the indirect object (IO) slot have an obligatory enclitic *-mu*.

g.   All predicates occurring in the final clause of a sentence take obligatory verb suffixes indicating person, tense, and mode in that order.

person suffixes are	*-ta*	'first person'
	-ra	'second person'
	-ki	'third person'
tense suffixes are	*-n*	'past'
	-m	'present'
	-k	'future'
mode suffixes are	*-po*	'declarative'
	-ne	'imperative'
	-ti	'interrogative'

h.   Any newly introduced participant or any change of actor is indicated by an obligatory noun as participant and requires a new sentence.

i.   A previously introduced participant as Direct Object is indicated by an obligatory pronoun as participant. Pronouns are optional in other clause constituents.

j.   If two actions in sequence have the same Indirect Object, only the first takes an obligatory participant as Indirect Object, the second never does.

k.   All quotes are direct quotes.

l.   Sequential actions within a sentence are connected by "and."

m. Sentences are not connected by any overt marker within a paragraph; that is, "and" does not occur between sentences.

n. A new paragraph is signaled by a focus on time or actor. In the first clause of a new paragraph the focus slot precedes the predicate and its modifier (Manner).

Mark 8:22–26—Span Chart

Time	Participants			Action	Manner	Location	Quote
	Actor	Goal–DO	Goal–IO				
	Jesus and disciples			arrived		Bethsaida	
	people	blind*	Jesus	brought		Bethsaida	
	people		Jesus	begged			to touch blind man
	Jesus	blind		took	by hand		
	Jesus	blind		led away		out of village	
	Jesus			spat		on blind's eyes	
	Jesus			laid hands		on blind	
	Jesus		blind	asked			if he (blind) could see anything
	blind's sight			began to come back			
	blind			said			I see men; they look like trees, but they are walking about
	Jesus			laid hands	again	on blind's eyes	
	blind			looked	hard		
now	blind			was cured			
	blind	everything		saw	clearly		
then	Jesus	blind		sent		to blind's home	
	Jesus		blind	said			Do not tell anyone in village

*blind = blind man

Chapter 32
Prominence

Additional Reading:

   Callow 1974: Chapter 4.

Prominence "refers to any device whatever which gives certain events, participants, or objects more significance than others in the same context" (Callow 1974:50).

A. Thematic prominence

Thematic material is material that develops the theme of a discourse, by contrast with background material, which fills out the theme but does not develop it. The theme of a discourse constitutes a progression, called...the time-line and the theme-line. (Callow 1974:53)

List the propositions which are the time-line of each passage. Then identify the propositions that carry the theme in each of the following passages.

Example: Col. 1:15–20

   (God's Son) exactly reveals (Greek: is the image of) God.

   He rules over everything. (He is the first-born of all creation.)

   He is (existed) before anything existed.

   He maintains all things. (He hold all things together.)

   He rules over the church. (He is the head of the body, the church.)

   He is supreme (Greek: beginning).

   He is the ruler (Greek: first-born).

Answer: (God's Son) exactly reveals God.

   All the other propositions describe God's Son showing him to be exactly like God, that is, "he reveals God."

(1)   Col. 1:21–23

(2)   Col. 1:24–29

(3)   Acts 3:1–10

(4)   John 14:1–7

B. Thematic function of relative clauses

The Greek relative clause has a wide variety of functions: one of these is thematic, that is to say, it carries information that is on the theme-line. An example of this is found in Col. 1:12–13, "Giving thanks unto the Father, *which* hath made us meet...*Who hath* delivered us...." In this case the relative pronoun, normally translated by English *who, which,* does not carry any backgrounding significance whatever, it simply serves as a participant-referent for the clause, and is then better translated by *he, it,* or the appropriate personal pronoun. (Callow 1974:59–60)

Study the relative clauses in the following sentences and decide which of them introduce a thematic proposition and which introduce a background proposition. If the proposition is thematic rewrite without using a relative clause.

(1) Acts 13:7
He was with the proconsul, Sergius Paulus, a man of intelligence, who summoned Barnabas and Saul and sought to hear the word of God.

(2) Acts 14:3
...speaking boldly for the Lord, who bore witness to the word of his grace, granting signs and wonders to be done by their hands.

(3) Acts 14:8
Now at Lystra there was a man sitting, who could not use his feet; he was a cripple from birth, who had never walked.

(4) Rom. 7:4
Likewise, my brethren, you have died to the law through the body of Christ, so that you may belong to another, to him who has been raised from the dead in order that we may bear fruit for God.

(5) 2 Cor. 2:14
...thanks be to God, who in Christ always leads us in triumph, and through us spreads the fragrance of the knowledge of him everywhere.

(6) 2 Cor. 8:16–17
But thanks be to God, who puts the same earnest care for you into the heart of Titus. For he not only accepted our appeal, but being himself very earnest he is going to you of his own accord.

(7) Col. 3:4
When Christ who is our life appears, then you also will appear with him in glory.

(8) 1 Thess. 5:9–10
For God has not destined us for wrath, but to obtain salvation through our Lord Jesus Christ, who died for us so that whether we wake or sleep we might live with him.

(9) 1 Thess. 5:24
He who calls you is faithful, and he will do it.

(10) 1 Tim. 2:3–4
This is good, and it is acceptable in the sight of God our Savior, who desires all men to be saved and to come to the knowledge of the truth.

C. Prominence with focus value

Focus is that type of prominence which acts as a spotlight, playing on the thematic material to bring some of it especially to the attention. In some languages, focus is an obligatory category and one cannot avoid using it. (Callow 1974:60)

Study the following and decide what participant, location, or concept is in focus and what is the theme of the passage.

Example: Col. 1:15–20
Answer: Christ is in focus throughout the passage.

(1)   Eph. 3:1–13

(2)   Eph. 5:25–33

(3)   1 Thess. 1:2–10

(4)   John 6:25–59

(5)   Luke 19:41–44

(6)   1 Tim. 3:1–7

(7)   1 Tim. 4:1–5

(8)   Heb. 6:20–7:3

(9)   Heb. 7:11–19

(10) Rev. 21:1–4

D. Focus of participants

...many languages assume that the participant functioning as agent is in focus, and that this is expressed grammatically as the subject of a clause. This creates considerable problems in translation, since Greek could have several different participants all featuring as agents (and sometimes all as grammatical subjects) in the space of one verse. A literal translation here would cause the readers considerable confusion as focus was apparently shifted rapidly from character to character. In Cakchiquel (Guatemala) it is natural to keep one participant in focus for several clauses, and therefore verses sound extremely unnatural if they switch focus from one participant to another and then back to the first again. In these cases Cakchiquel sometimes uses a passive construction so as to maintain focus on the first participant throughout. An example of this is found in Mark 9:31, "The Son of man is delivered into the hands of men, and they shall kill him." Here the Cakchiquel reads, "I, the Son of man will be delivered into the hands of men and *I will be killed,*" thus avoiding introducing "they" as grammatical subject of "will kill." (Callow 1974:62)

Rewrite the following so that only the one participant in focus (the italicized) occurs as the subject of the clause. The other participants will have to occupy other slots in the clause. It is all right not to keep focus on some participants in relative clauses.

Example: Mark 10:1–10
           And *he* [Jesus] left there and went to the region of Judea...he taught them. And Pharisees came up and in order to test him asked, "..." He answered them, "..." And in the house the disciples asked him again about this matter.

Answer: And he left there and went to the region of Judea...he taught them. And he was asked by the Pharisees who came up to him in order to test him asking, "..." He answered them, "..." Again in the house he was asked by his disciples about the matter.

(1)   Mark 14:10–11
      Then *Judas* Iscariot, who was one of the twelve, went to the chief priests in order to betray him to them. And when they heard it they were glad, and promised to give him money. And he sought an opportunity to betray him.

(2)   Mark 14:72
      And immediately the cock crowed a second time. And *Peter* remembered how Jesus had said to him...And he broke down and wept.

(3)   Luke 4:42–43
      And when it was day he *[Jesus]* departed and went into a lonely place. And the people sought him and came to him, and would have kept him from leaving them; but he said to them...

(4)   Acts 8:26–31
      But an angel of the Lord said to *Philip,* "Rise and go toward the south..." And he rose and went. And behold, an Ethiopian...was returning; seated in his chariot, he was reading the prophet Isaiah. And the Spirit said to Philip, "Go..." So Philip ran to him, and heard him reading Isaiah...and asked, "..." And he said, "..." And he invited Philip to come up and sit with him.

E. Identifying the theme propositions in Acts

Toussaint (1967:5) outlines the book of Acts as follows:

I.   The witness in Jerusalem 1:1–6:7
II. The witness in all Judea and Samaria 6:8–9:31
III. The witness to the extremity of the earth 9:32–28:31
        A. The extension of the church at Antioch 9:32–12:24
        B. The extension of the church in Asia Minor 12:25–16:5
        C. The extension of the church in the Aegean Area 16:6–19:20
        D. The extension of the church to Rome 19:21–28:31

Study the verse ending each section and identify the Theme proposition which indicates the close of each of these large units of the discourse. Notice what is in common in the last verse of these sections.

Chapter 33
The Communication Situation

Additional Reading:
   Shaw 1988.

A. Involvement of the narrator

Some languages make it obligatory that the relationship of the speaker to his material be specified at every point, as to whether he observed the events reported, knows them by hearsay, or has deduced them from evidence. In other languages this is not obligatory, but it is of relatively frequent occurrence.

Assuming that you are translating into a language which requires this specification of narrator involvement, study the following passages and try to decide if the speaker observed the events reported, knew them from hearsay, or deduced them from evidence.

Example: John 2:1–11
Answer: John probably observed the events reported, since it says that the disciples were there.

(1)   John 3:22

(2)   John 3:23–30

(3)   John 4:7–15

(4)   John 4:31–38

(5)   Acts 1:6–11

(6)   Acts 5:1–11

(7)   Acts 16:11–15

(8)   Acts 16:35–39

(9)   Acts 21:17–25

(10) Acts 21:26

B. Attitude of the speaker using vocative phrases

One function of the vocative phrase in the English and the Greek New Testaments is to show the attitude of the speaker toward the person to whom he is speaking. In each of the following, identify the vocative phrase and indicate the attitude of the speaker that is being conveyed.

Example: Acts 26:15
            Who are you, Lord?
Answer: The term "Lord" shows an attitude of respect.

(1)   Luke 12:32
      Fear not, *little flock*, for it is your Father's good pleasure to give you the kingdom.

(2)   Acts 26:25
      I am not mad, *most excellent Festus*, but I am speaking the sober truth.

(3)   Luke 12:20
      But God said to him, '*Fool!* This night your soul is required of you'

(4)   Gal. 4:19
      My little children, with whom I am again in travail until Christ be formed in you!

(5)   John 20:16
      Jesus said to her, "*Mary.*" She turned and said to him in Hebrew, "*Rabboni!*" (which means Teacher).

C. Functions of the vocative phrase

   Study this list of functions of the vocative phrase. Then study the passages below to determine which vocative function is in focus in the passage. A single vocative phrase may have more than one function.

   a. To show the attitude of the speaker toward the person to whom he is speaking.
   b. To make a personal appeal by focusing attention on an individual or group of individuals. Proper names are often used.
   c. To focus on certain qualities of an individual or group.
   d. For rhetorical or stylistic effect.
   e. To mark off the sections of the argument—to recall attention or to signal the beginning of a new subject.
   f. To focus on certain classes of individuals in the audience.

Example: Luke 12:20
          But God said to him, 'Fool! This night your soul is required of you...'
Answer: To show the attitude of the speaker.

(1)   1 John 4:7
      Beloved, let us love one another; for love is of God...

(2)   Acts 26:27
      King Agrippa, do you believe the prophets?

(3)   Matt. 17:17
      O faithless and perverse generation, how long am I to be with you?

(4)   Luke 13:34
      O Jerusalem, Jerusalem, killing the prophets and stoning those who are sent to you!

(5)   John 20:16
      Jesus said to her, "Mary." She turned and said to him in Hebrew, "Rabboni!" (which means Teacher).

(6)   Luke 7:40
      ...Jesus answering said to him, "Simon, I have something to say to you."

(7)   Eph. 5:22
      Wives, be subject to your husbands...

(8)   Matt. 23:13
      But woe to you, scribes and Pharisees, hypocrites!

(9)   1 Tim. 6:11
      But as for you, man of God, shun all this...

(10) 2 Cor. 6:11

Dear friends in Corinth! We have spoken frankly to you, we have opened wide our hearts. (TEV)

D. Changing vocative phrases to a different grammatical construction

It may be necessary to change the form of the vocative phrase in order to conform to the natural grammatical pattern of the receptor language. In many languages, vocative phrases that focus on particular qualities and thus carry information are translated by a separate clause or sentence. Rewrite the vocative in each of the following, using a nonvocative grammatical pattern.

Example: Matt. 6:30

RSV: ...Will he not much more clothe you, O men of little faith?

Answer: TEV: Won't he be all the more sure to clothe you? How little faith you have!

(1) Luke 19:17

And he said to him, "Well done, good servant! Because you have been faithful...you shall have authority over ten cities."

(2) Matt. 17:17

O faithless and perverse generation, how long am I to be with you?

(3) Luke 13:15

Then the Lord answered him, "You hypocrites! Does not each of you on the sabbath untie his ox...and lead it away to water it?"

(4) Matt. 6:30

...will he not much more clothe you, O men of little faith?

(5) Matt. 8:29

What have you to do with us, O Son of God?

E. Attitude of the speaker

The attitude of the speaker is reflected in the choice of words and grammar. Study each of the following to determine the attitude of the speaker. What specific words or phrases helped you make this decision?

Example: Mark 6:22

For when Herodias' daughter came in and danced, she pleased Herod and his guests; and the king said to the girl, "Ask me for whatever you wish, and I will grant it."

Answer: pride; words like 'pleased', 'whatever you wish'

(1) Mark 6:30

(2) Mark 7:6–13

(3) Mark 7:18–23

(4) Luke 24:19b–24

(5) Luke 24:25–26

(6) Acts 8:20–23

(7)   Acts 8:24

(8)   Gal. 1:6–9

F. Placement of the vocative phrase

In some languages the vocative must always come at the beginning of the sentence, but never within the sentence, since it would break the continuity of the main idea. Rewrite the following, making this adjustment.

Example: Acts 10:13
          And there came a voice to him, "Rise, Peter; kill and eat."
Answer: And there came a voice to him, "Peter, arise, kill and eat."

(1)   Luke 4:34
       "Ah! What have you to do with us, Jesus of Nazareth? Have you come to destroy us? I know who you are, the Holy One of God."

(2)   Luke 1:1–4
       [1]Inasmuch as many have undertaken to compile a narrative of things which have been accomplished among us, [2]just as they were delivered to us by those who from the beginning were eyewitnesses and ministers of the word, [3]it seemed good to me also, having followed all things closely for some time past, to write an orderly account for you, most excellent Theophilus, [4]that you may know the truth concerning the things of which you have been informed.

G. Aspects of the communication situation

Many aspects of the communication situation raise special problems for the translators. The location (differences in climate, topography, flora and fauna), the time in history when the material was written, and the occasion for writing. In each of the following there is a potential problem for the translator which may need some adjustment such as a classifier, implicit information made explicit, or a more descriptive phrase. Identify the potential problem and rewrite, adjusting for a tropical forest culture of the Amazon region of Brazil.

Example: Luke 12:54–55
          He also said to the multitudes, "When you see a cloud rising in the west, you say at once, 'A shower is coming'; and so it happens. And when you see the south wind blowing, you say, 'There will be scorching heat'; and it happens.
Answer: These descriptions of the weather are peculiar to Palestine and would sound strange to speakers of languages where the rain or the heat come from other directions. It would be possible to make the implicit information explicit by having Jesus say, "In this country,..." or "Here, when you see a cloud..."

(1)   Matt. 3:4
       Now John wore a garment of camel's hair, and a leather girdle around his waist; and his food was locusts and wild honey.

(2)   Matt. 3:5
       Then went out to him Jerusalem and all Judea and all the region about the Jordan.

(3)   Matt. 4:12
       Now when he heard that John had been arrested, he withdrew into Galilee.

(4)   Matt. 8:5
        And he entered Capernaum, a centurion came forward to him, beseeching him...

(5)   Matt. 13:33
        He told them another parable. "The kingdom of heaven is like leaven which a woman took and hid in three measures of flour, till it was all leavened."

(6)   Mark 10:16
        And he took them in his arms and blessed them, laying his hands upon them.

(7)   Luke 21:21
        Then let those who are in Judea flee to the mountains, and let those who are inside the city depart, and let not those who are out in the country enter it...

(8)   Luke 23:53
        Then he took it down and wrapped it in a linen shroud, and laid him in a rock-hewn tomb, where no one had ever yet been laid.

(9)   Acts 4:11
        This is the stone which was rejected by you builders, but which has become the head of the corner.

(10)   Acts 20:8–9
        There were many lights in the upper chamber where we were gathered. And a young man named Eutychus was sitting in the window. He...fell down from the third story and was taken up dead.

Chapter 34
The Information Load

Additional Reading:
    Callow 1974: Chapter 5.

A. Known and new information

Different languages present information at a different rate. A translation should communicate biblical information at a rate within the normal patterns of the receptor language. Identify the old and new information in the following passage by underlining the new information (Things and Events) and circling the old information.

> Luke 10:30–35
> [30]A man was going down from Jerusalem to Jericho, and he fell among robbers, who stripped him and beat him, and departed, leaving him half-dead. [31]Now by chance a priest was going down that road; and when he saw him he passed by on the other side. [32]So likewise a Levite, when he came to the place and saw him, passed by on the other side. [33]But a Samaritan, as he journeyed, came to where he was; and when he saw him, he had compassion, [34]and went to him and bound up his wounds, pouring on oil and wine; then he set him on his own beast and brought him to an inn, and took care of him. [35]And the next day he took out two denarii and gave them to the innkeeper...

B. Linking new to known information in discourse

The first time a Thing or Event is mentioned, new information is being introduced. Each time it is referred to again it is considered old information. In the passages below look for ways old information is signaled by doing the following:

> a. Take the first participant introduced and list the ways it is referred to in all further references. Then take the second participant introduced and do the same. In this way study how participants are referred to when newly introduced (new information) and how they are referred to when again mentioned subsequently in the text.
> b. List the Events that occur in the text in order. See if any Event is referred to more than once. The first time it will be new information. When it is referred to again it will be old information. Does the form used differ?
> c. What is said in the quotation does not need to be included in the analysis at this time.

First look for the new and old information and how it is signaled in the RSV. Then do the same with the passage in the language given below.

(1)   John 1:35–44 RSV
> [35]The next day again John was standing with two of his disciples; [36]and he looked at Jesus as he walked, and said, "Behold, the Lamb of God!" [37]The two disciples heard him say this, and they followed Jesus. [38]Jesus turned, and saw them following, and said to them, "What do you seek?" And they said to him, "Rabbi" (which means Teacher), "where are you staying?" [39]He said to them, "Come and see." They came and saw where he was staying; and they stayed with him that day, for it was about the tenth hour. [40]One of the two who heard John speak, and followed him, was Andrew, Simon Peter's brother. [41]He first found his brother Simon, and said to him, "We have found the Messiah" (which means Christ). [42]He

brought him to Jesus. Jesus looked at him, and said, "So you are Simon the son of John? You shall be called Cephas" (which means Peter).

[43]The next day Jesus decided to go to Galilee. And he found Philip and said to him, "Follow me." [44]Now Philip was from Bethsaida, the city of Andrew and Peter.

Tepehua back-translation:

[35]The next day again John was standing with two of his men. [36]And he again saw Jesus where he was coming and said to them, "Look at that man who is going to be like God's lamb." [37]And those two of John's when they heard what he said, well, immediately they followed Jesus. [38]And when Jesus turned around he saw those who were following him. He said to them, "What are you hunting for?" And they said to him, "Rabbi, where do you live?" Rabbi means teacher. [39]Well, he said to them, "Come. You will see where I live." And they went with him. They saw where he lived. Well, that day they stayed there with him since it was about four in the afternoon. [40]And those two who heard John's words and followed Jesus, well, one was called Andrew. He was the younger brother of Simon Peter. [41]Well, Andrew immediately found his real brother who was called Simon. And he said to his brother, "We have found the Messiah. That means we have found the Christ, the one of whom it was said that God would send him here." [42]And immediately he took him to where Jesus was. When Jesus saw him he said to him, "You are Simon. You are the son of Jonas. You will be called Cephas." Cephas and Peter mean rock. [43]When the next day came, Jesus said that he was going to the land of Galilee. There he came across the one who was called Philip. And he said to him that he should follow him. [44]Philip lived in the town of Bethsaida. It was the land of Andrew and Peter.

(2)   Acts 1:21–24

[21]So one of the men who have accompanied us during all the time that the Lord Jesus went in and out among us, [22]beginning from the baptism of John until the day when he was taken up from us—one of these men must become with us a witness to his resurrection." [23]And they put forward two, Joseph called Barsabbas, who was surnamed, Justus, and Matthias. [24]And they prayed and said, "Lord, who knowest the hearts of all men, show which one of these two thou hast chosen...

Aguaruna back-translation:

[21]"Because it says like that, we ought to look for another, 'Who it ought to be,' saying. [22]It should be one who beginning when John baptized Jesus, always was with Jesus, being one who was left by him when he went to heaven. When he is thus, with him we can tell 'Jesus truly rose,' saying." [23]When Peter said that, they said, "Let it be Joseph Barabbas, called Justus." When they said, others speaking said, "Let it be Matthias." [24]When they said that, they prayed to God, "Lord, you see the heart of each one. You being thus, 'who is it' you choose, 'It is he,' saying."

(3)   Mark 7:31–33

[31]Then he returned from the region of Tyre, and went through Sidon to the Sea of Galilee, through the region of the Decapolis. [32]And they brought to him a man who was deaf and had an impediment in his speech; and they besought him to lay his hand upon him. [33]And taking him aside...

Waffa back-translation:

[31]Jesus returned and came again from the town called Tyre, passed through the town called Sidon, passed through the big town called Decapolis and came and sat on the bank of Lake Galilee. [32]He sat, and the friends of a man who was deaf and could not talk got him and went to Jesus. They went, and strongly asked Jesus to touch him. [33]When they had asked him, Jesus taking him ...

C. Preview and summary

Preview and summary are also used to slow down the information load. Study the following passages and identify any propositions whose function seems to be to provide a preview or a summary. If any of the following passages do not have a preview or summary proposition, suggest a possible wording for such a proposition for the passage.

(1)   Matt. 1:18–25

(2)   Matt. 4:1–11

(3)   Matt. 9:1–8

(4)   Rom. 8:1–17

(5)   1 Cor. 13

D. Reducing the rate of information

Callow (1974:84–85) suggests that there are the following ways in which the receptor language may adjust the information load so as to have a slower flow of new information.

  a. Splitting an original construction into smaller units using repetition as linkage.
  b. Splitting an original construction into smaller units using implied information as linkage.
  c. Splitting an original construction into smaller units in such a way that no additional linkage is needed.
  d. Splitting an original construction into more units using semantically neutral words such as "there was."
  e. Descriptive phrase for unknown concept.

Following each passage given below is a back-translation from a specific language. Identify any occurrences of the above in the back-translation. There may be more than one in a verse.

Example: Rom. 6:23 For the wages of sin is death...
             Huixteco back-translation:
             Because the one who works for sin, he will be paid for his work. The payment of his work will be that he will be lost eternally.

Answer: a

(1) Luke 15:12
     Father, give me the share of property that falls to me.
     Kasem back-translation:
     Father, take your possessions and divide, result you give me my share.

(2) Matt. 8:4
     See that you say nothing to any one; but go, show yourself to the priest, and offer the gift that Moses commanded, for a proof to the people.
     Shipibo back-translation:
     See that you tell no one. Go your way to show yourself to the priest. So that they may know that you are healed, offer the gift that Moses commanded.

(3) Luke 10:31
     Now by chance a priest was going down that road...
     Kasem back-translation:
     There was a certain priest, he got up and came down that road.

(4) Acts 1:21–22
     So one of the men who have accompanied us during all the time that the Lord Jesus went in and out among us...must become with us a witness to his resurrection.
     Aguaruna back-translation:
     Because it says like that, we ought to look for another, "Who it ought to be," saying. It should be one who always was with Jesus...When he is thus, with him we can tell, "Jesus truly rose," saying.

(5)   John 2:11
       This, the first of his signs, Jesus did at Cana in Galilee, and manifested his glory; and his disciples
       believed in him.
       Tepehua back-translation:
       This thing to be marveled at Jesus did in the town of Cana in the land of Galilee. That is the
       first thing to be marveled at that Jesus did. In that way he showed to the people his power. At
       that time, then, his disciples believed on Jesus more.

(6)   John 2:9
       When the steward of the feast tasted the water now become wine, and did not know where it
       came from (though the servants who had drawn the water knew), the steward of the feast called
       the bridegroom...
       Totonac back-translation:
       And the chief tasted it, and it was wine, and he didn't know that it had been water and that
       the water had been changed to wine. Only the servants knew because they had put the water
       into water pots. Then the chief called the bridegroom.

(7)   John 3:1
       Now there was a man of the Pharisees, named Nicodemus, a ruler of the Jews.
       Ojitlan Chinantec back-translation:
       A man was named Nicodemus. He believed according to the law of the Pharisee people. And
       he was a head man of the Jews.

(8)   John 3:15
       ...that whoever believes in him may have eternal life."
       Tepehua back-translation:
       When I will have been thus, all who will have confidence in me won't be lost. They will have
       life forever up in heaven.

(9)   John 5:2
       Now there is in Jerusalem by the Sheep Gate a pool, in Hebrew called Bethzatha, which has five
       porticoes.
       Lalana Chinantec back-translation:
       In Jerusalem there is a large hole containing water where people bathe. It is near the gate in
       the wall which goes around the outside of town which is called the gate of sheep. They call
       the hole which contains water Bethzatha in the Hebrew language. There were five porches
       along the water.

E. Expected information

There is certain information that is only implied in the Greek but which may be expected in the receptor language and therefore needs to be added in a given translation if the translation is to sound natural.

> In many West African languages...any motion that took place must be stated. In the story of Moses in the bulrushes, Exod. 2:3 reads, "she took for him an ark...and put the child therein; and she laid it in the flags by the river's brink." Motion is implied in the last clause of the verse; Moses' mother had to go to the river to leave the child there. This is clear, were proof needed, from vv. 7 and 8. Moses' sister said, "Shall I *go* and call thee a nurse...?" She then *went* and called the child's mother. Thus it is obvious that their home was not right at the water's edge—motion was involved. In Kasem, motion is not normally implied, but stated, so the last clause of the verse becomes, "she *went* to the river's brink and laid it in the flags." This is not only more natural, and avoids confusion; it also spreads out the information in a more acceptable way. To attach both "in the flags" and "by the river's brink" to the single verb "laid" would be too heavy an information load in Kasem. (Callow 1974:87)

In each of the following passages look for events that are implied in the source language and which may need to be made explicit in the receptor language.

(1)   Matt. 2:7–8, 12
      Then Herod summoned the wise men secretly and ascertained from them what time the star appeared; and he sent them to Bethlehem, saying, "Go and search diligently for the child, and when you have found him bring me word, that I too may come and worship him." And being warned in a dream not to return to Herod, they departed to their own country by another way.

(2)   Matt. 4:1–2
      Then Jesus was led up by the Spirit into the wilderness to be tempted by the devil. And he fasted forty days and forty nights, and afterward he was hungry.

(3)   Matt. 9:9–10
      As Jesus passed on from there, he saw a man called Matthew sitting at the tax office; and he said to him, "Follow me." And he rose and followed him. And as he sat at table in the house, behold, many tax collectors and sinners came and sat down with Jesus and his disciples.

(4)   Mark 3:6
      The Pharisees went out, and immediately held counsel with the Herodians against him, how to destroy him.

(5)   John 2:9–10
      When the steward of the feast tasted the water now become wine, and did not know where it came from (though the servants who had drawn the water knew), the steward of the feast called the bridegroom and said to him, "Every man serves the good wine first; and when men have drunk freely, then the poor wine; but you have kept the good wine until now."

(6)   Acts 20:5
      These went on and were waiting for us at Troas...

(7)   Acts 24:24
      After some days Felix came with his wife Drusilla, who was a Jewess; and he sent for Paul and heard him speak upon faith in Christ Jesus.

(8)   Matt. 18:21
      Then Peter came up and said to him, "Lord, how often shall my brother sin against me, and I forgive him? As many as seven times?"

VI. The Translation Project

Chapter 35
Establishing the Project

Additional Reading:
  Barnwell 1986:217–230.

A.   Interview two or three translators who have completed or are now working in a translation project with the goal of writing a brief description of the project. Prepare your questions carefully first based on your reading of Larson and Barnwell. Then have an interview and write up your summary.

Chapter 36
Translation Procedures

Additional Reading:
   Barnwell 1980: Chapter 24.

A. Asoinda text (Saramaccan) (prepared by Catherine Rountree)

Using the material provided below, translate this text into idiomatic English.

Interlinear text

(1) *Naomi, I   de no baa?*
   Naomi you are no VOC

   Naomi are you there, brother?

(2) *I   de bumbuu no?*
   you are well   no

   You are well no?

(3) *Gaantangi fii   u dee   sondi i   manda da u baa.*
   great^thanks for^you for the^PL things you sent   to us VOC

   Great thanks for the things you sent to us brother.

(4) *Noo   na   panta tumusi   e?*
   CONN NEG fear   excessively hear

   And don't fear excessively, hear?

(5) *Wan   o   kumutu a   Tjalikonde.*
   we^NEG INCOMPL leave   from Tjalikonde

   We are not going to leave from Tjalikonde.

(6) *Noo   mi bi jei kaa   a fesi taa*
   CONN I PT hear already in front that

   And I heard already in front that

(7) *so Steli bi o   ko,*
   thus Steli PT INCOMPL come

   so Stanley was going to come,

(8) *ma mi feekete u piki   i*
   but I   forgot to inform you

   but I forgot to inform you.

(9) *Noo so.*
   CONN so

   And so.

(10) *Noo   mi bi manda Modensi faa   ko   fan ku   i*
CONN I   PT sent   Modensi for⌢to come talk with you

And I sent Modensi to come talk with you

(11) *fa   hii sondi de.*
how all things are

how all thing are.

(12) *Noo   mi sabi   taa*
CONN I   know that

And I know that

(13) *a   sa fan ku   i   hii sondi finifini.*
he can talk with you all things in⌢detail

he will talk with you all things in detail.

(14) *Noo   so.*
CONN so

And so.

(15) *Me   ko   a Foto moon fu de   an   musu pakisei taa*
I⌢NEG come to town more for they NEG must think   that

I did not come to town any more for they must not think that

(16) *mi kumutu a   di konde.*
I   leave   from the village

I left from the village.

(17) *Noo   a di kuutu   di   u go tu   konde bi ko.*
CONN at the meeting which we go two village PT come

And at the meeting which we went to two villages came.

(18) *Noo   de   bi meni taa*
CONN they PT think that

And they thought that

(19) *mi ta-koti   di konde,*
I   PROG-cut the village

I am cutting the village,

(20) *ma de   da mi pasi   u fan du   de.*
but they give me path/time to talk with them

but they gave me opportunity to talk with them.

(21) *Noo   mi piki   de   limbolimbo taa*
CONN I   inform them clear⌢clear that

And I informed them clearly that

(22) *na   mi.*
      NEG   me

      not me.

(23) *Noo   ma   sa   du so   wan gaan sondi sondo   di   pisi   sata   sabi.*
      CONN I^NEG can do such a   great thing without the piece water know

      And I cannot do such a great thing without the piece of water knowing.

(24) *Ma Steli, a   de u   di   lo   fu Awananenge.*
      but Steli she is of the clan of Awananenge

      But Stanley he is of the clan of Awananenge.

(25) *Noo   hen mbei   a   sa   du so   wan sondi.*
      CONN it   makes she can do such a   thing

      And that makes he can do such a thing

(26) *Noo   mi go deen   wan maun a   di   wooko.*
      CONN I   go give^him a   hand in the work

      And I went gave him a hand in the work.

(27) *Noo   so.*
      CONN so

      And so.

(28) *Noo   de   an   jaka   u moon fuu   kumutu a   di   konde.*
      CONN they NEG chase us more for^us leave   from the village

      And they didn't chase us anymore for us to leave from the village.

(29) *Hii dee   biibima de bumbuu.*
      all the^PL believer are well

      All the believers are well.

(30) *Noo   u   abi   begi   fanoudu   eti.*
      CONN we have prayer necessary yet

      And we have prayer need yet.

(31) *Hii sondi an   de limbolimbe eti?*
      all things NEG are clean^clean yet

      All things are not clear yet?

(32) *Ma u   sabi   kaa   taa*
      but we know already that

      But we know already that

(33) *wa   o   kumutu a   Tjalikonde.*
      we^NEG INCOMPL leave   from Tjalikonde

      we are not going to leave from Tjalikonde.

(34) *Kabiten Nelison ko   a Foto.*
      Captain Nelson came to town

      Captain Nelson came to town.

(35) *Noo   ma   sabi na un   ten mi sa   ko   a Foto eti*
      CONN I^NEG know at which time I   may come to town yet

      And I do not know at what time I may come to town yet

(36) *ma mi ka   ko.*
      but I   want come

      but I want to come.

(37) *Tee   mi ko*
      when I   come

      When I come

(38) *Noo   u   sa   taki moon fini.*
      CONN we can talk more in^detail

      then we can talk more in detail.

(39) *Wasi de a u aki fa u de,*
      Wasi is at us here as we are

      Wasi is with us here as we are,

(40) *Noo so mi ke   tjeen   ko   a di september 1983*
      CONN we I   want bring^her come in the september 1983

      and so I want to bring her in the September 1983

(41) *Ma me   saki undi u dee   daka eti.*
      but I^NEG know which of the^PL days yet

      but I do not know which of the days yet.

(42) *Noo Wasi hangi i   te na sondi.*
      CONN Wasi hungers you til not something

      And Wasi longs for you til it is not something.

(43) *A   tamanda   wan piki kasaba ku   wan piki alisi da i.*
      she CONT^sends a   little casava with a   little rice give you

      She is sending a little casava and a little rice to you.

(44) *Noo Malimbo an   ko   a Foto.*
      CONN Malimbo NEG come to town

      And Malimbo did not come to town.

(45) *Mi puu   en taa*
      I   removed her saying

      I removed her saying

(46) *di   hen mama o   ko   a Foto*
since/because her mother INCOMPL come to town

since her mother would come to town.

(47) *noo   me   ke   a   fika*
CONN I^NEG want she remain

then I did not want her to remain

(48) *noo   be a   ko   luku hen mama.*
CONN let her come look her mother

and let her come look at her mother.

(49) *Noo Sisa Edmelia liki   di palati u Sane.*
CONN Sister Edmelia received the tape of Sane

And Sister Edmelia caught the tape of Sane.

(50) *Noo   mi kisi   di biifi   ku   kii dee sondi di   i   manda da u tuu.*
CONN I   received the letter with all the things which you sent   to us all

And I caught the letter with all the things which you sent to us all.

(51) *Noo   so.*
CONN so

And so.

(52) *Duumundu o.*
Goodbye   INCOMPL

Goodbye.

Commentary notes

This is a letter written to Naomi Glock by a Saramaccan Bushnegro, Asoinda Hagbo. He is one of the leaders of the church in Tjalikonde. It was written early in 1983.

(1)   *baa* is a vocative which means literally 'brother,' but it is used loosely for anyone. It seems to be a feature for adding a gentle or friendly tone to the discourse, rather than a term of address.

(3)   'the things sent'—The specifics of the 'things' sent is not known.

(4)   *noo* is a connector which indicates logical links between clauses or larger units.
'hear'—This is a feature for giving mild emphasis.

(5)   'Tjalikonde'—This is a Saramaccan village on the Suriname River. It is a few miles south of the Afobaka Lake.

(6)   'in front'—i.e., beforehand, previously

(7)   Stanley—a Saramaccan Christian man, another leader of the Tjalikonde church.
'going to come'—i.e., move from the capital city back to the Saramaccan area.

(10) 'Modensi'—a Saramaccan Christian man, a third leader of the Tjalikonde church.

(15) 'they'—i.e., the non-Christian villagers of Tjalikonde and her sister village, Tutubuka.

(16)   'left from the village'—i.e., permanently.

(17)   'two villages'—i.e., representatives of two villages.

(19)   'cutting the village'—i.e., clearing ground to build a settlement.

(23)   'piece of water'—i.e., that area of the river. It includes several villages and several hundred Saramaccans.

(24) (25)   'clan of Awananenge'—The Awana clan has territorial rights in that area. Those rights include the right to clear an area and build a settlement on it.

(28)   'chase'—i.e., figuratively.

(31)   'not clear yet'—i.e., all the problems have not been solved.

(34)   Captain Nelson - the Captain or headman of Tjalikonde.

(39)   *Wasi*—a Saramaccan Christian woman, a friend of Naomi's.

(42)   'til it is not something'—an expression which adds emphasis to a statement.

(44)   Malimbo—Wasi's teenage daughter.

(45)   'removed her'—i.e., prevented her from going to town.

(45)–(48)   The meaning here is not clear. There are several possibilities.

    a. 'she' in (47) refers to Wasi. Asoinda did not want Wasi to remain behind while Malimbo went to town.

    b. 'she' in (47) refers to Malimbo.

        i. refers to Malimbo remaining in town. Asoinda did not want Malimbo to go to town and stay while her mother was in the village and then later return to the village while her mother was in town. This would mean that the two would be separated for a long time.

        ii. refers to Malimbo remaining in the village. Asoinda did not want Malimbo to go to town at this point and then later have to remain behind while her mother was away.

(49)   'Sister'—a title used by Christians for a female Christian.
Edmelia—a Saramaccan Christian woman of Tjalikonde.
Sane—a Saramaccan Christian woman living in town.

(50)   'caught'—i.e., received.

B. Dawson text (Saramaccan) (prepared by Catherine Rountree)

Using the material provided below, translate this text into idiomatic English.

Interlinear text

(1) *Mi ta-sikifi   di pampia aki a di 8 daka u di Bakajailiba.*
I PROG-write the paper here on the 8 day of the January

I am writing the paper here on the 8th day of January.

(2) *Naomi i   de no baa?*
Naomi you are no VOC

Naomi, are you there, brother?

(3) *Soo   umfa i   de?*
CONN how you are

So, how are you?

(4) *I   de bumbuu no?*
you are well   no

You are well, no?

(5) *We mi a' di meni   taa*
well I have the thought that

Well, I have the thought that

(6) *i de bumbuu e   baa.*
you are well   hear VOC

you are well, hear, brother.

(7) *Noo mi ke i   sabi taa*
CONN I want you know that

And I want you to know that

(8) *u   seei de bumbuu aki tu e.*
we self are well   here too hear

we ourselves are well here also, hear.

(9) *Gadu de ku   u ku bunuhati leti kumafa a de ku i   ala tu e   baa.*
God is with us with good^heart just like   he is with you there too hear VOC

God is with us with a good heart just like he is there with you there also, hear, brother.

(10) *Noo mi kisi   dee sondi dee i   manda da mi e*
CONN I caught the things which you sent   to me hear

And I received the things which you sent to me, hear the paper with the 5 guilders, and the songs also,

(11) *noo   mi wai   e   baa.*
CONN I   happy hear VOC

and I am happy hear, brother.

(12) *noo   hen dee njonku sembe a di keiki lei   dee kanda.*
CONN and the young people in the church learned the songs

And then the young people in the church learned the songs on the tape til they knew them well.

(13) *Hen de   kanda de   a di keiki*
and they sang   them in the church

Then they sang them in the church

(14) *noo   a suti   te na sondi.*
CONN it sweet   til not something

and they were sweet very much.

(15) *U wai   seei kaa.*
we happy self already

We are very happy, brother.

(16) *noo   fa u   de aki misikuma di libi ku   Gadu ko*
CONN as we are here I^sI^as   the life with God   come

And as we are here I see that the life with God becomes very sweet very much,

(17) *noo   mi si   taa*
CONN I   see that

and I see that

(18) *mi do   ta-konda di woutu   u Gadu*
I   come PROG-tell the message of God

I have come to tell the message of God with more power upon me also,

(19) *so seei hati u mi ko   de   moon suti.*
so same heart of me come to^be more sweet

and also my heart has become sweeter.

(20) *Noo   im ke   i   sabi taa*
CONN I   want you know that

And I want you to know that

(21) *a di jai liba   noo   3 sembe dopu   u   Futunaa*
in the year month CONN 3 people were^baptized from Futunaa

on January 3 people of Futunaa will be baptized,

(22) *so seei di Akaa u Gadu ta-naki*
so same the Spirit of God PROG-knock

and also the Spirit of God is knocking in many people's hearts for them to change their lives,

(23) *noo u   ta-begi   ta-futoou   Gadu go dou,*
      CONN we PROG-pray   PROG-trust God go arrive

      and we are praying, trusting God arriving,

(24) *ma noo te   i   ko   mi o-konda   wan gaan sondi da i   di   Gadu du.*
      but CONN when you come I INCOMPL-tell a   big thing to you which God did

      but then when you come I will tell a big thing to you which God did.

(25) *A bigi e.*
      it big hear

      It is big, hear.

(26) *We noo mi o-knoda   wan sondi ake da i,*
      well CONN I INCOMPL-tell a   thing here to you,

      Well and I will tell a thing to you here,

(27) *noo joo   wai   seei.*
      CONN you-INCOMPL happy self

      and you will be very happy.

(28) *Mi ke   i   sabi taa*
      I want you know that

      I want you to know that

(29) *a di 18 u di Bakajailiba noo   di womi Sonneveld ku   di mujee Kotensi, wan*
      on the 18 of the January   CONN the man Sonneveld with the woman Kotensi a
      mii   u Br. Siteeli o-toou.
      child of Br. Steeli INCOMPL-marry

      on the 18th of February, then the man Sonneveld and the woman Kotensi, a child of Brother
      Stanley, will marry.

(30) *Noo so wan gaan sondi e   baa.*
      CONN so a   big thing hear VOC

      And such a big thing hear brother.

(31) *Da so.*
      thus so

      Thus so.

(32) *Noo awaa mi o-bia   ko a wan oto sondi aki.*
      CONN now I INCOMPL-change come to one other thing here

      And now I will change, come to another thing here.

(33) *We nà di moni di   dee sembe bi manda da mi.*
      well not the money which those people PT sent to me

      Well, (is it) not the money which those people sent to me.

(34) *Noo hen we mi ke fan ku i fii   da de tangi da mi e   baa,*
CONN CONN well I want talk with you for^you give them thanks for me hear VOC
   di sf175
   the sf175

And then well I want to talk with you for you to give thanks for me hear, brother, the sf175

(35) *noo be i   da de tangi da mi.*
CONN let you give them thanks for me

and let you give them thanks for me.

(36) *Mi kisi   di moni.*
I   caught the money

I received the money.

(37) *Mi si   taa*
I   see that

I see that

(38) *fa u   miti te u paati de*
as we met til we parted there

as we met til we parted there

(39) *noo de an feekete mi moonso*
CONN they NEG forgot me ever

they did not ever forget me,

(40) *noo a bigi da mi e   baa.*
CONN it big to me hear VOC

and it is a big thing to me hear, brother.

(41) *Noo Masa Gadu musu mbei de   fendi bunu a di wooko de ta-du   deen.*
CONN Master God must make them find good in the work they PROG-do for^him

And Master God must make find good in the work they are doing for him.

(42) *Gadu musu naki   de   koloku noomo*
God must knock them luck   surely

God must surely knock them fortune,

(43) *noo be i   seei fan ku de da mi tu fa i si sondi ta-waka   aki.*
CONN let you self talk with them for me too as you see things PROG-walk here

and let yourself talk with them for me also as you see things are walking here.

(44) *Noo ee wan sembe sa   hakisi taa*
CONN if a   person should ask   saying

And if a person should ask you saying

(45) *we unmeni   sembe so di keiki de   sa abi?*
      well how^many people so the church there can have

      well, and how many people might the church there have?

(46) *noo   i   piki   taa wan 75 so.*
      CONN you answer that one 75 so

      And you must answer saying 75 thus.

(47) *We noo me   a' sondi   u taki moonso e   baa.*
      well CONN I-NEG have something to say   more   hear VOC

      Well and I do not have anything to say more hear, brother.

(48) *Be i   de bumbuu u te i   sa toona ko   baka*
      let you be good   of til you may return come back

      Let you be well until you may return come again,

(49) *noo be i   da i   tata ku i   mama gaan odi.*
      CONN let you give your father and your mother big   greetings

      and let you give your father and mother big greetings for me.

(50) *Taki da de   taa*
      say to them that

      Tell them that

(51) *te   di juu dou*
      when the hour arrives

      when the hour comes

(52) *noo mi o-si   de.*
      CONN I INCOMPL-see them

      then I will see them.

(53) *A sa de a Saana.*
      it may be in Suriname

      It could be in Suriname.

(54) *A sa be na Ameeka.*
      it may be in America

      It could be in America.

(55) *A sa de tu a hembe*
      it may be also in heaven

      It could also be in heaven

(56) *noo woo   wai ku u seei te tjika.*
      CONN we^INCOMPL happy with we self til enough

      and we will be very happy with ourselves.

(57) *Noo   i   piki   de   taa*
CONN you inform them that

And you inform them that

(58) *di wooko di   i   ta-du aki*
the work   which you PROG-do here

the work which you are doing here,

(59) *noo   a suti   da Gadu poi*
CONN it sweet   to God   exceedingly

and it is very sweet to God,

(60) *noo   be de   lusu i*
CONN let them loose you

and let them loose you

(61) *be i   toona ko   baka.*
let you return come back

let you return come back.

(62) *Fa Gadu paati i   ku de   u wan pisiten   de*
as God   parted you and they for one piece^time there

As God parted you and them for a little while there

(63) *noo   Gadu o-solugu   da de.*
CONN God   INCOMPL-care^for for them

God will care for them.

(64) *Be de   an panta poi   e.*
let them NEG fear   exceedingly hear

Let them not be overly afraid, hear.

(65) *Mi ta-begi   Gadu da i   mama*
I   PROG-pray God   for your mother

I am praying to God for your mother,

(66) *noo   mi ta-biibi   en tu fa a   toona ko   bete.*
CONN I   PROG-trust him too for she return become well

and I am trusting Him also for her to become well again.

(67) *Noo   da so e!*
CONN thus so hear

And so!

(68) *Lesi a Psalm 34:19–21.*
Read in Psalm 34:19–21

Read Psalm 34:19–21.

(69) *Duumudu e   baa.*
Goodbye hear VOC

Goodbye, Sister.

(70) *A tan   so.*
it remains thus

It remains so.

Commentary Notes

This letter was written to Naomi Glock by a Saramaccan Bushnegro, Dawson Petrus. He is the leader of the church in Futunaa. At the time Naomi was in the United States caring for her mother who was recovering from an operation.

(2) *baa* is a vocative which means literally 'brother', but it is used loosely for anyone. It seems to be a feature for adding a gentle or friendly tone to the discourse, rather than a term of address.

(7) *noo* is a connector which indicates logical links between clauses or larger units.

(9) 'with his good heart'—refers to the graciousness and goodness of God toward men.

(10) 'catch'—receive

(14) *te na sondi*—an expression which adds emphasis to a statement.

(16) *di libi ku Gadu*—refers to our relationship and fellowship with God.

(19) *so seei* is a connector which links clauses of equal rank.

hati in this passage refers to the spirit or inner being of a person.

(21) *jai liba*—'year month' = January

'three people baptized of Futunaa'—this construction is unusual. The usual word order is: three people of Futunaa were baptized. The reason for the unusual order here is not clear. There are several possibilities:

    a. The author made a mistake. (AB)
    b. The author added the last phrase 'of Futunaa' as an afterthought. (CD, EF, GH)
    c. The author had an unknown reason for the unusual order. (IJ)

(22) 'knocking in many people's hearts' refers to the influence or work of the Holy Spirit in people's inner being.

(23) 'trusting God arrive'—the focus of this expression seems to be the continuation of the process rather than reaching the goal.

(33) The word order of this clause indicates that 'the money', the object of the sentence, is emphasized.

(34) *noo hen we*—these connectors together indicate that a very important statement is about to follow.

(38), (39) (38) seems to express the idea that they met and got acquainted, and even though they parted again, the result of the meeting was that they did not forget him.

(40) 'it is a big thing to me'—an idiomatic expression for being impressed by something.

(41)   'Master God must make them find good in the work'—This is not an imperative for God but more like a blessing or well-wishing for the parents to prosper in their work.

(42)   'knock them luck'—bless/be gracious to

(56)   'til enough'—an expression for indicating exceedingly or very much.

(57)   *piki*—answer/respond/inform

(60)   'let them loose you'—does not necessarily indicate that the parents were holding on to her.

(64)   'let them not be overly afraid, hear'—This does not necessarily mean that the author knew that the parents were afraid.

(66)   *bete* 'better'—fully recovered.

(70)   *A tan so*—Amen.

C. Alekano text: "The Bicycle"

Instructions

A.   Read through the text once or twice just to try to get the general drift of the story.

B.   Read through the text again, trying to find answers to the following questions:

1. Identify the writer or writers. (It was dictated by one named individual to another named individual: but there is something tricky occurring in the text.)
2. What can you say about the situation in which it was written?
3. List stylistic features different from English.
4. List what appear to be idiomatic expressions and their probable meaning. List any other words which seem to be used with extended meanings.
5. List passages which contain flashbacks.
6. List places where it appears that implied information would need to be added to give understanding to those not familiar with the setting and circumstances.
7. List places where you need more information (i.e., you need to do "exegesis" by asking someone familiar with the language and the culture).

(1)   I and Izape went to (where) they staked payment (for) our bodies.

(2)   Going we stayed looking.

(3)   Izape and additional councilmen having come along I came along later.

(4)   He red man having given me a bicycle, after he came in a car, mud having become his bicycle, he gave (it) to me.

(5)   After he gave (it) to me, taking (it) I came along.

(6)   Big rain having struck, turning around again, having taken (it) and gone down I struck (it with) water.

(7)   Having struck (it with) water, the rain having struck I stayed in a house.

(8)   As I was, after it burned clear, taking (it) I came along.

(9)   Time having been finished, I having ascended on bicycle, ascended on bicycle, as I was coming along, with-bows men took at my hands.

(10) Having taken, having said "From where are you?", taking me and coming along they spoke saying, "You will sleep in the house (where) they habitually sleep cool."

(11) Having spoken, they gave a rope to the bicycle in a house.

(12) Having given (it), they said, "You also will sleep in that house."

(13) I said, "No."

(14) Having said "No", they struck at my ears, it is two and it is additional time.

(15) Having struck at my ears, taking my ears again they twisted.

(16) Having done thus, taking me ascending, after speaking talk in a rope it went in a red man's house.

(17) Red man not being, his red man's child, he having spoken talk it came.

(18) After it came, the with-bows men spoke saying thus:

(19) "Be your name!" they having spoken, I having been-given them my name, they burned-put a carving.

(20) They burned-put saying the house place is at Wanima.

(21) They spoke saying thus:

(22) "You, not fleeing, morning quickly as the sun is rising come!" saying they said.

(23) After they spoke, in darkness slowly slowly coming coming I came to house.

(24) After coming I spoke-gave to the councilmen's with-bow man Izape saying thus.

(25) After speak-giving him, he spoke saying, "morning and-Wanimapi we will go."

(26) Speaking having spoken, I having descended, after I spoke-gave to Wanimapi, go in I slept.

(27) Today morning we (2) went.

(28) As we went, Gitene and Bunulo coming, having taken at our bodies, additional we went.

(29) Our going Gitene returning having come, we only, those with Gunulo and Maima, only we, it is two it is additional man, we went.

(30) As we went, from at the road at (where) red man Ziosi's house burned, below, the red man having taken (and) put us, he went.

(31) Going, he having left us at Noti Koloka, Gunulo returning having come to his woman, having come he spoke thus:

(32) "It having sickened my boy, taking him in the medicine house I will go", having spoken, having stayed, we, and Maima, we (2) went in ground.

(33) Going going entering in the medicine house, Wanimapi and additional red man having spoken talk talk, a red man taking us, coming, we (2) having asked about red man Lekesi's woman, taking us he came.

(34) That woman not being, additional red woman being, we having remained speaking with that woman and another red man, as they were staying we (2) went to an office.

(35) After going, in the carving getting house, I having said "Maima, you be outside!" I going up, after they burning had thrown a carving, it came from my house.

(36) Going up, after I getting (it) had descended, we (2) having gone down, after we ascended in the doing prosecution house, we (2) having gotten Wanimapi's girl he bore day carving, having descended, coming, we having entered additional house, a doing prosecution house, we did a search for additional with-name man, a red man who is always taking stones from the local people.

(37) He not being, additional red man Masta Talaiva being, we spoke-gave to him.

(38) He spoke saying thus:

(39) "You going speak to the with-bow men's father!", having spoken, going we (2) spoke.

(40) He spoke saying thus:

(41) "It is now finished, go to house!", having spoken, as we were, Gitene having come, Napaneha threw a carving thing from at the road down there.

(42) Taking-giving (it) to Gitene, counting it on the road we came hearing (it).

(43) Coming coming, at the Asalo-clan's bridge, as Loisie was taking the little girl's wearing cloth (and) going, we having met, Gitene running around went.

(44) The (2) having went, we (2) came.

(45) As we were coming, red man Loli taking us, turning around, coming, after they taking-throwing-throwing the coffee in Kalia Wasoni, coming along in the car, taking coming along and having left the car at (the) doing prosecution house, he having gone and gotten a carving thing (and) come, having entered the car, taking driving (it), after he said "we will now go to house," coming coming, after he left us at the road that comes along to the houses(s), as we (2) came along, as Hekaguno was coming from in garden, having taken-joined (as), additional coming, Gohogole and Namaneha taking a knife and coming, having put it, as they (2) gave her stone, as they were putting file (to) the knife, coming along, after we saw, entering, after I spoke saying in the house "as you are saying-giving-giving me talk, as I was burning-putting-putting a carving, from our staying after the two men had just gone, we (2) ourselves stayed with only Maima as he kept saying-giving-giving to me."

Chapter 37
Testing the Translation

Additional Reading:
   Barnwell 1986: Chapter 29.

A. Apeninge text (Saramaccan) (prepared by Catherine Rountree)

   Using the material provided below, translate this text into idiomatic English.

Interlinear text

(1) *Katolina mi ke   fan ku   Veni Pai wan soni.*
     Katolina I   want talk with Veni Pai one thing

     Catherine, I want talk to Veni Pai about something.

(2) *Biga   wan   sa   na un   juu ten langa a de a Saamaka.*
     because we^NEG know at which hour time long he is in Saramacca

     Because I don't know how long he is in Saramacca.

(3) *A kande   a ko   de aki te a ko   a mujee.*
     it perhaps he comes is here til he comes to woman

     Perhaps he comes to be here til he comes to have a woman.

(4) *Mujee bee   abi en libi.*
     woman family has it living

     The woman's family has its ways.

(5) *Aki Saamaka   i   mujee bee, i   mai   abi en fan.*
     here Saramaccan your woman family your mother-in-law has her talk

     Here is Saramacca, your woman's family, your mother-in-law has her talk.

(6) *I   mai   ju o-lesipeki   i   mai.*
     your mother-in-law you INCOMPL-respect your mother-in-law

     Your mother-in-law, you will respect your mother-in-law.

(7) *I o-lesipeki   i   pai,   i   suwaki.*
     you INCOMPL-respect your father-in-law your sister-in-law

     You will respect your father-in-law, your sister-in-law.

(8) *Pee lafu.*
     play laugh

     (You will) play, laugh.

(9) *Ja   musu saanti   en.*
     you^NEG must sass/insult her

     You must not sass or insult her.

(10) *I   feni   soni*
      you obtain something

      You obtain something;

(11) *i   da   sembe.*
      you gave people

      you give to people.

(12) *Sembe feni*
      people obtain

      Other people obtain;

(13) *a   da   i,   i   mujee   bee.*
      he gives you your woman family

      he gives to you, your woman's family.

(14) *I   libi   ku   pizii.*
      you live with pleasure

      You live with pleasure.

(15) *I   nango   a   kamian*
      you CONT^go to place

      You go places;

(16) *dee   oto   takule   kilikilikili   ta-du   soni   fanjanfanjanfanjan.*
      the^PL others CONT^run (ideophone for running) CONT^do something disorderly

      the others run around doing things disorderly.

(17) *Ja   mumu libi so.*
      you^NEG must live so

      You must not live thus.

(18) *I   musu libi ku   lesipeki.*
      you must live with respect

      You must live with respect.

(19) *I   musu libi ku   paadon.*
      you must live with pardon

      You must live with pardon.

(20) *Noo   i   ku   mujee bee   o-kai.*
      CONN you with woman family INCOMPL-fall

      You and the woman's family will fit together in harmony.

Commentary notes

In an attempt to escape the evils of Western culture, a young American man spent six months living among the Saramaccan. After he had been there for some time, Apeninge, an older Saramaccan woman gave him this advice.

(1) In such advice-giving situations, it is customary to direct the statements to a third party. In this text, the discourse is directed to Catherine, but is intended for Veni Pai. Veni Pai is present, listening.

(3) *Mujee*—woman/wife

(4), (5) The Saramaccans have many rules and regulations about the behavior between in-laws. Many of the rules concern how they speak to each other.

(8) Part of the speech behavior includes a lot of friendly joking and teasing.

(9) *saanti*—includes any remarks they consider disrespectful. It includes many things we would consider "smart remarks" and many things we would consider acceptable.

(10) Meat from hunting and fishing and other food or goods from town are customarily shared between relatives, friends, and important or needy people in the village.

(15), (16) A group of young people or children can be very rowdy and rough in their play, chasing each other about the village, wrestling, yelling, etc. This is considered ill-mannered by the adults.

(19) *paadon*—pardon = forgive, respectful, well-behaved.

(20) *o-kai*—refers to things that fit together or please or suit each other.

Noo is a connector which combines propositions and larger units into various logical relationships. (Here it marks the conclusion.)

B. Comprehension questions

Check your translation with unconditioned native speakers (at least two) and record the answers your receive.

Genre questions

1. What kind of speech is this? Story? Sermon? Legal Document? Advice? Scolding?

2. Do you think it was written or said orally only? Why?

3. Do you think the speaker is a man or a woman? Old or young? Why?

4. Do you think the speaker is a native speaker of English? Why? Why not? How much education? Why? Does he/she know how to express himself well or not? Why?

5. Do you think he was in a hurry? Why? Why not?

6. Do you think this was said or written to an adult, youth or child? Why?

Overview

Tell me in your own words as much as you can remember of what I just read.

Thematic questions
(Ask only those not answered in overview response.)

1. Who is this addressed to? (Victor)

2. What does Catherine have to do with it? (She is a third party to whom the remarks are directed by, they are actually for Victor.)

3. Why do that? (It is a custom of the speaker's people.)

4. What does the speaker say to Victor? (You may get all of the story here OR how he should treat his in-laws.)

5. Why does the speaker want to tell him all that? (He/She thought he might take a wife there someday and wanted him to be prepared.)

6. So, what was it she wanted him to know? (There are many rules about how one treats their in-laws.) Specifically? (One must speak respectfully to them especially his mother-in-law.) What else? (He must share things with them.) What else would he do or not do? (When going places should behave himself and not act like the others.)

Detail questions

1. About the way a young man speaks to his in-laws, can you give me more details about how that should be done? (no sass, insults, rather joking)

2. What kind of things do you think they share? (Just be sure you get a reasonable answer.)

3. Specifically what is it "the others" do that he is warned against? (Running around, being rowdy and disorderly.)

C. Identifying adjustments that have been made in a translation

Identify as many translation adjustments that have been made in the following translation as you can. This is a back-translation into English of the translation into Tepehua. Compare with the RSV. Prepare comprehension questions for checking this Tepehua translation with unconditioned native speakers.

John 1:35–44 (Tepehua)

[35]The next day again John was standing with two of his men. [36]And he again saw Jesus where he was coming and said to them, "Look at that man who is going to be like God's lamb." [37]And those two men of John's when they heard what he said, well, immediately they followed Jesus. [38]And when Jesus turned around he saw those who were following him. He said to them, "What are you hunting for?" And they said to him, "Rabbi, where do you live?" Rabbi means teacher. [39]Well, he said to them, "Come. You will see where I live." And they went with him. They saw where he lived. Well, that day they stayed there with him since it was about four in the afternoon. [40]And those two who heard John's words and followed Jesus, well, one was called Andrew. He was the younger brother of Simon Peter. [41]Well, Andrew immediately found his real brother who was called Simon. And he said to his brother, "We have found the Messiah." That means we have found the Christ, the one of whom it was said that God would send him here. [42]And immediately he took him to where Jesus was. When Jesus saw him he said to him, "You are Simon. You are the son of Jonas. You will be called Cephas." Cephas and Peter mean rock. [43]When the next day came, Jesus said that he was going to the land of Galilee. There he came across the one who was called

Philip. And he said to him that he should follow him. [44]Philip lived in the town of Bethsaida. It was in the land of Andrew and Peter.

John 1:35–44 RSV

[35]The next day again John was standing with two of his disciples; [36]and he looked at Jesus as he walked, and said, "Behold, the Lamb of God!" [37]The two disciples heard him say this, and they followed Jesus. [38]Jesus turned, and saw them following, and said to them, "What do you seek?" And they said to him, "Rabbi" (which means Teacher), "where are you staying?" [39]He said to them, "Come and see." They came and saw where he was staying; and they stayed with him that day, for it was about the tenth hour. [40]One of the two who heard John speak, and followed him, was Andrew, Simon Peter's brother. [41]He first found his brother Simon, and said to him, "We have found the Messiah" (which means Christ). [42]He brought him to Jesus. Jesus looked at him, and said, "So you are Simon the son of John? You shall be called Cephas" (which means Peter).

[43]The next day Jesus decided to go to Galilee. And he found Philip and said to him, "Follow me." [44]Now Philip was from Bethsaida, the city of Andrew and Peter.

CPSIA information can be obtained at www.ICGtesting.com
Printed in the USA
BVOW06s0850120314

347335BV00005B/12/P